The Petroglyphs of Mu

"One site stands out as greatly significant in our understanding of the emergence of civilization in the Pacific. That place is the enigmatic site of Nan Madol on the eastern shores of the island of Pohnpei in Micronesia. Carole Nervig not only throws new light on this mysterious place but finds its precursor in Pohnpaid, adding considerable knowledge to what we know about this much understudied part of the ancient world."

ANDREW COLLINS, AUTHOR OF *GÖBEKLI TEPE*

"In her beautifully illustrated new book, *The Petroglyphs of Mu,* Carole Nervig provides a vivid, firsthand account of little-known sites and traditions from the Pacific island of Pohnpei that may hold the key to unraveling the mystery of Nan Madol and its unique megalithic architecture; all of this against the background of prehistoric transoceanic journeys and the possibility of a lost Pacific culture of the last ice age."

MARCO VIGATO, AUTHOR OF *THE EMPIRES OF ATLANTIS*

The Petroglyphs of Mu

Pohnpei, Nan Madol, *and the* Legacy of Lemuria

Carole Nervig

Bear & Company
Rochester, Vermont

Bear & Company
One Park Street
Rochester, Vermont 05767

Text stock is SFI certified

Bear & Company is a division of Inner Traditions International

Cataloging-in-Publication Data for this title is available from the Library of Congress

ISBN 978-1-59143-447-4 (print)
ISBN 978-1-59143-448-1 (ebook)

Printed and bound in the United States by Lake Book Manufacturing, Inc. The text stock is SFI certified. The Sustainable Forestry Initiative® program promotes sustainable forest management.

10 9 8 7 6 5 4 3 2 1

Text design by Virginia Scott Bowman and layout by Debbie Glogover
This book was typeset in Garamond Premier Pro with Acherus Grotesque, Gill Sans MT Pro, ITC Legacy Sans Std, Myriad Pro, and Sabon LT Std used as display fonts

If not otherwise noted, illustrations and plate pictures are either from the author's personal collection or in the public domain. Every attempt has been made by the author to clarify the ownership of illustrations used in this book. Any oversights or omissions brought to the author's attention will be corrected in future printings.

To send correspondence to the author of this book, mail a first-class letter to the author c/o Inner Traditions • Bear & Company, One Park Street, Rochester, VT 05767, and we will forward the communication.

Contents

Access to the Divine Feminine

Barbara Hand Clow

The time line for artistic human cultures has been pushed back fifty thousand to one hundred thousand years by recent discoveries that are revealing what life was like for our ancestors. For example, we now have a solid date for the most recent magnetic reversal, which caused a pole shift forty-two thousand years ago. This date comes from an analysis of ancient kauri trees that were preserved in sediment in New Zealand for more than forty thousand years. Scientists are using the rings of these trees as a Rosetta stone to correlate their voluminous records of Earth's environmental cycles over one hundred thousand years of cave deposits, ice core analysis, and peat bogs.

What was it like for living people to experience a pole shift that would have rearranged landmasses and submerged many coastlines? Some researchers, including me, think that the pole shift precipitated a cataclysm that was the cause of the Neanderthal extinction, the sudden widespread disappearance of figurative art in caves, and the subsequent emergence of the Cro-Magnon people.

We need to reach further back in time to resonate with our ancestors' world. If we do so, we'll realize we wouldn't be here now without their creativity and brave striving. Carole Nervig penetrates the veils of time in this wonderful book as she explores deep secrets hidden in one of the most mysterious and ancient sacred sites on Earth: Pohnpaid on the island of Pohnpei in Micronesia. *The Petroglyphs of Mu* is her study of the symbols she found there, which she believes were the language of the Great Goddess. Long ago the people of Pohnpei revered the goddess and the land, and many still do today. Her book makes me wonder whether Mu emerged soon after the pole shift forty-two thousand years ago? Maybe Mu came to be when the artistic and deeply intuitive Neanderthal people were fading away? Or perhaps Neanderthal legacies passed to new cultures that emerged at that time? The eminent Neanderthal researcher Stan Gooch thought that's what happened. Gooch wrote about the reverence for the Great Goddess that the Neanderthals displayed at their lunar-based sacred sites. Gooch says the Neanderthal legacy was the "mother civilization" that worshipped the Pleiades and Orion.

Carole Nervig's discovery and interpretation of the Pohnpaid petroglyph site is a significant contribution to the search for antediluvian or pre-Flood cultures. Her findings and conclusions awaken our sensitivity to the world as it existed more than fifteen thousand years ago. For many years I've followed the exploration of antediluvian sites by such eminent researchers as James Churchward, Charles Hapgood, Graham Hancock, Andrew Collins, Gregory Little, Stephen Oppenheimer, and Stan Gooch. Now, Carole Nervig joins these pioneers with her discovery and analysis of the Pohnpaid petroglyphs that are tangible links to long-lost Mu.

When I peer into the deep past, the time before the cataclysms that submerged Mu and Atlantis, left-brain academic techniques take me only so far. I welcome Nervig's book because of her ability to combine intuitive research with all the increasingly sophisticated analytic tools, such as improved dating techniques (including kauri tree analysis), and geodetic, navigational, and astronomical analysis. Nervig refers to her exploratory process as "connecting the megalithic dots."

Yet why would anybody go to all this trouble? Well, it's not just curiosity. Based on my own research into the last twenty thousand years, as articulated in *Awakening the Planetary Mind,* we need the stories of our ancestors because they remind us to treat our planet with respect. Eco-sensitivity awakens in us as we consider the Motherland at a time when humans were in harmony with Earth. When we examine the early to mid-Paleolithic awakening that transpired approximately one hundred thousand years ago, our intuitive and feminine awareness expands.

In *Awakening the Planetary Mind,* I describe a syndrome that alienates us from Earth, which I call "catastrophobia." This paralytic fear embedded in the human mind twelve thousand years ago nearly terminated human life on Earth. I think the memory of what happened to Earth only twelve thousand years ago is lurking in our minds like a time bomb that will explode if we don't face and process it. Recovering the memory of the Motherland, Mu, seems to ease our unprocessed inner fear.

We need to know the story of our planet to reconnect with the great people who existed in this realm earlier than twelve thousand years ago. If we don't, we are plagued by pervasive and blinding amnesia, we've lost the Divine Feminine, and we even may be missing extraterrestrial connections that could enlighten us. The recovery of the Motherland, Mu, possibly the first enlightened culture, could help us restore normal male/female balance on Earth. Nervig restores Mu's spiritual power by showing that its symbols are still sacred today. Mu inspires us to embrace the Goddess, the primeval, enlightened soul of the Motherland. Besides a balance between the sexes, Nervig demonstrates that Pohnpaid's stones, petroglyphs, and energetic grid systems remind us of our responsibility to Mother Earth. When we embrace Earth, we find the Goddess.

To access ancient memory, Nervig notes, "a petroglyph is worth . . . a thousand voices." This resonates because when I see petroglyphs, I hear sounds and voices that are just a step beyond my physical hearing. If I slow myself down and trace a petroglyph with my fingers, something emerges that feels true. I'm excited by Nervig's descriptions of the petroglyphs and the clues that are in the rocks near where she found them. These symbols link us to cosmic sources (even extraterrestrials, if you like). Sacred sites are encoded with signals that access other worlds, and once you start picking them up, you're never quite the same. These signals are in the archaeoastronomy of the sites, in the geometry of the standing stones and other rock sculptures, and in the petroglyphs themselves. Nervig compares them with symbols found all over our planet in sacred cultures that still exist today.

The Pohnpaid petroglyphs suggest that the people who created them were in contact with other realms; this was important to them. And Pohnpaid is exceedingly valuable because it has so many petroglyphs, which is very unusual in Micronesia. I think Nervig's conclusions are timely because we are getting very close to linking to other worlds and dimensions in *our* time. The ancient ones used these symbols to contact cosmic realms, a skill we need to recover ourselves.

Assuming that contact with other realms at sacred sites was and is important, *how* do we do it? During my visits to these sites with a variety of groups, I was the teacher/leader, and as such I had to be especially adept at tuning in to the sites to translate any intelligence I detected. My process is as follows: First I wander the site in order to locate its strongest source of power and subtle energy. Once I pick up signals that feel magnetic and/or electric, I slow my mind and body down to the cellular level—the second dimension in my cells that records waves of knowledge. While receiving this information, I maintain total openness to animals, other beings, and synchronicities, and a link is made to the site's core energy. So far I've been the most successful when I remind myself that these sites are *interdimensional portals*. That is, sacred sites are dimension openers, places where other realms, higher or lower, are inhabited by intelligent beings that hold the stories of time.

Petroglyphs at sacred sites such as Pohnpaid represent a library of universal symbols that awaken inner knowledge. Today's libraries contain accounts of world history that go back only about five thousand years. Sacred sites with identified astronomical alignments, stone monuments, and petroglyphs are similar to modern libraries, but their symbols may go much further back than five thousand years. Ubiquitous symbols are found in all ancient cultures that studied the sky to glean the astronomical information it proffered. Based on this global data bank, Nervig's study of the Pohnpaid petroglyphs establishes them as the originating symbols of the Motherland, Mu. Their equivalents are still found in current sacred cultures, such as the treasured symbols of India that recede back into antiquity and the sacred symbols of most indigenous groups still extant in the modern world today.

Pohnpaid has some archetypal symbols that predate the sinking of Atlantis, which Nervig believes was a colony of Mu. I agree with her, for her thoughts on Mu as the originating culture ring true. I think Mu reaches back to forty-two thousand years ago, and that the remnants of Atlantis I described in *Awakening the Planetary Mind* are the remnants of Atlantis after the cataclysms. I strongly suspect Oceania was the central location of Mu and that it was more submerged than Atlantis.

Regarding the symbols, Nervig notes that they have no geographical or cultural boundaries and are not subject to quantitative or third-dimensional analysis. Based on my own terminology, these symbols are multidimensional and cosmic. Meditating on them helps us release buried trauma and access hidden memory. My Cherokee grandfather exposed me to many symbols because he wanted me to dedicate my life to helping people heal repressed fear. Later I was exposed to symbols when I taught at sacred sites. They fascinated me as I struggled to penetrate their meaning, yet it has only been during the past ten to twenty years that these symbols have really opened up for me.

To offer a taste of how exciting this kind of research is these days, the explorer and code breaker Genevieve Von Petzinger has identified thirty-two symbols she found in Neanderthal cave art in Portugal and Spain. The graphic communication system of geometric markings she analyzed goes back one hundred thousand years. Like Von Petzinger's book *The First Signs*, Carole Nervig's dedication to decoding the Pohnpaid symbols is a significant contribution to understanding the ancient symbolic language of our ancestors. These symbols tell us what people were thinking about and how they were orienting themselves to the cosmos.

Nervig says Mu is the *point of origin* of the archaic matriarchal tradition. Since so little has remained of the matriarchal Mu, most researchers believe that patriarchal Atlantis invented archaeoastronomy, sacred symbols, and the myths. As we find Mu in our times, the origins of feminine spirituality link to the Pleiades. Indeed, many cultures on Earth believe their ancestors came from the Pleiades star system, the progenitor of the human race. Being part Cherokee, I was taught and still believe that I came to Earth from the Pleiades. This makes me wonder whether the Pleiades is the Motherland.

Nervig thinks she found a petroglyph of the Pleiades star cluster at Pohnpaid and plans to confirm it by revisiting the site. I personally have found the Pleiades depicted all over the world at ancient sites and suspect that Mu was a Pleiadian culture. Significantly, Pohnpei Island is also home to the world-class sacred site Nan Madol, as well as Kahnihmueiso, which is underwater and in the future may reveal much about Mu. Nervig says we should think of Mu not just as a *specific landmass*, but also as extensive *time frames, time lines, or phases* of a primordial enlightened civilization *of all races*. This is a fabulous depiction of Mu.

Nervig goes on to say that it was an enlightened civilization that existed over a vast expanse of time and multidimensional realities, and before its submergence, it was geographically originated in the Pacific Ocean but was culturally diffused outward through its survivors and colonies. She believes Mu and Atlantis were different civilizations that coexisted over a long period of time, yet Mu predated Atlantis. This new paradigm is slowly capturing the attention of many researchers.

I felt Mu to be the progenitor culture during two journeys I took to the Indonesian islands of Sulawesi and Bali. Tana Toraja is a major sacred site on Sulawesei that has huge standing stones and gigantic rooms that have been hollowed out of huge basalt stones. I think the oldest layers of Tana Toraja originated during the time of Mu. The existence of Mu will never be proven with left-brain scholarly study only, yet much will be coming forth eventually as the result of underwater lidar or other new technologies. Any discoveries are difficult because the vast evidence testifying to Mu's existence is on the ocean floor. As for other physical remains of Mu, rising seas submerged most of it, yet some mountaintops remain, which today include the islands of Pohnpei, Sulawesi, and Bali as well as Easter Island, all other Pacific islands, and Australia.

We have the power to feel inner knowledge when we visit these sites, and in Tana Toraja on Sulawesi, I could really feel the less dense and delicate sensibility of Mu, the gateway to the feminine and the Pleiades. Carole Nervig's depth of feeling about Pohnpei, her knowledge of the Pohnpeian culture and language, and the openhearted welcome given to her by the indigenous people of Pohnpei make her the best guide to this mysterious, sacred site.

Enjoy this book as you allow its mystical symbols to sink into your heart and soul.

BARBARA HAND CLOW

BARBARA HAND CLOW is an internationally acclaimed ceremonial teacher, author, and Mayan calendar researcher. Her numerous books include *The Pleiadian Agenda*, *Alchemy of Nine Dimensions*, *Awakening the Planetary Mind*, and *Revelations from the Source*. She has taught at sacred sites throughout the world and maintains an astrological website, **www.HandClow2012.com**.

Prelude

A HUMBLE REQUEST

As is *tiak en sapw* protocol, both an apology and a request for clarification is offered here for any and all misinformation or interpretations about Pohnpei and Nan Madol in these pages. Because this writing is undertaken by what Pohnpeians consider an "outsider," I make no claims of authority in Pohnpeian cultural protocols or history. I am only an analytical observer. The following examples reflect the proper traditional language and respectful attitude of my endeavor to present all perspectives. I thank the authors of these extracts for their expertise.

> *Ahi soaipoad rorowei likin ihmwa-mwail. Ma emen mwahngih, e nekkainenela pwe pereki meh i pwapwa pwa.* "My words are placed before you who have listened. Those among you who know better should correct my errors." (recorded in writing and translated by Hanlon 1988)

We would like to add our confession and a request to those who read this: *Keipwenih pohn mwoalen wahu pahn kupwuren Erekso ko Pohnpei uh. Re ketin kupwurehkin kiht at tungaol elep lepin sepwil en, pwe sen kak warohng patoh pahn kupwurahr nan doadoahk wet. Eri ihr me ketin mwahngi, en ketin karonge oh kainenehla audepen doadoahk wet pwe pirakih me se pwahpwa.* "We are humbled by the honor of you royalty in Pohnpei. Please follow us to invite listeners knowledgeable of the subject to come forth and correct our mistakes, in that we realize that the little we know needs to be corrected." (recorded in writing and translated by Panholzer and Mauricio 2003)

I have yet to gain the maturity and sufficient wisdom to interpret, explain and—more importantly—properly and effectively use Pohnpeian history. I will also preface this discussion with a salutation in the form of an honest confession, a definition and a parting request. Conventionally, every local historian, or soupado, begins a narrative with a respectful salutation (*kemwetimwet*) and ends the narrative with a parting request. With due respect for these conventions, I salute you and those who will read this paper with the confession that *pirakih me I pwa, me ese nek kainenehla,* or "my story is not straight—those who know more should make it straight." My parting request is *ai soai pwoat rohrohwei,* or "my story is carried forth." (recorded in writing and translated by Mauricio 1998)

Acknowledgments

To my sister, Jeri McGiverin, armed with her professional experience, who waded through the swamp of my unending drafts. Her willingness, generosity, and encouragement that my book was worth pursuing gave me the confidence to proceed.

To recognize those no longer in the physical realm whose presences overshadowed me during my writing process:

To James Churchward for his wealth of information on Mu, the lost continent of the Pacific; and to Norman Paulsen and Andres Boulton Takra, who introduced me to Mu;

To Pohnpeian historian and knowledge keeper Masao Hadley for inspiring me along the investigative path of Pohnpei oral history;

To my former PATS student turned historic preservation official Emensio Eperiam, whose dedication to Pohnpeian archaeological sites accompanied me on many investigations and provided support in accessing these sites;

To Hawaiian kahuna Hale Kealohalani Makua for his everlasting spiritual support;

To astronomer/astrologer Nick Anthony Fiorenza, who for years freely shared his knowledge of the start over Pohnpei;

To *Isopahu Nanmwarki* Kerpet Ehpel, who acknoweledged my concepts, believed in my mission, and bestowed unlimited access to all sacred sites of Madolenihmw;

To all Pohnpeian historians, who kept the oral histories alive for generations; and to all anthropologists, archaeologists, and historians, still among us and not, especially Arthur Saxe, whose findings and records enabled me to establish a background for my interpretations, and in some cases provided photographs.

And now for those still with us whose contributions and support ensured the creation of this book:

To the board members of the Nan Madol Foundation, who by their endorsement allowed me to pursue my work on Pohnpei: Emensio Eperiam, Nelson Pelep, Rufino Mauricio, and especially Nickolson Solomon, who organized a critical meeting with the Nahnmwarki of Madolenihmw, Governor Marcelo Peterson, and officials, where I shared photographs of the yet unknown petroglyphs;

To Barbara Hand Clow for graciously persevering through a thousand pages of manuscript to advise me, then offering to write the foreword, and to my editor, Kayla Toher, who performed professional miracles with enormous dedication;

To all of my GoFundMe donors, who allowed my 2018 return to Pohnpei to share my petroglyph findings with Pohnpeians, as none had seen them, and to my niece Kelly Kienzle, who inspired me to crowdfund;

To countless dear friends, who listened to my endless procrastinations for decades, yet patiently urged me on . . . with a special thanks to Marlene Durliat Newman for her support at many levels; and to all my Pohnpeian friends and colleagues who over the years offered their friendship and support during my sojourns on their island;

To Maria Grazia Fanelli Stephens of Kosrae Pacific Treelodge Resort on Kosrae for her generous support along with Takasy Salik Waguk of Kosrae Jungle Tours;

To the many photographers and illustrators who gifted their work to the public domain, creative commons, or this project—thank you;

Kalanganan kumweil to my Lohd Pah family from my days in the Peace Corps, to *Soulik en Lohd* and his wife *Kedinlik en Lohd* for sharing Lohd legends, and to Morleen Thomas *Nahleio dolen Madolenihmw* and Papiano Tihpen *Nahnawan dolen Madolenihmw,* who drove me to Pohnpaid where we macheted our way to the petroglyphs.

Enough Legendary Smoke to Confirm Ancient Fires

Life can only be understood backwards; but it must be lived looking forwards.

Sören Kirkegaard, *Journals*

In light of recent and continually growing evidence of cultured civilization from as early as fifty thousand to seventy-five thousand years ago, and in locations that were not previously considered "advanced," we have been forced to rethink mankind's past. This often results in the confirmation of cultural diffusion rather than isolated local spontaneous generation.

To understand these antediluvian enlightened ones, it is critical to look beyond mere anthropological identification, archaeological documentation, migratory routes, and time frames. Examination of the interrelationships within their networks of sacred sites and their systematic functionality is essential to understanding this bygone world.

Identifying and interpreting the traditional, spiritual, visual, architectural, astronomical, navigational, geomantic, and geodetic knowledge embedded in the Pohnpaid petroglyph site, a part of Greater Nan Madol—as a component of these global networks of sacred sites—is my contribution toward connecting such megalithic dots.

Resemblances of the virtually unknown Pohnpeian petroglyphs documented herein are not limited to Oceanic art but match those of advanced historical civilizations in the Americas, Europe, Asia,

1

and Australia, as well as the megalithic structures of Nan Madol. My "rediscovery" of these "out of place" petroglyphs at Pohnpaid lit a fire under my keyboard, and publishing news of their very existence became my priority. Later, under separate cover, I will share my interpretations of oral histories and discoveries of sacred geometries and geodetic alignments embedded within Nan Madol.

My overall intent is to first share my analysis of oral histories and unpublished findings relative to the Pohnpaid petroglyph site. My second intent is to establish the origins of these enlightened cosmologies and global earth energy systems as legacies from the Motherland of Mu with the hope that these understandings may guide us to a more nurturing relationship with Mother Earth. *The Petroglyphs of Mu* is not meant to be an academic treatise, despite its wealth of meticulously researched evidence. One of its goals is to motivate interested parties everywhere to continue to deepen the investigation of Mu.

HOW TO READ THIS BOOK

As you will see as you make your way through *The Petroglyphs of Mu,* it contains many words and phrases that have a variety of different spellings. This is due to the fact that the Pohnpeian language was originally an oral one, resulting in varied spellings developing over time, with different spellings for different districts of the island. Even the present-day language features these spelling variations. To clarify this for the reader, I have added the original and/or variant spelling of any given word or phrase in question in parentheses or brackets, where appropriate.

You will also find that the syllable *mu* is prevalent in many indigenous words this book contains. To my mind, this is significant, for it underscores the profound and extensive connection that these ancient people had with the Motherland. The sheer quantity of these words with meanings relating to primordial creation, Mother Earth, Goddess, Deity, serpents, water, land, or fertility prove more than incidental and should not be dismissed. I have italicized these syllables at first mention of the associated word in the text to help them stand out.

Although decades of rigorous research have preceded this book, particularly its objective content, it is not meant to be a conventional academic exercise of building measurable evidence toward only one irrefutable verdict, especially regarding time lines. Rather it is an in-depth probe of *both fact and legend,* designed to decipher the significance as well as the functions of megalithic sacred sites of Pohnpei and the Pacific and explore how they are linked via their systematic and potent locations.

Functioning within this context I occasionally propose a multitude of rationales or interpretations of any given megalithic or sacred site, rock art, or their respective alignments. Some of these interpretations may be conflicting and others quite outside the box, and consequently I am often and intentionally raising more questions than I am answering.

As they say, where there's smoke there's fire. And I say that when consistent and extraordinary smoke emerges, the presence of a modicum of fire is inevitable. My expectation is that I have presented sufficient smoke to elicit further investigations into the whys, hows, and whens of these Micronesian mysteries. It is then up to the reader to connect even more dots than I, and in doing so, to draw their own conclusions.

I remain optimistic that this book will generate enough fire to avoid being summarily dismissed by conventional archaeologists, geologists, and historians, as well as that the book will light an investigative fire under those seeking fresh evidence to validate the emerging alternative scenarios of our civilization's true past . . . one that's becoming significantly older by the day.

More than just its contents, the medium or formatting of its contents is another type of message embedded within this book. In historical or archaeological accounts, the message is all too often that of a patriarchal scientific fundamentalism (scientism, macro-Newtonianism), to the *exclusion of any or all other paradigms* or considerations. Central to this concept is the arrogance that possibilities outside of this third-dimensional, "observable and repeatable" realm cannot be proved, and therefore cannot be real. Even Einstein's authority was not able to squelch such chauvinism. Fortunately, today's quantum perspective is forcing this attitude and reality to change. The following chapters lend equal credence to both the unseen and the seen; the matriarchy and the patriarchy; and metaphysics and physics—which we now know are practically inseparable in light of such advances in the areas of quantum mechanics, fractal nonlinear resonance, and multidimensional realities, for instance.

My specific stylistic approach to creating dynamic equilibrium between "masculine" and "feminine" concepts is *demonstrated literally by the book itself.* This is accomplished by the juxtaposition of odd-numbered chapters on right-brain, subjective, narrated personal transformational events with even-numbered ones containing left-brain, descriptive documentations of actual oral histories, physical places, and various phenomena. The chapters validate and enhance each other by their consistencies and serendipities, providing more fertile and in-depth understandings while posing new questions for the reader to ponder. They also provide a deeper look into my emotional and spiritual journey that led to becoming an author.

Should you choose to focus only on "factual" information without the context of the personal narrative, the even-numbered chapters will provide this half of the picture. For a more nuanced and holistic experience of the book's message and contents, the subjective narratives in the odd-numbered chapters should not be passed over.

Decades ago, the renowned Lithuanian archaeologist and anthropologist Marija Gimbutas, and later the social scientist Riane Eisler, became pioneers in creating an awareness of our need to restore matriarchal/patriarchal *balance*—a balance that has no social *dominators* (a word coined by Eisler). In their writings, both women demonstrated how past cultures accomplished this balance with enlightenment and success.

Giving equal credence to intuition and non-third-dimensional phenomena is what most of academia has always systematically ruled out. It is evident that the exclusively patriarchal paradigm has not created a harmonious planet, despite its scientific achievements. The ability to perceive the *value* of both feminine and masculine perspectives and experiences offers an option of bringing our world into balance. Perhaps it is time learn from our past—and to approach the future with open minds and hearts.

KALAHNGAN EN KUMWAIL (THANK YOU ALL)

CAROLE NERVIG, *LIH EN EIR**

---

*Woman of Eir, the honorific title of Lohd Pah bestowed upon me while in the Peace Corps; Eir is the mythical land to the south of Pohnpei where its first migrations originated.

1

Pacific Petroglyphs in the Room

SCHMOOZING IN PARADISE

I ordered seafood spaghetti.

This dish had nothing to do with Italian cooking. I was in Pohnpei, and my friends and I were escaping into the air-conditioning of the "seedy yet upscale by island standards" Palm Terrace restaurant, where the only authentic Italian ingredient might be garlic.

This expat favorite consists of lots of soba noodles curled in a deep, plastic Japanese bowl, with garlic that is not *usually* from a shaker, chopped fresh scallions, salt, world-renowned Pohnpei pepper, and small cubes of grilled tuna caught that morning. It was the most "meat-and-potatoes" entrée on the menu, a must for Americans craving some kind of normalcy in the laid-back yet unpredictable tropics.

I was at the Palm Terrace with a group of Pacific regional environmentalists. They were conferencing here at the capital of the Federated States of Micronesia for the week. Earlier that day I had made a presentation to them about Nan Madol, the largest archaeological complex in the Pacific Ocean, highlighting its need for both environmental and cultural preservation.

Nan Madol is a dark and brooding city of canals that encompasses nearly one hundred man-made, black basalt islets floating on the blue waters off Pohnpei's shore. Rufino Mauricio, former director of the National Archives, Culture and Historic Preservation for the Federated States of Micronesia, estimated 750,000 metric tons of rock was used to

5

construct both the perimeters of these artificial islets and the columnar basalt structures that were stacked upon them. Such imposing edifices, one reaching over forty feet, were created without the use of pulleys, levers, or metal. Even though it is the most famous megalithic complex in the Pacific and now a UNESCO World Heritage Site, its origins remain mostly mysterious. Aside from the lame classification of Nan Madol as having a mortuary-residential function (a component of most sacred sites worldwide), there is scant evidence of its deeper purposes.

Desperate for answers, conventional archaeologists, alternative historians, and alien visitation proponents have birthed rather fantastic and illogical theories about its construction and existence. The answer, if and when it is finally gleaned, will probably be a hybrid of all, incorporating, most importantly, Pohnpei oral history.

A grant of $250,000 was in the offing. I, as sole fundraiser for the Nan Madol Foundation, was making a plea for this sacred city and its protection, a cause to which I was evidently addicted. Some of the visiting group of environmentalists in the audience had asked me to join them for dinner.

I lived on a small, isolated island where all social life revolves around drinking *sakau,* the Pohnpeian version of kava, or Budweiser, into the wee hours . . . night after night. Thus the prospect of dinner with a group of professional, educated, and articulate Aussies and New Zealanders sounded like a peak experience.

About halfway through the meal Ronald started asking me about petroglyphs. A professor at Australian National University but *not* in anthropology, his avocation was Pacific petroglyphs.

Due to my role as director of the Nan Madol Foundation I was knowledgeable about Pohnpeian archaeological sites. He rightly figured I would know where to find them. Indeed, I had shown the sites to several groups over the years. Yet not wanting to trek out to Madolenihmw District in the stifling heat and humidity just to show him what I thought at the time were fairly insignificant petroglyphs, I pooh-poohed them.

Ronald was a friendly old chap, with the typical Aussie adventurous spirit. He grilled me incessantly about these petroglyphs. Perhaps the scarcity of rock art in the mid-Pacific had ignited his enthusiasm.

I eventually caved. But not without first negotiating a "must have air-conditioning" rental car for the two-hour drive to the site near the Lehdau River, just past the village of Sapwalap in the southeast of the island. We scheduled our little escapade for the following Saturday, my day off.

DESTINY PREVAILS

We were a good hour into our adventure on the rough gravel road when Ronald finally showed his true colors. His petroglyph passion was based in esoteric foundations! I didn't see this coming—a professor and all.

I had been slipping him little hints of the spiritual and esoteric motivations for my work with Nan Madol. Not only was it one of the *major* sacred sites of the planet, it also, according to some oral histories, had been constructed by twin giants who used *mwanamwan* (spiritual power or magic) to fly the stones into position.

But I wasn't prepared for *his* revelation—although that sweet-and-sour shock that accompanies synchronicities wasn't a new experience for me.

Sweet because synchronicities validate that I am not alone on my path. There is a Source energy that is really working with me, covering any lapses in faith that might lead me astray from my personal spiritual path.

Sour because if Source is in charge, there are no excuses, no limitations, *no one to blame but myself for not living my destiny.*

Sour as in *fear*. Fear about the attempt to even contemplate or comprehend that such grace, such orchestration of events on my spiritual path, could even exist at all.

I recovered gradually as he shared that he was part of an obscure esoteric brotherhood of which I was aware. He was no new age bliss ninny. His spiritual group was heavy-duty and authentic . . . and he had a Ph.D. to boot!

It was like a scene from the *Unveiled Mysteries**—secret

---

*This details the synchronistic events that led Guy W. Ballard (pen name Godfré Ray King) to Mount Shasta, where he began his encounters and eventual dictations with the Ascended Master Saint Germain.

brotherhoods making contact with me and all! He asked for anonymity about his spiritual persuasion, which he received from me. I have changed his name in this book and in other instances where it might be mentioned.

Once I had recovered from the shock of his true spiritual identity and exactly why he was drawn to our esoteric rendezvous, a deep conversation ensued about sacred places and petroglyphs and their ultimate meaning and purpose. As we spoke, I felt us shifted to other levels of consciousness where we were uniting and remembering The Plan to have this encounter. I felt humbled and honored to be participating in something much greater than me.

DROUGHT DISCLOSURES

As Ronald and I made our way around Pohnpei's perimeter and its only road toward Madolenihmw, the southeast district of the island, I noticed the effects of the current and highly infrequent drought. The typically lush jungle and canopy of monkeypod trees looked thirsty and confused by the lack of rainfall on an island whose interior receives more than four hundred inches of rain a year. The humidity, man's foe but the rain forest's ally, had not subsided one bit.

For fun, the local kids had been lighting matches just to see the normally impossible sight of a brush fire racing through a couple of acres. Consequently, here and there along the road were unusual displays of open space and brown scorched fields and stumps with no vegetation. Fortunately, streams everywhere stopped these fires in their tracks before any serious damage ensued. So no one bothered to put them out.

We passed the village of Sapwalap, parked the car off the road near the Dauen Sapwalap, and shed any unnecessary layers of clothing. We left our air-conditioned oasis, loaded our water and cameras, and headed down the unmarked footpath to the petroglyph site less than a mile away near the Lehdau River. According to legend, both the Dauen Sapwalap and the Lehdau River had been "dug" by the magician Lapoange, with his penis, no less! (The name *Lapoange* may also appear in the text as *Lapone* and *Laponga*.) We were no doubt treading on sacred—or at least fertile—ground.

We made our way to the *known* petroglyph rock outcrop site, which was about eighteen feet (five meters) in height, with a gently sloping surface covering almost one hundred square feet (thirty square meters). As mentioned, I had been here many times before, often leading groups to the site, and I would normally start my tour by pointing out the gigantic Takai en Pahsu "vagina" stone.

A Pohnpeian friend and former head of FSM Tourism had called my attention to this smooth anthropomorphic fertility stone a few years prior on our way to the outcrop. A precise cavity was chiseled into its eroded upper surface, disrupting its sensual curve (fig. 1.1; plate 1). While inspecting the boulder, he also shared that its mythohistoric origin was connected to the god Lapoange. He explained that this stone was believed to represent Lapoange's wife's genitals. Her body had fallen apart when Lapoange turned her into stone and this was the only part remaining.

The megalith called me to touch her, and I wanted to feel her mwanamwan, her power (fig. 1.2; plate 2). Afterward, my friend explained that women would touch it to become pregnant. Fortunately, I had no such luck.

Fig. 1.1. Takai en Pahsu fertility stone, Pohnpaid meadow.
Photo by Carole Nervig, 1992.

Fig. 1.2. Author with Takai en Pahsu, Pohnpaid, 1992.

Suddenly, I was compelled to eat one of the white ginger blossoms growing nearby. Go figure. This was before aromatherapy was hip. It would be years before I researched why I had eaten this aphrodesiac spontaneously. Interesting timing—my urge to eat this after touching the fertility stone.*

But this time with Ronald . . . something else was different. Was I looking at the same stone I had seen so many times before? Was I disoriented?

No, it wasn't the stone. It was the jungle around it. Gone. The kids had burned it off (fig. 1.3; plate 3).

I saw for the first time an entire field of huge stones, some at least twelve or fourteen feet high! They had peeked out from the lush vista in the past but had never revealed their gigantic size or configuration. There were dozens.

---

*White ginger *(Cananga odorata)* is also known as ylang-ylang, which means "flower of flowers." Magical uses: peace, love, and sex spells. Aromatherapy uses: to alleviate frigidity, impotence, insomnia. Key qualities: powerful sedative, calming, euphoria-inducing, and narcotic when used in large quantities.

Fig. 1.3. Portion of burned Pohnpaid boulder field. Photo by Carole Nervig, 1992.

Never had I seen *this* before! Initially Ronald, never having seen the site's original vegetation, didn't understand my state of shock. My usual route was to the left fork in the path, to the outcrop, not to the right.

The lack of natural camouflage had revealed a configuration of basalt boulders, megaliths that formed what appeared to be a double circle. *Stone circles in the Pacific?* No one had ever mentioned anything about this place before. But then how could they? The area had always been choked with vines and underbrush, diminishing their true size and camouflaging their numbers . . . not to mention their other extraordinary secrets.

I wandered about in a daze. Ronald had gone off to one side of the site and was poking around at some vegetation. He yelled at me to come at once and see some kind of a garden. Garden? Who cared? We were discovering a megalithic site and he was going botanist on me?

At his insistence, I joined him, but there was no word about greens; it was a trick. He told me to turn around and look to the north.

I was stunned. A huge stone, and *I mean huge*—or, should I say, a megalithic sixteen-foot phallic rock—was lying on its side (fig. 1.4;

Fig. 1.4. Pohnpaid phallic monolith.
Photo by Carole Nervig, 1992.

plate 4). It was without doubt of a phallic shape and a good match for the female stone near the path. No wonder a fertility theme was associated with the area.

My left brain countered that it could also be a fallen solitary upright, or an ancient sculpture of a turtle or a sea creature deteriorated beyond easy recognition rather than a cyclopean lingam.

Then I saw them.

A Site to Behold

The entire exterior of the sixteen-foot-long megalith was covered with petroglyphs! Incredible. Nothing like the familiar petroglyphs I had been intending to show Ronald. There were more glyphs on this one rock than on the entire outcropping of the well-known rock art site nearby, the one we'd originally been headed toward.

We both rushed to the astonishing rock.

Overload. My mental *and* emotional circuits were blown. We were being allowed to see what the jungle had hidden all these years.

There were hundreds of shapes and symbols on the phallic rock,

Fig. 1.5. Author with the Pohnpaid phallic monolith, 1992.

some familiar, but the majority not. These new motifs were certainly more complex than the glyphs upon the well-known rock outcrop nearby. Most of the designs were sophisticated, completely unlike the simple yet elegant stick-figure petroglyphs found throughout Polynesia. Until this moment of discovery, there were no other known petroglyphs on Pohnpei and exceedingly few in all of Micronesia.

An equilateral cross, outlined twice, caught my initial attention. But there were more of these enveloped crosses; some were outlined once, some three times (figs. 1.6 and 1.7, p. 14; plates 5 and 6). The same symbol was carved in several locations around this rock. The equilateral crosses were much older than the Russian expedition of 1828, or the occupations by Germans in 1865, Spaniards from 1887 to 1889, or Japanese from 1914 until the end of World War II, and therefore not of a Western religious nature. My intuition was betting that perhaps some of them even predated Nan Madol and Lapita cultures.

These patterns were not easily assigned to any one particular culture. We saw a whole section of connected shapes and symbols that resembled intricate Mayan motifs. Perhaps their complexity could be

Fig. 1.6. Double-enveloped cross on the phallic monolith, Pohnpaid.
Photo by Carole Nervig, 1992.

Fig. 1.7. Triple-outline enveloped cross and sun, Pohnpaid.
Photo by Carole Nervig, 1992.

Fig. 1.8. Grids on the phallic monolith, Pohnpaid.
Photo by Carole Nervig, 1992.

a result of layering one stratum of glyphs over another. Another out-of-place symbol featured a design that called to mind the style of the renowned artist Piet Mondrian, combining lines or rectangles (fig. 1.8; plates 7 and 8).

My mind was reeling. Fortunately, Ronald had enough sense to start taking photos. I followed suit, hoping it would bring me back to Earth.

With Ronald's ample grip to assist me, I leveraged my way to the top of the "male rock," about six feet off the ground.

Luckily I had worn tennis shoes instead of *zories,* the official footwear of the tropics. It usually required a few months before one became proficient in negotiating Pohnpei mud in flip-flops—fine for the beach, but disastrous in mud. Telltale brown-spotted calves always indicated *mehn wai* (foreigners), expats, or other assorted unacclimated nonlocals.

As we looked down from the top of the lichen-covered boulder, our feet were surrounded by a maze of abstract circles and shapes. One section of interlocked triangles formed some sort of a grid area

Fig. 1.9. Pyramid-runway motif on the phallic monolith, Pohnpaid. Photo by Carole Nervig, 1992.

evoking a maplike or geodesic feel. The entire surface was enmeshed with unrecognizable marks and motifs.

I focused in on one distinctive pattern, a pyramid or triangular shape with parallel lines dividing it in half. Most Southeast Asian, Mexican, and Central and South American pyramids have stairs, so that was my first impression. However, it also gave the impression of a runway, Nazca style, as seen from above (fig. 1.9; plate 9).

A boat or canoe-shaped inscription appeared nearby (fig. 1.10; plate 10).

Who had made this site and carved more than five hundred images

Fig. 1.10. Boat motif on the phallic monolith, Pohnpaid.
Photo by Carole Nervig, 1992.

in these rocks? When? Why? Again, I sensed its origin predated Nan Madol, whose oral history is accounted for by present-day Pohnpeians. No one had ever spoken to me of these "new" petroglyphs before—no archaeologists, no historic preservation people. No one.

In the months to come, I would speak with the landowners of the site. They were aware of the large stones and their reputation for fertility but gave no special significance to the multitude of strange petroglyphs that covered more than twenty megaliths or boulders on the land they owned. They knew there were some markings, but they seemed of little consequence to them.

Similarly, Emensio Eperiam, my former student from my days with the Peace Corps, and current historic preservation officer and board member of our Nan Madol Foundation, was in disbelief about my new findings. This was 1992, prior to any site documentation, and I had to personally escort him to Pohnpaid before he believed me. Once there, he was speechless.

But back to the stones, which had more secrets to reveal.

CELESTIAL MARKERS

Feeling overwhelmed by this mystery and not wanting to use all our film at once, Ronald and I began to inspect other nearby boulders.

Sure enough, the nearest one had not only more rock art covering its surface but a precise circular basin carved into its top surface. This water-filled bowl was surrounded by geometric configurations, many of which were symmetrical (fig. 1.11; plates 11 and 12). That they were archaeoastronomical calculation devices was a definite possibility. It brought to my mind other "water mirrors" used by the ancients to track the movements of the stars. Were these geometric symbols used to mark or compare the distance a star reflection traveled in relationship to the adjacent basin edge?

It was sweltering. With no shade, the relentless sunshine drained us from the inside out . . . not to mention the 1000 percent humidity. The only effective way to quench my insatiable thirst was with a fresh coconut or several cold beers, neither of which were forthcoming. How had I ended up in the tropics? And almost right on the equator, no less. At least there were no snakes!

Fig. 1.11. Astronomical basin and surrounding inscriptions, Pohnpaid, 1992.
Photos by Carole Nervig, 1992.

I prayed for clouds as an adrenaline rush propelled me onward. The next stone was perhaps five feet across and again covered with glyphs.

Just when I thought I could no longer be shocked, there it was! Could it be for real?

Half of a winged sun disk. Impossible. But unless I was hallucinating, it was right before my eyes!

Talk about validation. After all the years of trying to piece together seemingly unrelated tidbits of esoteric or circumstantial evidence to prove the existence of an advanced prehistoric mother culture in the Pacific, finally something *tangible* had surfaced. With no apparent connection to Pacific cultures of recent centuries, these vestiges of an advanced civilization, possibly of navigator-priests, could not be disputed.

Fig. 1.12. Winged sun disk stone, Pohnpaid, outlined at right for clarity.
Photo by Carole Nervig, 1992.

The smoking guns were etched in stone, for Christ's sake.

Now maybe what I was looking at wasn't *really* a winged sun disk per se. But it *was* a double circle divided into twelve segments, which might represent the astronomical zodiac (fig. 1.12; plate 13). A winglike shape extended from the right side of the circle. Within the wing were "supports" or "trusses" at ninety-degree angles to each other. Hanging down from the wing were a series of geometrical configurations.

The ninety-degree angles caught my attention.

These angles had meaning, perhaps functioning as mathematical propulsion "corners" for space traveling or shifting between the third dimension to higher ones. Was this some sort of galactic map or resonance diagram to assist its viewers in remembering moreso than contemplating or calculating? I knew this configuration but couldn't articulate its message at the time. (See "Winged Disks" on page 195 for a discussion of interdimensional travel via ninety-degree angles.)

When Ronald caught up with me, he was astounded as well by the nature of these designs, a far cry from the recognizable Pacific motifs with which he was familiar.

No longer able to express himself in words, he grounded himself by the methodical clicking away of photographs. They would provide material evidence not only of this amazing encounter, but of our sanity.

Once again, he motioned to another rock, and I struggled through the charred brush in my sneakers (what I would have done for some good hiking boots!) to confront another medium-size stone.

It featured another star theme . . . or at least a flying one this time.

Fig. 1.13. Pleiades stone, Pohnpaid, outlined at right for clarity.
Photo by Carole Nervig, 1992.

I remember seeing seven of the starlike shapes, but were they birds, airplanes, or the Pleiades? There was a circle in the center of each (fig. 1.13; plate 14), and their curved appendages gave an indication of motion.

No definite answers were forthcoming. We stumbled on.

THE MEGA FINALE

Drunk on discovery, I made my way through some of the sparse underbrush to the center concentration of gigantic megaliths. Most of these did not house visible petroglyphs, but they had their own mysteries. They were perhaps remnants, though by no means small, of an inner circle of stones or some sort of primeval, purposeful configuration (fig. 1.14;

Fig. 1.14. Inner stone circle, Pohnpaid (note the adult on the right).
Photo by Carole Nervig, 1992.

plates 15 and 16). They were difficult to discern, but there appeared to be about a half dozen of them. Eight to fourteen feet high (at least the portion of them that was on the ground), they towered above me.

Dwarfed by their masses, Ronald and I pondered their proximity to each other. Could they have originally been in a perfect circle, dislodged by ancient typhoons or earthquakes, shifting out of formation over time by their own instability?

One thing we were sure of: they were *ancient*. Proof? There was none. Some things are recognizable only in the gut, with that knowingness that no amount of logic can deny. Proof would come later.

They were ancient, as in having been erected *before* the accepted migration time line and routes agreed upon by those academics who study the Pacific. This find was a paradigm buster and I was thrilled.

But who had been on Pohnpei back then? There was certainly no mention of this site in the *Book of Luelen,* the premiere oral history of Pohnpei, and the only one to date that speaks of the first canoes to arrive on Pohnpei.

There was something bizarre about these stones besides their size and dissimilarity to other large stones that had been found around the island. It was their shape. As well, they featured unnatural notches, laser-like convolutions, and smooth flat areas that appeared here and there—lending the stones a fecund but high-tech feel.

Where had I seen this before?

Oh, yes. The smooth indentations were like the "vagina stone" we had previously passed, near the path to the other well-known petroglyph outcrop. They did have a similar look and feel to the vagina stone, but they were larger. Clearly they were all part of a gigantic complex.

I looked at the stones of the inner circle with new eyes. There were no other phallic rocks around, but those indentations could be symbols of female anatomy. A closer look at a couple of these female parts revealed small notches and bumps placed in very provocative configurations that convinced one that sexuality and fertility could have been a focus of this entire site at some time.

The energy and look of these stones brought to mind the "birthing stones" of Kukaniloko near Wahiewa, which in my opinion is one of the most powerful sacred sites of Oahu. It was at this site that Hawaiian *ali'i* (royalty) were born and passed hand-to-hand, individual by individual, over the mountain and to the shore for "baptism." I have often wondered what the site at Kukaniloko might have been in more ancient times and whether or not it was limited to birthing (perhaps not unlike Pohnpaid).

Later I was to receive confirmation of the fertility aspect from the family who owned the land and lived next to the site. They willingly shared this knowledge about the site, but when asked, they couldn't recall when it had last been utilized, nor any other details for that matter.

Well, okay. So fertility was part of the picture. Before I even began to sort this out, however, I was face-to-face and magnetized by . . .

A rock.

It was another huge one, but it was all wrinkled and oozing with smooth "bowls" carved over its top. The base portion looked very much like pahoehoe, the smooth lava that looks like cake batter pouring into its pan. This particular stone was unlike all the others. Yes, it could be a chunk of pahoehoe lava, broken off and distributed in proximity to the other smooth megaliths, but it had a distinct look of being carved. In all the years I had spent exploring Pohnpei, I had never seen anything quite like this formation (fig. 1.15; plate 17), and I certainly had never seen any pahoehoe.

GANESHA IN THE ROOM?

The boulder resembled something else as well: an elephant's trunk. Where had I seen this before? I wracked my brain for memories while the rock's strange vibration took hold of me. It was not one of power or malevolence, but a feeling of comfort and familiarity. A vibration I felt I should have *remembered*.

It wasn't until sometime later that validation of my familiarity with this stone revealed itself to me.

I had been given a photograph of this very stone years prior. While going through my file of old Pohnpei photos, I came across two snap-shots that were given to me by my Pohnpeian shaman friend. One was an unknown Pohnpeian elder or shaman, the other, a strange-looking basalt rock with a long protrusion. Evidently the two pictures were somehow related. He insisted I take both photos but refused to explain why and only said, "These are for you." The old photo he gave me was

Fig. 1.15. Elephant megalith, inner stone circle, Pohnpaid.
Top: Photo by Carole Nervig, 1992. *Bottom:* Photo provided by Pohnpeian elder.

shockingly similar to the elephant stone at Pohnpaid. Could this possibly be one and the same stone? How could my friend have known that it would be part of my future discoveries?

In the meantime, I was fixating on what an image of an elephant was doing on Pohnpei. To my knowledge, there are clearly no accounts of elephants in Micronesia. Despite the incredible accomplishments of the ancient Pacific navigators, I could not conjure up an image of an elephant cruising on an outrigger canoe!

My mind scoured its contents, desperate for clues about who might have created this place.

Perhaps Ganesha worshippers had carved an image of their cherished elephant god for this site. I knew of pachyderm motifs and sculptures found in Mexico, another location not frequented by these enormous mammals. Does this mean the Hindus were here, as well as Mayans . . . or perhaps there was common source to explain all?

As I left the central grouping of megaliths and made my way to Ronald, I contemplated the layout of the complex again. In the center were the gigantic, unusually formed megaliths, including the "elephant rock," which had perhaps formed a more precise inner circle at one point. Time had taken its toll on the outer circle. Many of its rocks were scattered out of circular alignment, but I was convinced that we had come across an ancient stone circle site in the Pacific. *A Micronesian Stonehenge?*

I shared my theory about the circles and elephant rock with Ronald. He mumbled an "uh-huh" but said no more. We were both still in a state beyond words, silenced by the honor of glimpsing this forgotten secret of the jungle, serendipitously opened for us briefly by the fires of drought.

Exhausted and sweaty, we retreated to the air-conditioned rental car. The ride home skirting Pohnpei's mangroved coast was quiet; our mood was of contemplation and surrender to the day's monumentality. Should I have been better emotionally prepared for this serendipitous find? But that's exactly the point. If I could have prepared for it, *it wouldn't have been magic.*

DILEMMA

What was going through my mind was: *Why me? What should I do now?* I was filled with the heaviness of responsibility. *Was this secret to be shared or protected?*

One thing I did know was that this site had not been *disturbed* by modern-day human activity, even if others had come across it. It was still active, alive, and potent. Intuitively I felt that I would have to answer to its powers if I did the wrong thing.

Ronald picked up on my concerns, my somewhat irrational feeling of somehow being responsible for these Pohnpeian sacred places. We agreed on the likelihood of past-life connections that were triggering my reaction. Had I not protected them before? Perhaps I had helped create them? My emotions were fueled by thoughts of my accountability in exposing their existence to the world. Would my spiritual integrity perish if I published news of these findings? Would tourists or archaeologists destroy the site's integrity, its mwanamwan (spiritual power)?

Or would the petroglyphs be even better preserved and understood, with more light shed on them?

I relinquished any need for immediate resolution of my dilemma as regards *timing* or *time*. Clarity, as I have experienced it, often comes with patience.

I felt lighter already, more centered.

I looked at the big picture of our miraculous day. Here was this guy Ronald bugging me about sightseeing some petroglyphs that I'd seen dozens of times before. I had resisted, but he was relentless, and destiny was in control. When I surrendered, not only did I have the discovery of a lifetime, but also one accompanied by a closet mystic who, like myself, recognized this rendezvous as destiny and magic.

2

Legends of Pohnpaid and Takaieu

Contradiction Reigns

UNLIKELY BEDFELLOWS

Grains of truth found in indigenous lore are finally being given serious consideration by geologists, and with proven success. In 2007, *Myth and Geology*, the first collection of peer-reviewed scientific papers discussing the geological reality behind some myths and legends, was produced and edited by Luigi Piccardi and W. B. Masse and published by the Geological Society of London.

In another publication Masse elaborates on reasons for the delay of the development of "geo-mythology," an exploration by scholars from various disciplines of the potential of the storylines of myths to yield data and lessons that are of value to the geological sciences.

To say that science has not looked favorably upon attempts to glean meaningful historic information from oral history and mythology is to grossly understate the contempt that some scientists have for such endeavors. Indeed, physicists and astronomers who were active in the early 1960s understandably are still upset when confronted by anything bearing a resemblance to the infamous theories and claims of Immanuel Velikovsky (Grazia, et al. 1966) . . . However, part of the blame for the sad state of myth as an explanatory tool must also rest on the shoulders of the ethnologists, folklorists and other scholars who most closely work with myth. The study of mythology for the last 100 years has been dominated by classical (e.g. Graves 1960), structural (e.g. Levi-Strauss 1969), and psychological (e.g. Campbell 1981) approaches. Although these approaches have produced fascinating insights into the nature and meaning of myth and have helped to highlight the critical role that myth has played in non-Western and early Western culture and society, they have misled generations of scholars by their assumption that myth lacks a meaningful foundation in the processes and events of real history.

Recent studies are beginning to revise our thinking with respect to the relationship between myth and history (Vitaliano 1973; Baille 1999; Mayor 2000; Barber and Barber 2005; Masse and Piccardi, in press).

The work of geologist Russell Blong (1982), which discusses a previously undocumented seventeenth-century Plinian style volcanic eruption in Papua New Guinea, is singled out as an exquisite example of the use of mythology to complement and enhance the findings from physical geology. By collecting and analyzing the environmental details in myths about the "time of darkness" from widespread villages and tribes in and around the tephra fall, Blong documented aspects of the nature and duration of the eruption that were otherwise enigmatic in the physical record. Blong demonstrated that no set of myths from a given village or tribe contained all of the pertinent environmental details, but rather each set had just a few details, a situation likely representing individual and local circumstances and a natural response of people reacting to major natural disaster. (Masse 2007, 40; citations from original article)

That geological events (volcanic eruptions, earthquakes, tsunamis, and cosmic impacts) on Pohnpei and Oceania have given rise to myths and oral histories must be considered. In some circumstances they underlie the sacred and cultural values of its landscapes, rocks, and geological formations.

Factors other than geology also need examination when attempting interpretation of the whys and whens of Pohnpaid and its partner site in the Kepine area, Takaieu Peak. They begin with confusion derived from its multiple names and dual physical locations and are then complicated by multiple variations of its oral history generated by a series of migrations, each adding their own layer to the legends. And last, the inherent secrecy and sometimes downright trickery of the Pohnpeian culture must be taken into account.

THE MANY NAMES OF POHNPAID

Pohnpaid is the largest petroglyph complex in the northern tropical Pacific region, and as was the case in many sacred places, the Pohnpaid petroglyph site was likely utilized by a variety of migrating groups over a vast expanse of time. Occupations *preceding* Pohnpeian oral histories may provide additional *layers* of material content still unrecorded, although vestiges of these older events could still have survived into legends recounted today. Throughout modern and prehistoric times, Pohnpei has been occupied by identified as well as unknown peoples. To be understood, the site of Pohnpaid, like no other in Micronesia, or in the Pacific, must take any and all of these possibilities into account.

> *The beginning of wisdom is to call things by their right names.*
>
> CHINESE PROVERB

Due partially to the enduring Pohnpeian belief that to tell all you know leads to your death, it is not surprising that both its name Pohnpaid* (aka Pohnpaip, Takai en Intolen, Tilen, Indenlang, Takaien, Takai nin Talang) *and* its oral history have disparate versions. When recited, details of these accounts can be altered slightly and often intentionally, so that no one hears the "whole truth."

Cultural anthropologist Glenn Petersen concludes that these variable name origins are a result of Pohnpeians maintaining intense secrecy especially around the esoteric naming of their sacred landscapes and sea-

---

*The name Pohnpaid will be used exclusively in this publication for all components of the petroglyph locations to avoid confusion, even though certain legends will utilize some of the other names mentioned here. Also, of utmost importance, Pohnpaid is not the same as Pohnpei, the name of the entire island.

scapes, thus protecting the power of place. He has even authored an article specifically on the Pohnpeian virtue of purposeful concealment of the truth, "Kanengaman and Pohnpei's Politics of Concealment." He writes:

Knowledge of the names of hills and rivers and channels remains esoteric and closely shielded today; the confusion inherent in the multiple versions of the origin myths can in part be traced to attempts to safeguard the power that inheres in these names. These names connect the people of modern Pohnpei to the creation. (Petersen 1990)

David Hanlon explains further:

Put another way, markers of the past are all about—overhead, underfoot, on the land, and in the sea. Indeed, the focus of history extends beyond animate beings. On Pohnpei, the reef, forests, mountains, hills, rivers, streams, boulders, and rocks all have histories. (Hanlon 2004)

Confusion over Pohnpaid naming and its oral histories runs rampant. As we've mentioned above but bears repeating here, the name Pohnpaid, pertaining to the site, is very similar to Pohnpei, the name of the entire island. Second, the Pohnpaid site is known by numerous different names, as noted above, some likely due to foreign migrations. And/or third, the site is made up of two components that are separated by physical distance: a terraced outcrop of metamorphic rock and a nearby meadow scattered with enormous metamorphic boulders. Then there is the inherent Pohnpeian cultural secrecy, which can cause minor and major variations not only in the site name but also, more importantly, in its oral histories.

Add to this mix a culture that admires those who can "pull a fast one" by manipulating or tricking someone. This is considered a hallmark of leadership and a trait to be admired with no shame, even today. This is not to disparage Pohnpeians; our Western cultural bias passes this judgment about cleverness versus deception.

A favorite story told to the author by more than one Pohnpeian provides a perfect example.

In the old days a man wanted to buy a particular house and had several conversations with the owner about its cost. Instead of offering the full price, he filled a basket with $1 bills amounting to half the asking price and presented them to the owner. When the owner saw the basket overflowing with the bills, he grabbed it immediately and consummated the deal. He was not cheated; he was outsmarted.

Case in point. Were Pohnpeians trying to "pull a fast one" on archaeologists about a Pohnpaid rock shrine—or just livening up their tales for the tourists? Was obscuring or altering the truth a way for Pohnpeians to claim the power and protect the knowledge of their site from foreigners? Or were they just being pranksters?

Academically published descriptions of a "shrine" located in the middle of the four cupules on the Pohnpaid outcrop could be an example of just that. The reported shrine consisted of small rocks upon which a large, flat basalt stone was placed. Likely recycled from offsite, the flat "sakau stone" would have been used in the sakau making process in which roots were pounded upon it. As documented by the author's photographs, none of these stones were present at the time of her numerous visits to the site beginning in 1970 and continuing intermittently until 1995.

Why modern-day Pohnpeians would enhance this spot with a sakau stone and/or altar is questionable. The vistas from the top might be enhanced by the drinking of sakau, but a descent from the top while intoxicated could be dangerous. This concoction of a pepper plant root and the inner bark of the hibiscus primarily affects motor skills, sometimes paralyzing the extremities, making for a difficult climb down. It would also be inconvenient to get the sakau trees or roots, hibiscus branches, and water to the site. It should be kept in mind that social drinking is a foreign concept when it comes to sakau. The goal is to become *sakaula* (inebriated); otherwise why bother? Anyone who has partaken would agree. Perhaps tour guides embellished Pohnpaid's drama by conjuring visions of the sacred root being pounded and imbibed on the "patterned blanket turned to stone."

There is no historical evidence or oral account that attests to this site being used for sakau in the past. However, this does not preclude some type of ceremony having taken place here in times gone by. On the contrary, it is quite likely that rituals of some sort were observed here. Perhaps they weren't even of Pohnpeian origin, nor necessarily involved with the drinking of sakau. Here we have one more example of the challenge of ascertaining the truth in Pohnpeian mythohistory.

Another overlooked plausibility for Pohnpaid's variety of names and legends is the fact that *currently* the site is, as previously mentioned, physically comprised of *two separate geological components*: the solid basalt outcrop (approximately sixty-five by twenty-seven yards) that slopes down toward the Lehdau River and the boulder field, which is about seventy-seven yards north on a plateau edged by ravines. Enough

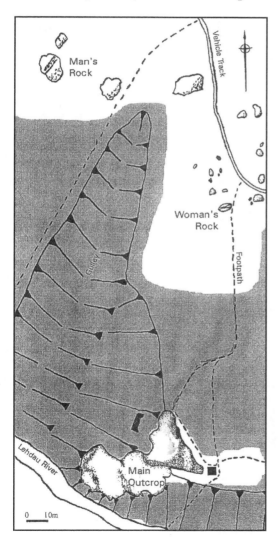

Fig. 2.1. Pohnpaid site plan with Takai en Pahsu (Woman's Rock) and hind end rock (Man's Rock). Image by Paul Rainbird, 1999.

distance separates the two locations to make it quite feasible they could be differentiated by name, historical accounts, or dates of origin.

The first to differentiate between the site's two parts—the *metamorphic outcrop* and the *boulder field*—was Paul Hambruch during his 1910 German Sudsee scientific expedition to Pohnpaid (and in his 1911 publication). His description of the site, "four boulders plus a large field or clearing," was pivotal, as the preponderance of legends *do not* make this distinction. Although the historic preservation office was made aware of the boulder field by this author in 1992, most Pohnpeians, and no archaeologists until 1997, had reported a separate glyphed boulder field. Even then, the *entirety* of Pohnpaid's rock art was not documented. Nor was a probable configuration of stone circle(s) recognized. However, Hambruch states this distinction clearly.

The possibility also exists that both sites are connected by even older megalithic secrets, now buried under the jungle's soil, that bridge the only two segments *known* today.

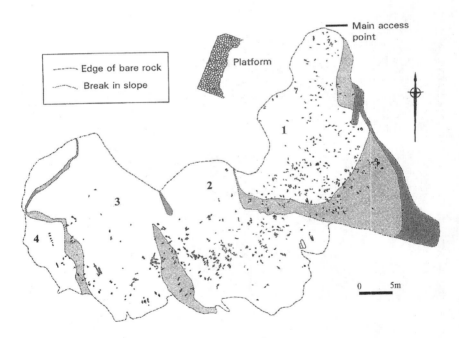

Fig. 2.2. Petroglyph map of the main outcrop at Pohnpaid.
The dots show the location of petroglyphs.
Image by Paul Rainbird, 1999.

Fig. 2.3. Lateral view, outcrop, Pohnpaid.
Photo by Carole Nervig, 1992.

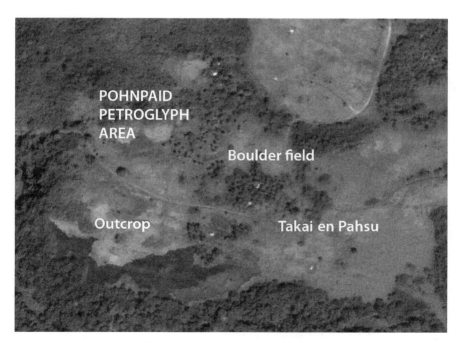

Fig. 2.4. Pohnpaid petroglyph site.
Map by the author using Google Earth.

NOMADIC NAVIGATORS

That Pohnpei has had continual foreign influences is irrefutable. That some are prehistoric is probable. Perhaps they are even earlier or concurrent with material proof of early inhabitation in other parts of Micronesia. Radiocarbon-dated pollen from cultivated taro from the fifth to sixth millennia BCE was found on Belau (Athens and Ward 2001, 172). To include the Pohnpaid site in this time frame is hardly unreasonable as ancient Carolinian navigators, or unidentified predecessors, routinely crisscrossed large expanses of the Pacific.

The following 1882 quote from the *Eureka Daily Sentinel* quite possibly references Pohnpaid, not Nan Madol, as its megaliths "stand among the woods," not on the reef: "Thousands of years before there was a race of people among those islands who built great temples to their unknown gods, carved idols, and hewed the rock into massive shapes . . ."

The ever-helpful Maria Grazia Fanelli Stephens brought my attention to this when she came across the following story, which she posted on Facebook. She explained: "While reading some old newspapers, I came through this article published in The Sentinel, on Nov. 10, 1882. Not sure if a tale or history but for me, it could reinforce the theory that this part of the Pacific was hosting an advanced civilization which expanded all the way to a bigger land to the East (Kataulap)." What follows is the 1882 story from the *Eureka Daily Sentinel* that she posted:

> There are old mysterious building at Ponape, the builders of which belong to a race long since extinct . . . They stand among the woods, like the deserted cities and temples of Central America, a riddle insoluble . . . An old missionary told her how, thousands of years before, there was a race of people among those islands who built great temples to their unknown gods, carved idols, and hewed the rock into massive shapes, and who then passed away into silence and oblivion, leaving a mystery behind them, whose secret no one will ever discover.

These alien influences, whether ancient Pacific gods/goddesses, demigods/demigoddesses, survivors of deluge catastrophes, megalithic master builders, seafaring sun worshippers, or historical Spaniards,

Russians, Germans, and missionaries, complicate oral histories as they may become hybrids with no single identifiable source.

Author and anthropology professor Glenn Petersen notes that Pohnpeian oral histories are quite open to the acceptance of foreign influence, and Paul Rainbird, an archaeologist from the University of Wales, concluded that Pohnpaid "incorporates multiple meanings" and a "variety of origins." Rainbird's 1997 archaeological documentation (and corresponding 1999 publication) of the Pohnpaid site with archaeologist Meredith Wilson of Australia National University is the most extensive to date. They attribute deviant oral histories to "ruptures in community historical consciousness" due to migrations from outsiders. Or perhaps these ruptures are of a more geographic or catastrophic nature, such as the impact from a comet, or floods . . . or merely the passage of time.

Adding to the confusion of site names and migration time lines surrounding Pohnpaid is a plethora of oral historical accounts.

However, in exploring these often conflicting meanings and origins, common themes and symbols do emerge. They range from fertility, vaginas/clams, giants/dwarfs, brothers/twins, and construction events by foreigners to stolen patterned blankets, flying rocks, and people who shape-shift into stones, all of which lend a bit of fire to Pohnpaid's smoke screen.

MORE THAN FERTILITY?

The element of fertility is a predominant theme attached to Pohnpaid to date, largely because of the presence of a petroglyph "mother goddess," a "phallus," and especially "vagina" megaliths.

Whatever the origins, their sexual potency and mwanamwan are carried through to present time in the form of warnings of becoming pregnant just by touching Takai en Pahsu, the "female" stone that sits at the edge of the Pohnpaid meadow. In Pohnpeian language, *pahsu* means "clam," but it is also slang for "vagina." Legends describe the origin of Takai en Pahsu, at Pohnpaid and elsewhere, as the vagina of a mythical woman from the sky who broke into pieces (fig. 2.5, p. 36).

Variations exist regarding the origins of Pohnpaid's Takai en Pahsu, but consensus tells us that a beautiful woman or goddess came from the

Fig. 2.5. Takai en Pahsu "vagina" stone, Pohnpaid.
Photo by Carole Nervig, 1992.

sky, hidden in a rock. On Earth, she came out only at night and fled back into her rock if anyone approached her. Many men desired her. Some versions tell of her being eaten by these men, leaving behind only her vagina (some say buttocks; see plate 24).

A more obscure and grotesque version is that a male giant was angry at a female so he stabbed her in the vagina with a sword and what was left was the vagina stone. This hints at a rather sensational imagination, and perhaps was fabricated and presented to tourists (rather than the oral history) to amuse them.

Curiously, there is not just one Takai en Pahsu on Pohnpei Island; there are *two* others at Pohnpaid alone. A second smaller one very close to the road is literally shaped like a clam, with scallops (plate 19); the third and largest is at least sixteen feet in height and, as such, is more impressive than the other two (plate 16).

Located within Pohnpaid's inner stone circle, the gigantic pahsu megalith is undocumented to date, with the exception of this publication. Due to its anonymity, there are no *specific* legends associated with it, but it is clearly connected to other pahsu accounts. Curiously, it bears precise "technical" markings that don't resemble conventional petroglyphs per se, or any other known glyphs at this site. These inci-

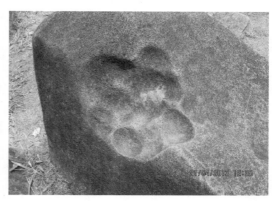

Fig. 2.6. Takai en Pahsu with incisions, part of the inner stone circle. Photo by Carole Nervig, 1992.

Fig. 2.7. Incised rock in Gunung Padang, Indonesia, similar to those etched on Takai en Pahsu, inner stone circle Pohnpaid. Photo by Danny Hilman Natawidjaja, 2013.

sions appear to represent female genitalia and are inscribed in an appropriate position on the enormous stone. While not possible to see in figure 2.6, these chiseled incisions somewhat resemble those found at Gunung Padang (fig. 2.7), the vast megalithic site of columnar basalt in Indonesia that has subterranean layers dating back to 8000–5000 BCE. (Note that both the Nan Madol and Gunung Padang sites consist of columnar basalt, an uncommon material for megalithic structures, making them likely related.)

A fourth Takai en Pahsu is found in remote Lohd Kousapw near the old sawmill, according to *Soulik en Lohd* Joseph Thomas, about ten miles as the crow flies away from the Pohnpaid petroglyph site. Thomas related a similar story line for the Lohd Pahsu, thus linking these locations by their almost identical oral histories. He said:

Long ago a beautiful woman came to Lohd from the sky. All the men wanted her. When they finally caught her, they ate up all of her parts except her vagina, which turned into a stone.

Also in Lohd Pah, but at its shore, is another more obscure legend-ary site also concerned with fertility or birthing. Pahsus (vaginas) are involved but in this case they are more literally interpreted as "clams." Nevertheless, creation is involved.

Thomas explained that the "sea creatures" of ancient Lepinsed (now known as Lohd) were once seashells or clams, called *likapisihno*. When they became abundant on the shores of Lohd, they transformed into humans. The area (near Takai en Mwahng) where they transformed (or shape-shifted) was considered taboo. If anyone entered this place, they would experience bad magic of some sort.

Luelen Bernart elaborates on the likapisihno legend and confirms the island of Air/Eir as the departure point for the first canoe to Pohnpei and the birthing of humans from sea creatures. Other tradi-tional versions with similar themes could be the result of varying inter-pretations relating to clan or location, or could be due to confusion over time. However, migrants from the south are considered the earliest to have arrived on Pohnpei. "The Story of the Creature Clan" legend, according to Bernart (1977), goes like this:

> There is a land that is named Air *(South)*, (aka Eir) from which the first canoe to come to Pohnpei came. There is a lagoon beside the land—which is the Southern Harbour. The lagoon is full of the kind of sea creature called Likapjino [clam]. It was this kind of creature which gave birth to people, and these people were the beginning of the clan Masters of the South. And when the lagoon became full of them and they appeared at the surface of the water they then turned into people. Now these people had no land of their own where they could construct their residence. This is why they went here and there looking about for a place to stay. Their name was Masters of the South, and they are the ones who are multiplying around Ponape at this time.

The likapisihno or "birthing" clamshell legend that connects Lohd Pah and Pohnpaid is not the only link. During the author's 2018 visit to Pohnpaid, she was shocked to find a previously undocumented boulder shaped exactly like a clam (fig. 2.8; plate 19). More exceptional were the "scallop" petroglyphs upon its surface (fig. 2.9) that mimic those of

Fig. 2.8. Author with "clam" boulder.
Photo by Morleen Thomas, 2018.

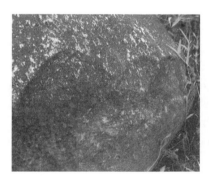

Fig. 2.9. Scallop detail, clam boulder, Pohnpaid.
Photo by Carole Nervig, 2018.

an actual clamshell! An unlikely combination perhaps, but potentially significant, considering the antiquity of both sites. And again, ancient Lepinsed (now Lohd) was, according to Bernart, said to be the landing place for the first canoe, and the Pohnpaid site is so old that none are aware of its existence, or its components.

And who knows how many other such stone vaginas are hiding in the rain forests of Pohnpei?

Fig. 2.10. Many are familiar with the *Birth of Venus* by Sandro Botticelli (painted in the mid-1480s), which depicts the goddess Venus arriving on shore in a shell after her birth.

The prevalence of the Takai en Pahsu stones and stories could be vestiges of a primeval female or goddess era on Pohnpei. Because the Pohnpaid site is older than Nan Madol, its oral histories of the matriarchy or *balanced* goddess/god culture could have been lost over time or with the takeover by the Sahu Deleur dynasty. It would not be the first time history was rewritten by patriarchal conquerors. In the same way, the worship by ancient Pohnpeians of the freshwater eel goddess, Ilake, was replaced by the patriarchy with its worship of the aggressive saltwater eel, Nan Somohl.

An exceedingly less conventional possibility would be that Pohnpaid's function was as an ancient breeding ground between extraterrestrials and humans. All versions are consistent that the woman/goddess in the pahsu legends *came from the sky,* with her vagina playing a significant role in the scenarios.

Other Pacific Islanders refer to their ancestry from the stars, or the Mu Motherland, or even a combination of the two according to personal communication from Maori women. So why not Pohnpaid? Such antiquity might also explain why there are no other legends about the Pohnpaid meadow of megaliths; it's just that old.

A similar case might be considered based on a Dogon alien "fish god" symbol. Perhaps it traveled from Motherland Mu outward to return later, or perhaps a *similar experience* on the far side of the world created a similar symbol.

FISH—OR AQUATIC HUMANS?

Two so-called fish petroglyphs are found upon Pohnpaid's phallic monolith. Fish they may well be, but literal or symbolic? Considering Pohnpaid's dominant themes of fertility, creation, and beings from the skies, were these motifs merely symbolizing fishing?

Pohnpei oral traditions describe ancient beings that inhabited the sea. Some of these "sea creatures" sprouted from clams or sea cucumbers, and others were half fish, half human, literally. Although referring to distant neighboring Yap, historian Luelen Bernart (1977) differentiates three locations for Yap Island: one beyond or of the horizon; one in the sky; and one under the sea, where "inhabitants are like fish, one end human and one end fish."

Pohnpeian Bernart's description fits the legendary Nommo, amphibious extraterrestrial(s) from Sirius and progenitor(s) of the African Dogon tribe; Matsaya, an avatar of Vishnu that saved humanity after the Deluge;

Fig. 2.11. Fish or turtle petroglyphs on the phallic rock, Pohnpaid.
Photos by Alexandra Edwards, 2017.

and Oannes/Dagon, the amphibious alien Babylonian god. If amphibious gods inhabited Africa, India, and Yap, then why not Pohnpei? Further, dismissal of fish-shaped petroglyphs as merely references to fish or fishing shrines is common, especially in Pacific cultures. Although valid in many cases, a site such as Pohnpaid with its myriad sacred and profound symbols requires a deeper look into their possible meanings. The fish glyphs recall the Dogon symbol for their amphibious creator god Nommo, who is always depicted *vertically* rather than in a horizontal swimming position, just as at Pohnpaid. This comparison may be a stretch, but the first beings to inhabit Pohnpei Island were perhaps amphibious, half human and half fish, as were the Dogon amphibious gods.

Yet how does this all relate to the simple fish petroglyph at Pohnpaid?

Besides the more literal images of the amphibious Oannes/Dagon at left, the Dogon tribe used a stylized graphic to symbolize the Nommo, their amphibious deity(s). An intriguing aspect of the Dogon was their detailed knowledge of the binary Sirian star system, only recently confirmed by astronomers, demonstrating their scientific sophistication and accuracy.

The Dogon explain that the oldest inhabitants of Earth were amphibious "sea creatures." As related previously, Pohnpeian oral tradition also refers to "sea creatures" giving birth to people of the first clan.

On the more scientific side, the evolution of humans from the ocean was first proposed in 1960 by marine zoologist Alister Hardy, explains Elaine Morgan in *New Scientist* (2002), followed by Desmond Morris in *The Naked Ape* (1967), Elaine Morgan in *Descent of Woman* (1972) and *The Aquatic Ape* (1982), and naturalist David Attenborough on BBC Radio (2016). Since the date of Morgan's last book, *The Naked Darwinist* (2008), the theory keeps floating. Krill (2017) reminds his readers:

> Textbooks on human evolution have been either ignoring or ridiculing the aquatic ape theory for the past 50 years. Nevertheless, it might be valid. We should not forget that textbooks on geology ignored or ridiculed the theory of continental drift for about 50 years, before it suddenly became part of the new paradigm of plate tectonics.

Fig. 2.12. A carving of Oannes or Dagon, the amphibious Babylonian god.
Public domain image courtesy of Zorger.

Fig. 2.13. Vishnu as Matsaya, a fish avatar, savior of humanity after the Deluge.
Image from an unknown artist, thought to be circa 1820.

Fig. 2.14. Nommo: amphibious extraterrestrial progenitors of the Dogon in Africa.
Illustration by Marcel Griaule and Germaine Dieterlen, as shown in Temple 1998.

Fig. 2.15. Evolution of humans.
Image by Allan Krill, 2017.

This is considered fringe theory by mainstream academia, whose protests seem to be more reactive than responsible. Did aquatic beings arrive from the stars as such, or did they evolve over time, or neither? Answers may lie in a combination of Darwinism, Aquatic Man theories, and indigenous mythologies. Unless science takes these seriously, we may never know. As Krill (2017) says:

> Paleoanthropologists should not let their orthodox beliefs keep a scientific theory of human evolution from becoming generally known and properly tested.

The widespread and consistent amphibian accounts could be considered as evidence of a global Motherland, sharing origins and archetypes. Are we to believe the consistent and specific accounts of ancient "savages"—their nymphs, mermaids and mermen, sirens, and aquatic gods—or dismiss these accounts as being mere myth?

The fish petroglyphs and their potential links to original creation, birthing, and aquatic aliens are subtle and obscure proof of Pohnpaid as a fertility site; certain male body parts turned into stone are not as subtle.

PHALLIC PRESENCE AT POHNPAID

Recall that Pohnpaid meadow also lays claim to what strikingly resembles a monolithic penis (fig. 1.4, p. 12). Despite the fact that this phallic stone is totally covered with impressive petroglyphs, no specific oral histories about it exist, nor does it have a name. If it were not so old, and because it is so impressive, surely the ribald Pohnpeians would remember its legends or at least give it an official name, as with the female counterpart Takai en Pahsu.

Due to the male rock's location near Takai en Pahsu, the "vagina" stone(s), it might be deduced that a legendary male suffered the same fate as the females.

Some oral traditions, although vague, claim that a magician punished the group of both men and women who created Pohnpaid by turning their parts to stone. The magician remains unnamed and the deed of the men and women unknown.

That said, specific oral histories do refer to the ancient magician Lapoange, who, as mentioned earlier, dug the Lehdau River channel "with his penis," making it only as far as Pohnpaid. There is no

Fig. 2.16. Detail of the phallic monolith, Pohnpaid.
Photo by Carole Nervig, 1992.

legendary recollection of him leaving his mighty genital behind, or that it had turned to stone. The only reference to Lapoange's demise was that his rivals, the boys *Mu*anlap and *Mu*antik (aka Mwohn*mwu*r and Sarapwahu, or Moni*mu*r and Jarapuau),* who created the outcrop petroglyphs, took his magic from him. There was no mention of his male parts, only Lapoange shape-shifting his entire body into stone. There are no cultural indications as to the identity or location of which stone was originally Lapoange. One account recalls:

> And the boys then threw stones on the man as well, and really made him sink, but he came up again at certain places and turned into stone himself, for he no longer had any magic, for the boys took his power from him. The end. (Bernart 1977)

In his 1891 book *The Caroline Islands*, historian F. W. Christian suggests a possible identity or origin of the name Lapoange.

> The name Laponga recalls the Lampongs, a tribe of Sumatra, distinguished among its less civilized neighbours by the possession of *Untang-untang*, or hieroglyphic records of ancient law (Cf. Ponapean *Inting* to write). This fact may have spread the use of the word *Lampong* as a generic term for wizard in these parts of the Malayan area. (Christian 1967)

Christian provides not only a possible origin of the lineages of Lapoange, but a linguistic tie to two variations of the many place-names of the Pohnpaid petroglyph site, Inting en Takai (meaning "writing on rocks") and Indenlang (meaning "writing"), and more importantly, a hint to their possible significance and meaning as "hieroglyphic records of ancient law"!

Presently this "male" boulder is found lying in a horizontal position, but it could have once stood vertically. If originally vertically upright, its

---

*As mentioned in the introduction to this book, the frequent use of *Mu* and *Mwu* as a prefix or syllable of names in Pohnpeian as well as other Oceanic and Pacific Rim languages is a legacy from the submerged continent and civilization of Mu. Again, I have italicized these syllables in the first mention of the associated word to help them stand out in the text.

shape would not necessarily have had a sexual context. However, considering this phallic monolith is located in the midst of what is considered by many to be a fertility site, it is highly probable that it did. Until its surroundings are inspected, its initial position remains undetermined, along with any hidden petroglyphs on its underside.

AN ARTICULATION OF TECHNOLOGY

The size and character of these Pohnpaid megaliths seem out of scale with *conventional* human fertility artifacts. More fitting functions include extraterrestrial "birthing" into the Earth's dimensions from a far distant past; genetic engineering; a strategic outpost of Kahnih*mu*eiso (sometimes spelled *Kahnihmweiso* outside of this book), the underwater city off Nan Madol; or a megalithic marking of a geodesic grid "navel" . . . rather than for just crops or human fecundity. Subsequent Pohnpeian culture(s) would be limited in articulating such sophisticated phenomena; such legends are their attempt. Perhaps the thread of fertility was a way to simplify its once complex function(s) of creation at Pohnpaid.

ALWAYS THE BROTHERS; SOMETIMES TWINS

In 1983, archaeologist Takeshi Ueki of Brown University and Madison Nena, former Trust Territory of the Pacific Islands historic preservation officer, recorded the *only* oral history of Pohnpaid that ascribes the builders of Nan Madol—the giants Ohlsipha and Ohlsopha—to creation of the Pohnpaid site. Of the many oral histories taken by various individuals, Ueki and Nena's is the sole account to mention them. That and the fact that it is quite recently recorded casts doubt on the identification of Ohlsipha and Ohlsopha as the specific brothers responsible for the petroglyph site. In addition, it is the *only* version out of many in which Nan Madol is mentioned specifically in connection with the rock art site. Ueki and Nena (1983) state:

> Olsipha and Olsopha, the builders of Nan Madol, stole a blanket from Kiti Municipality and carried it to the petroglyph location where it turned to stone, decorations and all.

Brothers, indeed; builders, no.

According to oral histories, brothers Muanlap and Muantik (aka Mwohnmwur and Arapahos, or Monimur and Jarapuau), the "magically potent" sons of Lienlama, "a woman before the canoe came from downwind Katau," were responsible for making the Pohnpaid petroglyphs from a "blanket" stolen from Kitti. Some accounts mention a woman inside the blanket. Olsipha and Olsopha, arriving on Pohnpei later, completed Nan Madol *after* the magicians Laopango and Muanlap and Muantik created noteworthy landforms in the vicinity (Pohnpaid, Takaieu, and Lehdau Channel). Certain accounts state that these same brothers paddled a piece of stone, like a canoe, to Pohndolen Imwinsapw near what is now Tahio, adjacent to Takaieu Peak.

The brothers' "house" at Pohnpaid sounds more like a megalithic site than a conventional thatched structure. Its "doorway" was an unconventional one in which they "disappeared" to "travel"—in other words, an interdimensional portal or tunnel.

> Takai en Intolen (stone with writing) consisted of four boulders plus a large field or clearing. The "house" at the site belonged to Muantik and Muanlap [small Mu man, big Mu man]. They decided to venture to foreign lands and closed the door on the rock/house and were not seen again. (Hambruch 1910)

Many sacred sites around the world are considered "portals" to other worlds and/or other dimensions. That they "closed the door" of the magical entrance/exit of the site hints of such an interpretation. Pohnpeian lore recounts that knocking with small stones on the outcrop where the door is located produces a hollow resonating sound, as if a cavity exists beneath its surface.

The *Pohnpei Ecotourism Travel Guide* also credits two brothers for Pohnpaid's creation, but with different names, Mwohnmwur and Sarapwahu, from Kitti:

> Their [Mwohnmwur and Sarapwahu] mischief began to escalate gradually until one night (when) they stole a bed sheet that one of the villages had prepared as a gift for the chief. But they soon found

out that the bed sheet was too large to hide in their house. After discussing what to do, they rushed into the jungle to the East, bringing the sheet with them. There they found Madolenihmw, a village rumored to be haunted with ghosts that no one dared to approach. No one will find it if we hide it here, they thought.

Meanwhile, just outside the village of Madolenihmw, a ghost named Lapango [Lapoange] was roaming around. As Lapango [Lapoange] was walking, he suddenly spotted a big stone and remembered the ancient legend about a chief who turned his wife into this very stone as punishment for her adultery. Lapango [Lapoange] was suddenly tempted to change something into a stone using magic too. So Lapango [Lapoange] changed some fermented breadfruit into a stone using his magic. He was so delighted with this that he turned a pandanus nut into a stone as well. Lapango [Lapoange] was even more pleased and wanted to change much bigger things into stone.

While thinking he bumped into some unfamiliar thing covering all the plants. It was the very sheet Mwohnmwur and Sarapwahu had stolen and hidden there. Lapango [Lapoange] decided this was perfect, so he chanted an incantation and turned the sheet in to a huge rock mountain. Today this mountain is named Pohnpaip.

Other oral reports during fieldwork by Rainbird include:

A late middle-aged man said his father told him they had been made by "oriental" people. A neighboring landowner explained that his father had told him that the site was a place of "ghosts" and that boulders in the vicinity were the remains of people who had turned to stone. (Rainbird 2002b)

Several accounts insist that the creators of Pohnpaid's inscribed landscape were foreigners:

While the creators of these petroglyphs are unknown, it is believed that they were carved long ago by visitors from another land. (Official Federated States of Micronesia website)

David Hanlon (1988) recounts:

Masao Hadley in his interview with me on June 21, 1983, at Meshihso in Madolenihmw described the two as boys who reached the island from foreign shores, drew pictures of the people and things they had witnessed during their travels, and eventually departed Pohnpei to resume their journeys.*

Emensio Eperiam, former Pohnpei historic preservation officer and oral history coordinator (who was first shown the Pohnpaid site by the author), began investigating the site and its hundreds of petroglyphs after his initial visit of 1992. He reported that elders said, "Indians [meaning people from India] were responsible."

The preponderant appearance of two brothers, some say twins, in not only Pohnpaid's past but that of all of Pohnpei Island, suggests the possibility of reference to the constellation Gemini, the Twins. Ancient cultural navigation, with its focus on astronomy, was essential for Micronesians to travel the vast Pacific. Their intimate knowledge of the stars and their movements, matching if not excelling that of other cultures of antiquity, could easily have been included or adapted to these legends. Examples abound worldwide of myths interchanging the gods with stars and/or giving human identities to celestial bodies.

At the very least, the "flying" and "sky" aspects should turn our heads to the heavens so that we may better understand this site.

MAGIC BLANKETS AND MAPS

Given that the flying blanket or sheet theme is one of the more consistently attached to the inscribed landscape of Pohnpaid, it is worth exploring its symbolism, which is both supernatural and possibly extraterrestrial, including creating sacred space.

A magic carpet or flying carpet is defined as a legendary carpet that can be used to transport persons instantaneously or quickly to

---

*The author was given similar information by Pohnpeian historian and knowledge keeper Hadley during her series of interviews with him about Pohnpei's oral histories in 1970 but only recorded those legends relevant to Nan Madol.

their destination. According to *Brewer's Dictionary of Phrase and Fable:*

> Whoever sitteth on this carpet and willeth in thought to be taken up and set down upon another site will, in the twinkling of an eye, be borne thither, be that place near hand or distant many a day's journey and difficult to reach.

The literary traditions of several other cultures also feature magical carpets. In most cases they fly or levitate rather than instantly transport their passengers from place to place. This again reinforces the possible "portal" connection with Pohnpaid.

Given that magic carpets can be seen as symbolic for teleportation, interdimensional and extraterrestrial travel is consistent with other ritual phenomena often linked with sacred sites, and portals or stargates. The legendary reference to "closing the door on the stone house" to "continue their travels" appears to reinforce the inter- or multi-dimensional aspect of this location. If extraterrestrial travel is occurring, the carpet could then refer to an actual rectangular craft or similar mechanism.

Portals, closing doors on stone houses, and distant travels could also refer to shamanic journeying in which the shaman "travels" in an altered state to other dimensions in order to retrieve information or for healing. Interpretation of rock art based on shamanism, San ethnography of South Africa, and the neuropsychological basis of altered states of consciousness has been successfully claimed by Jamie Hampson (2016), who followed David Lewis-Williams's approach. Such perspectives should not be overlooked at Pohnpaid.

Because many of the Pohnpaid glyph motifs are also found in the Americas, this site and its legends could be related to Native American practices or universal shamanic journeying experiences such as the following:

> The rocks where shamans depicted their visions were considered a portal into the spirit realm. Some Native American peoples speak of seeing a portal opening before them in the rock; at other times, they see only rocks. Entry into the spirit world may be spoken of

as going underwater. Once inside the rock, the California shaman passed through a tunnel, guarded by dangerous animals, an equivalent of the vortex. After being instructed in a "large house" filled with "wealth," the Initiate emerges some distance from where he entered the earth; he is now accompanied by his newly acquired animal-helper. He then begins to heal people. (Whitley 2000)

A flat blanket with patterns might also be a "map" of its creator's travels, portraying incidents of seafaring or multidimensional or stellar destinations or experiences. Directions, alignments, locations, or celestial phenomena could be indicated as well as historical documentation of a "plan" or "route." The word *sheet* is often interchanged with *blanket* in these legends, with the former more conducive for conjuring an image of a paper map with writing rather than decorations of a blanket, especially for those unfamiliar with seeing paper. Take these examples from Wilfred Buck, an Opaskwayak Cree:

Star woman came down from that hole in the sky and she brought with her *the original star blanket*. The original star blanket had seven points on it to represent the seven stars right here—the Pleiades, the Seven Sisters. This is where they say human beings originated from. (emphasis added)

The Cree in what is now Canada refer to the Pleiades as *Atchakos Ahkoop*, the Star Blanket, which was given to the people by *Atchakos Iskwew*, Star Woman. The seven points of the star blanket were symbolic of *Pakone Kiisic*, the Hole-in-the-Sky. In Cree legend, *Atchakos Iskwew* was a being of energy and spirit called Atchakos Iskwew who was able to traveled [*sic*] through realities. Wilfred Buck describes the "Hole-in-the-Sky" as a wormhole, allowing spirits to travel. (See Volker, n.d.)

As mentioned previously, certain versions of the Pohnpeian "stolen blanket" legend note that a woman was inside this stolen blanket. This is one more possible link to the Pleiades, star women, or spiders—and the female energy connected with weaving the geomagnetic resonance grid of the planet. Weaving imagery could represent this concept at the

Fig. 2.17. Paddle/weaving peg, Pohnpaid outcrop. Similar pegs used for weaving are known in the Caroline Islands of the Pacific.
Photo by Carole Nervig, 1970.

Pohnpaid outcrop *if* these petroglyphs are actually meant to be literal weaving pegs (fig. 2.17) such as those used in the Caroline Islands of the Pacific.

Also worth consideration is the "blanket" as representation of a grid system of the planet, galaxy, or cosmos rather than a conventional map. If viewed or conceptualized in a flat plane or folded or collapsed as a blanket might be, these grid lines or energetic filaments might take on the visual properties of a blanket/sheet. Not only does one of the Pohnpei global grid lines run through the Pohnpaid site, but Pohnpei Island itself is a major node or "navel" on the planetary Earth grid, if not the galactic and cosmic grids. "Throwing a blanket down," as recounted in the Pohnpaid legends, might allow a line(s) to be established, thus supporting travel to and from, upon that line(s).

Turning a blanket/grid into petroglyphs could be a way of explaining in prehistoric terms and of preserving a map in stone for future

Fig. 2.18. Grid detail on the phallic monolith at the boulder field, Pohnpaid;
it may represent a blanket of the cosmos.
Photo by Carole Nervig, 1992.

generations (fig. 2.18)—*a map of where its creators came from; a map of where they were going.*

SOUNDSCAPES

Sound vibration is another element associated with consciousness-raising, ritual, sacred space, planetary energy grids, and portals. Resonance affects consciousness, alters brain waves, and is an inherent component in ceremony and "earth acupuncture" worldwide. Advanced knowledge of acoustical science is demonstrated in megalithic sites such as Malta, Newgrange, Baalbek, and Chavin de Huantar in Peru, to name only a few. Sims (2013) states that "acoustic phenomena has long been linked to the production and distribution of rock art."

And whenever gigantic megaliths are involved, the possibility of levitation of the stones by acoustics and/or magnetics is always present. Construction of nearby Nan Madol is no exception.

Archaeoacoustics is the use of acoustical study within the wider scientific field of archaeology. This includes the study of the acoustics at archaeological sites, and the study of acoustics in archaeological artifacts. Over the last forty years it has become increasingly obvious that studying the sonic nature of certain areas of archaeology can help us understand ancient cultures. Archaeoacoustics is an inter-disciplinary field, it includes various fields of research including: archaeology, ethnomusicology, acoustics and digital modeling. (Evans 2017)

Children living near the Pohnpaid outcrop are always happy to demonstrate the varying tones created by banging its surface with rocks. This resonant spot, which may indicate a cavity underneath, lies at the legendary "door of the house" that Muantik and Muanlap entered/closed prior to their final departure to foreign lands.

Rainbird (2002a) argues that much of the social significance of such places, which he termed *soundscapes,* might lie in the "noise of their manufacture" and particularly through transmitted "high frequency" rhythmic sounds.

Pohnpeian culture is no exception when it comes to sound, as their primary ceremony even today incorporates rhythmic pounding of reso-nant basalt during sakau preparation. This hypnotic pounding can be heard at great distances, serving as a communication tool announcing its preparation as well as creating a trancelike state of mind for those about to consume this slightly narcotic drink.

Although there is no hard evidence per se that sakau was made on top of the outcrop, considerable sound would have been produced in just creating the petroglyphs themselves, also producing an altered state in their artist. Reviewing the work of Hampson, Russell (2019) comments:

The process of making rock art was just as important, if not more so, than the product itself. He [Hampson] also considers carefully the inter-actions of the artists with the rock face and reflects on con-cepts of somatic transformation and embodiment theory to explain why rock art was produced.

Of more significance in the consideration of sound waves at Pohnpaid is that sound, as well as information, was embedded into petroglyphs as they were created by Lemurian cultural legacies. The

Mu and their descendants *touched and felt the petroglyph vibrations and listened to stories recorded into their motifs.*

An example of how *cymatic* or acoustic information stored within select petroglyphs might have been accessed in the past, not only for communication purposes, but also to create and/or teach language, is demonstrated in the following "channeled" text. Although fictional, the following account may embrace more than just a particle of truth. Utilization of similar acoustical elements may well be the case with certain Egyptian hieroglyphs, or at the least at the time of their creation. Perhaps it is time to test petroglyphs for such acoustic possibilities, especially those of a more symbolic rather than pictorial nature.

> It didn't take her long. She spied the wiggly symbol [glyph] beneath the bird [rock art drawing] first, and impulsively fingered it. The sound translation zinged through her fingertips—weak as yet, Sumpter could tell, but she was getting it. It took her only a few seconds to connect the sounds she was getting from the symbol, with the drawing of the bird above.
>
> It would be a while before he could explain that the symbols were embossed with sound—not the drawings themselves, as in the earlier ones she'd seen, because if all the paintings identified themselves audibly, then there would be no built-in reason for pupils to learn the written characters. (Roberts 1995)

Regardless of how sound was actually created, utilized, or experienced at Pohnpaid, it is only one of many components identifying it as a sacred site or other dimensional portal.

ARAMAS LAPALAP, ARAMAS TIKITIK, AND THE MU

Pacific lore has often linked giants and diminutive supernatural beings with sacred sites, megaliths, stonework, and interdimensional portals. Pohnpei is no exception.

Suffixes of *tik* and *lap* refer to "large" and "small" in Pohnpeian language. References to Muantik and Muanlap (Mwahntik and Mwahnlap, Semen Pwei Tikitik and Semen Pwei Lapalap, etc.) corroborate other Pohnpeian oral histories that include giants and pygmies. The *aramas tikitik* (little people) who presently inhabit the nearby Takaieu Peak area provide more compelling evidence of truth in these legends.

Historian F. W. Christian details a "cemetery" for the *sokolei,* aramas tikitik, or *kichin aramas,* the "dwarf negritos . . . dark of skin and flat nose," shown to him by oral historian Litak en Na (Joe Kehoe) on a ridge behind Nan Tamworohi (Ta*mu*eu). Buried in vaults a mere four feet in length, these deceased little people originally "dwelt in the land before the coming of the Liat (cannibals) and Kona (giants)" (Christian 1967). He elaborates:

> We suddenly came upon a low breastwork of stones enclosing the object of our search, which turned out to be a cemetery in the shape of an irregular or broken parallelogram, as can be seen from the sketch plan. Six graves were found in the lower enclosure and three on a platform raised five feet above the level of the ground. All were little vaults not exceeding four or four and a half feet in length— roofed in with massive slabs of basalt—the graves of the Chokalai, Kichin-Aramach or Little Folk, woodland elves, answering to

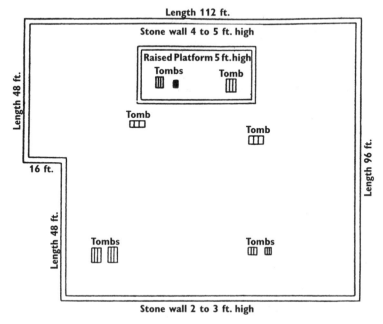

Fig. 2.19. Graves of the Chokalai, "little people," Madolenihmw, Pohnpei.
Illustration from Christian 1967.

our own pucks and pixies, to the Trolds, Cobolds, and Dwarfs of the Teutonic peoples, and to the Patupaiarehe of the Maoris. Ethnologists would style them dwarf Negritos. These, according to Ponapean tradition, were the little dwarfish folk who dwelt in the land before the coming of the Kona and Li-ot, the giants and the cannibals. (Christian 1967)

Albert Helgenberger, a Madolenihmw schoolteacher, gave the following explanation to Rainbird and Wilson. It connects the *same* mythical brothers and the *same* magician (this time as a giant) responsible for the petroglyphs, the river "channel," and the creation of Takaieu, the mountain component of the Pohnpaid alignment complex.

At the same time as people were being turned to stone, a mythical character name Lapone [Lapoange] lived in the area. Lapone was able to change his form and in a competition with two boys became a giant. The contest was for Lapone to dig a channel from one side of the island to the other before the boys could build a mountain to the clouds. Using his penis to dig the channel, Lapone only made it as far as the petroglyph outcrop before the two boys, using magic rather than brute force, had completed their task. The present Lehdau River flows in the channel created by Lapone. (Rainbird and Wilson 1999)

Lapoange, the magician who was often a part of the same "two boys stealing a blanket" legend, was able to shape-shift himself into a giant. Using his magic, he turned their inscribed blanket into the petroglyphs. Lapoange was also connected to Takaieu, the pyramid-shaped mountain near the Pohnpaid petroglyph site, via the following oral tradition in which he breaks the "mountain to the clouds" into the peak of Takaieu.

Lopango [Lapoange], Weni and Wena [Muantik and Muanlap] had a competition (or contract). Lopango was to dig a canal; Weni and Wena were to build a mountain. When Lopango's canal was halfway finished, he turned back to see the boys. He saw the mountain had already reached the sky. He became angry, and he picked up a flat piece of stone and threw it at the mountain. The mountain broke into pieces. The peak of it fell down and made the tall peak known as Takaiuh, the standing rock. These men then became enemies. At last the two men killed Lopango, the loser. (Blackburn 1967)

So that explains the connection to giants, but what about the little people? Perhaps the little people, referred to with the suffix *tik,* were the descendants of mischievous dwarfs. Historian David Hanlon explains that these dwarfs were identified by the Pohnpeian named Silten as *Sokele,* one of four groups of nonhuman or subhumans who came from "under the earth" to inhabit Pohnpei. Silten (n.d.) stated, "The Sokele were (or are—some suggest they still live on Pohnpei) mischievous dwarves."

Since the 2004 discovery of a new hominoid, *Homo floresiensis,* on Flores Island in Indonesia, the existence of three-foot-tall pygmies in Oceania can no longer be refuted. Updates made in 2017 by Australian National University's Debbie Argue and her team found that *Homo floresiensis* evolved before *Homo erectus* (the first hominoid to grow tall) from one of the earliest species of humans 1.7 million years ago. In the *Journal of Human Evolution,* Argue estimated that they arrived on Flores Island almost two million years ago and survived until about thirteen thousand years ago before they became extinct. Or did they?

Sightings continue of these *orang pendek* (short fellows) in Indonesia and Malaysia to the present day. According to the *Telegraph,* a British expedition spotted an *orang pendek* in Sumatra in 2009. During the 1900s when Vanuatu was known as New Hebrides, sizable pygmy tribes were reported throughout northeastern Santo.

Less well known and smaller than the Flores individuals, but sharing some of their features, were the human skeletal remains of at least twenty-five miniature *Homo sapiens* who lived circa fourteen hundred to three thousand years ago. These remains were found on Chelechol ra Orrak in the rock islands of Belau, Micronesia, by Lee Berger of the University of Witwatersrand, South Africa, in 2008. Although the researchers are uncertain how tall the islanders were, they believe a fully grown male would have weighed around forty-three kilograms (ninety-five pounds) and a female just twenty-seven kilograms (sixty pounds). Because they were found piled together in Ucheliungs Cave and Omedokel Cave and dated to a historical time of rising seas, it was initially surmised by some that they were drowned together while trying to

Fig. 2.20. Lovoni *bête* (priests), Ovalau, Fiji. Photo from the 1800s from the Fiji Museum.

survive the rising waters. Contrary to this notion, it is commonplace for Hawaiians and other Pacific Islanders to bury their dead in caves and lava tubes. This could also be the case for these Belauan caves. Rising sea levels or hiding in caves for any other reason is irrelevant to explanations of these burials being found in caves. Burials are still burials and small bones are small bones. This new evidence of "little people" brings their reality even closer to Pohnpei than other examples.

One characteristic that ties the little people of Oceania together is their connection to stone construction. The Hawaiian Menehunes were famous for creating unbelievable amounts of work after dark, finishing lengthy stone walls or massive structures in just one night. Similarly, the "Pohnpei little people" were linked with megalithic stone sites and the "Takaieu little people" with the stones from the sky and the pyramid monolithic marker of Takaieu.

BIG MEN, SMALL MEN IN OTHER CULTURES OF THE WORLD

Tribes of very short people or pygmies are found elsewhere in Oceania: in Vanuatu, New Guinea, the Philippines, the Solomon Islands, and

Australia, as well as around the world in Bolivia, Brazil, Africa, and Southeast Asia.

New Guinea and New Britain mythohistories have their versions of the "big man/small man" as well: Kulabob, the big man and technologically advanced navigator, and Manup, the small. Manup is a dark and short, stocky figure, which Stephen Oppenheimer in his book *Eden in the East* relates to populations of native Negrito pygmies of Southeast Asia.

Japan is not without its own accounts of little people, and it is open to considering current alternative history theories that indicate the existence of Mu and inhabitants of a now submerged continent in the Pacific. Among Japanese legend are the Koropokkuru, a race of little people that lived in Japan *before* the Ainu arrived. The Ainu describe the Koropokkuru dwarfs or pygmies as short, agile, and skilled at fishing. In 1879, Edwin S. Morse published his finds in *Traces of an Early Race in Japan,* establishing the shell heap mound, or Kjoekkenmoedding, in Omori, near Tokyo, as being the home of an "unknown neolithic race that predated the Ainu."

The Ainu are believed to have descended from the Jōmon-jin people, who lived in Japan from the Jōmon period from circa 14,000–300 BCE. According to *The Return of the Ainu,* "One of their Yukar Upopo, or legends, tells 'The Ainu lived in this place a hundred thousand years before the Children of the Sun came'" (Sjöberg 1993). In appearance, the diminutive people of Pacific lore vary from smooth-skinned to hairy; from dark-skinned to light-skinned to red-skinned; from two feet

Fig. 2.21. Koropokkuru sculptures at the Hokkaido Museum of Northern Japan. Photo by Carole Nervig, 2018.

to four feet tall. The accounts even include some redheads. All such descriptions suggest a diverse stock of these pygmy groups of Oceania.

Further evidence of big and small men is shown in footprint petroglyphs around the world. A *petrosomatoglyph* is an image of human or animal body parts in rock. They occur all over the world, often functioning as an important form of symbolism used in religious and secular ceremonies. Some are regarded as artifacts linked to gods or cultural heroes. Images of footprints were a way of claiming space, akin to an "I was here" sign, and sometimes were executed to mark the spot of a visitation by a "god."

Recall that Muantik and Muanlap (Mwahntik or small Mu man and Mwahnlap or big Mu man) are cited as creators of the petroglyphs, or at least of throwing the "blanket" down on the ground. The foot-like petrosomatoglyph at the Pohnpaid outcrop is much smaller than the average Pohnpeian foot size. This is significant because Pohnpeians are of relatively small stature compared to Caucasians. This depiction could be symbolic, or literal if belonging to one of the aramas tikitik. Could the footprint belong to Muantik or Muanlap? (Muantik is more likely due to his smaller size, but who knows how small either of their feet were.)

Footprint motifs considered similar to those of Pohnpaid can be found elsewhere in Micronesia, specifically on Tarawa Atoll, Kiribas. However, the Kiribas prints are literally gigantic while the Pohnpei ones are much smaller than adult size. The Kiribas prints are discussed by Rainbird (2004):

> The engravings reported by I. G. Turbott, 1949, consist mostly of footprints pecked out of the rock. The old men had told him that

Fig. 2.22. Footprint on the outcrop, Pohnpaid.
Photo by Carole Nervig, 1970.

they were places where giants, their names remembered for the most part in oral history, had stood during various "historic" events. Indeed that these are footprints of giants is certainly consistent with their size: the largest has twelve toes and measures 1.35m (about 4.5 feet) in length. It is said to be the right foot of Tabuariki, an ancestral giant commonly mentioned in stories.

David Hanlon's *Upon a Stone Altar* recounts another big man/small man phenomenon originating from a different but nearby and quite significant locale, Mal Island. On the southwestern perimeter of Greater Nan Madol, Mal Island is the home of the mythical figures Semen Pwei Tikitik and Semen Pwei Lapalap. These brothers traveled far and wide acquiring much worldly knowledge. Only Semen Pwei Tikitik survived their journeys, and he returned to kill one of the oppressive Sahu Deleur rulers of Nan Madol.

According to an earlier cycle of myths told to Glenn Petersen by Ioakim David of Uh, the Pali seafarers from Ulithi Atoll of Yap were the earliest people to inhabit Mal Island. They not only predated the Sahu Deleur builders of Nan Madol but also were prehistoric navigators, astronomers, and master planners who first laid down its master plan aligned from this same island of Mal.

So now we have the big/small man theme interwoven with advanced technology from foreign exposure and Mal Island, whose inhabitants, *if predating Nan Madol,* could be one and the same as the Pohnpaid petroglyph creators. In this scenario, Semen Pwei Tikitik and Semen Pwei Lapalap would be their descendants who maintained the giant/pygmy lineage in their names.

More credibility is given to the mythic "big man/small man" concept by an explosion of documentation worldwide, and specifically from Oceania.

Legends of giants are abundant on all Pacific islands. Material evidence is also documented, for example:

• During World War II, shinbones over three feet long were unearthed at a coastal watch tower construction site on Rotuma, Fiji.
• Japanese archaeologists found a three-and-a-half-meter-long grave on the atoll of Nukulaelae on the nation of Tuvalu, which villagers said was of a giant.

- According to Martin Doutré, author of *Ancient Celtic New Zealand,* when pre-Polynesian Lapita skeletons were found, just like the pre-Maori skeletons that were once abundant in New Zealand burial caves or sand dunes, examination and forensic tests were prohibited. Similarly, in 2002 when a complete, six-foot-six-inch Lapita skeleton was found alongside Lapita pottery on the Fijian island of Lomaiviti, this was the *politically correct* result: "Patrick Nunn, the supervisor of the archaeological team analyzing the remains at University of the South Pacific would not comment. [He said,] 'We have decided to keep our find under wraps'" (according to *News24,* South Africa, on July 14, 2002).
- According to a local New Zealand newspaper, an eight-meter-tall skeleton was found in 1875 seven feet below the surface at Saltwater Creek spit, Timaru, New Zealand.
- The Dutchman Jacob Roggeveen reached Rapa Nui (Easter Island) in 1722 and found living giants. Bahrens, one of his men, recorded giants of such stature that seamen could stand upright between their legs.
- Hawaiian genealogist Delthia Mahiai claimed skeletons were recovered from a cave in the southern Kona Hills of the Big Island of Hawai'i. The male was twelve feet tall and the female was ten feet tall, both with red hair.

Despite the increase of material evidence, resistance to the reality of giants and little people is still endemic in anthropological circles. Tiny tools were recently found at the site of a six-thousand-year-old geoglyph of a moose in the Ural Mountains of Russia. The site had been discovered by satellite in 2011. The conclusion about the small size of the tools was that *children* from a lost civilization helped adults construct this enormous moose image from rocks. Children? Why not pygmies? Especially if it was a "lost civilization"?

Although Pohnpei per se has no pygmy skeletons yet, it does have oral accounts of its diminutive inhabitants, as do other Micronesian islands, and they sound very similar to the oral legends of Mu in Hawai'i. Fijian legends associated little people seen by children as being the original inhabitants of Fiji. In 1931 historian Thomas Williams wrote:

A very old Fijian, native of Viti Levu, talks to me of these little gods, with as strong a faith in them as a Highlander has in fairies . . . "When residing near the Kauvadra, I often hear them sigh," said the old man, and his face brightened up as he proceeded: "They would assemble in troops on the tops of the mountains and dance and sing unwarily. They were little. I have often seen them and heard them sing." (as cited in Tarte 2014)

Pohnpei also has material evidence of "giant" skeletons, and joins a plethora of other locations *throughout the world* that are now providing concrete specimens of the same in addition to oral accounts.

Most famous was the 1907 discovery made at Nan Madol by the German governor Victor Berg, who found giant-sized bones, supposedly of the warrior Isokelekel. Son of the thunder god Nan Sapwe and of "virgin birth," demigod Isokelekel (or Idzikolkol) and his 333 warriors conquered the oppressive Sahu Deleur dynasty of Nan Madol circa 1628 CE. Afterward Isokelekel was "lifted" into a "hovering canoe," where he was anointed by the god Luhk as first in a lineage of enlightened rulers and was instructed to establish a new social order in Madolenihmw that continues to this day. These bones, thought to be Isokelekel's, were found in the *lolong* (stone burial chamber) on the islet of Pehi en Kitel. In 1928 the Japanese excavated Isokelekel's alleged tomb and found bones larger than those of modern Pohnpeians, according to Masao Hadley, among many others.

Of course, Ohlsipha and Ohlsopha, builders of Nan Madol, are often described as giants—sometimes also as twins, sometimes as black, but always as brothers.

Prolific are the references to the inland giants who occupied the mountains of Pohnpei in days gone by. Being cannibals, they were not well received, although they are progenitors of certain present-day clans.

According to Ken Rehg, former associate professor of linguistics at the University of Hawai'i at Mānoa, in his work, *The Pohnpean Language Dictionary*, one legend, amidst the profusion of Pohnpei origin myth variations, has even attributed the creation of the island itself to a giant, Maukuk, who assisted Pohnpei's establishment upon Pohnnamweias, a piece of coral that juts above the water on the reef.

Or, according to Hambruch (1911), "work on the island was

completed when giants used their bodies to create the reef, shore and island." Maukuk was cited as one of the giants.

Perhaps the most consistent theme of Pohnpaid is what is *never* addressed in its legends: *the actual glyphs, what they mean, and why they were made.* The absence of such documentation in the legends leads to the logical conclusion that the petroglyphs were created in such antiquity that their origins were long forgotten by Pohnpeian mythmakers.

ALL A MATTER OF TIME

Not unlike other significant rock art sites, the inscribing of Pohnpaid's surface and erection of its stone configurations likely encompass untold centuries. Sacred space and purpose attracted its users across time and across cultural changes.

Distinction should be considered between the outcrop and the adjacent bouldered meadow when considering the chronology of Pohnpaid. The boulders in the high grassy area to the northeast have a greater preponderance of sophisticated glyphs than those found on the stone outcropping. They (the gylyphs found on the boulders) consist of more enveloped cross patterns and a "winged sun disk." Star motifs, anthropomorphs with halos, abstract rectangles, and so on abound. Cruder or more utilitarian glyphs of such things as fishing lures, paddles, and swords, among other objects, dominate the top of the outcrop. Clearly this does not preclude overlap, and the sophistication of the designs at either location could be a function of their older age. In other words, perhaps the earlier inhabitants were more advanced and/or their designs might be related to ceremonial activities that transpired at the sites.

Contrary to academic, published time lines for Pohnpaid, the meadow boulders and stone circles of its first phase were most likely in place by *at least* 8000–7000 BCE, contemporary with Kahnihmueiso and Namket, the ancient and now submerged cities under and beyond Nan Madol. Rising sea levels at various intervals could have prompted the creation and/or proliferation of the inland Pohnpaid petroglyphs (and later Nan Madol) to "mark the spot" of this sacred portal vicinity composed of Pohnpaid, Kahnihmueiso, and Takaieu Peak.

According to the author's conversations with Pohnpeian historian Masao Hadley, Lapoange was a famous giant god who lived at Pohnpaid *before* Nan Madol existed. Micronesian historian Luelen Bernart concurs. That Pohnpaid—which is connected to other accounts of the boys, with Lapoange—also *predated* Nan Madol is implied. From "The Story of a Woman (before the Canoe Came from 'Downwind Katau')":

> There was a woman who was named Lienlama. She lived in Jalapuk. She gave birth and had two children, two sons. The name of one was Jarapuau, and the other was Monimur. The woman was born in Salapwuk . . . Lapoñe [Lapoange] said to the two, I hear that you are two magically potent children. The two replied "Yes, why?" Lapoñe said, "Let us have a race with work to see who will be the fastest." So the boys built up the mountain while Lapoñe made the channel of Letau. (Bernart 1977)

As mentioned earlier, radiocarbon dating from Belau, Micronesia, revealed the following:

> Eight grains of pollen from a probable introduced cultigen, the giant swamp taro Cytopsperma chamis-sonis, were dated to the 5th to 6th millennia BP and held as "evidence [which] appears to be the "smoking gun" establishing human agency at a very early time. (Athens and Ward 2001)

Another indication that Pohnpaid predated Nan Madol is found in an obscure and curious article from 1837 in *Sailors' Magazine*. A reprint from the *Hobart Town Courier* in Tasmania, it reports finding Nan Madol, but also refers to "far greater" ruins. Located about eight miles inland, these rocks were covered with "figures." The area was inhabited by a "different social system," one where work was not done exclusively by women, suggesting a more advanced culture of masculine/feminine balance.

> Amongst the Caroline Islands, only six weeks from Sydney, is Ascenion [sic] (about 11 degrees north latitude), discovered very

lately by his Majesty's sloop-of-war Raven. Mr. Oug, now a resident of this Colony, some years back remained there for several months, and we have our information from a friend, who conversed frequently with Mr. Oug on the subject. On the above named island of Ascension, the language of the inhabitants is more harmonious than in the other islands of the South Seas, a great many words ending with vowels. There are at the northeast end of the island, at a place called Tamen, ruins of a town, now only accessible by boats, the waves reaching to the steps of the houses. The walls are overgrown with bread, cocoanut, and other ancient trees, and the ruins occupy a space of two miles and a half. The stones of the edifices are laid bed and quoin, exhibiting irrefutable traces of art far beyond the means of the present savage inhabitants. Some of these hewn stones are twenty feet in length by three or five each way, and no remains of cement appear. The walls have door and window places. The ruins are built of stone, which is different from that occurring in the neighbourhood. There is a mountain in the island, the rocks of which are covered with figures, and there are far greater ruins eight mile in the interior. The habit of these islanders exhibit traces of a different social system; the women do not work exclusively, as is the custom in the other islands . . . Asked about the origin of these buildings—the inhabitants say, that they were built by men who are now above (pointing to the heavens).

A later or second phase of Pohnpaid corresponds to painted pottery radiocarbon-dated to 2630 BCE, found in a burial cave in Sengall Ridge, Koror, Belau. The particulars of this were published in 2002 by Felicia Beardsley and Umai Basilius, providing more documentation of ancient inhabitation of Micronesia.

Validation of an 8000–7000 BCE origin for areas of Pohnpaid via conventional archaeological mechanisms becomes complicated if not impossible but not improbable at this point in time. Significant consideration should be given to the fact that only at about 6000 BCE did sea levels approach their current position.

No professional or extensive attempts to investigate the waters *inside or outside the reef* for either Pohnpeian sunken city—Kahnihmueiso or Namket—have been made to date, nor have there been any subterranean probes at Pohnpaid or Nan Madol. Use of state-of-the-art instruments including magnetometers, airborne laser detection systems, ground-penetrating radar arrays, electromagnetic sensors and lasers, and submarines or marine robotic vehicles is definitely in order in light of the documentation of "legendary" underwater cities in the Gulf of Cambay, India. BBC News reported in 2002 "that archaeological remains discovered 120 feet underwater in the Gulf of Cambay off the western coast of India could be over 9,000 years old."

Discovery of the submerged megalithic Yonaguni Monument off the coast of Yonaguni, in the southernmost of the Ryukyu Islands, Japan, lends further credence to these sunken city legends, not to mention the 13,800-year-old Haida Gwaii stone structure found under four hundred feet of water off Queen Charlotte Islands, British Columbia, in 2014.

Once Kahnihmueiso and Namket were submerged, only Pohnpaid and Takaieu survived as part of their original complex/alignment until Nan Madol was built in various phases to mark their submarine location.

However, *some* of the petroglyphs might have been more recent additions during Pohnpaid's estimated second phase of 4200–3000 BCE, created after their underwater city components disappeared and well *before* the completion of Nan Madol. This art is contemporary with similar motifs in the Pacific Rim and beyond, for example, the numerous enveloped crosses found in Melanesia (fig. 2.23).

Aside from Pohnpaid, Melanesia's rock art is the most prolific in the western Pacific. Specifically, its enveloped cross glyphs have been

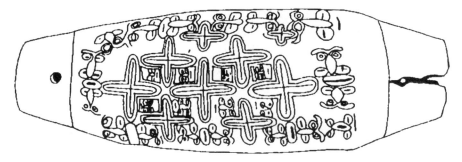

Fig. 2.23. Traditional Kanak wooden door lintel,
New Caledonia in the South Pacific.
Image by Christophe Sand, 2012, after an illustration by G.-H. Luquet, 1926.

dated from 2000 to 1100 BCE by Matthew Spriggs in *The Island Melanesians* in 1997. Others, according to Paul Rainbird and Meredith Wilson's 1999 report (including Roger Green and David Roe in personal communication with those authors, and Specht and Bosden 1997 as cited by those authors), consider this motif part of the Lapita designs starting at 3500–3300 BCE in Melanesia.

The remarkable elephant in the room is that Pohnpaid legends all relate to *who* created them, *not what they mean*. Never do interpretations of their symbolism accompany the oral histories. This allows for the probability that whoever *made* them predated the legendary accounts in such antiquity that their identity and the purpose of the glyphs have long been forgotten.

COMET CONNECTIONS?

It is intriguing that the enveloped cross motif is *not limited* to the western Pacific as some state. Examples are found worldwide, including in California, New Mexico, Arizona, Wyoming, Idaho, Chile, Venezuela, Argentina, Bonaire, and Cuba.

The juxtaposition of two enveloped crosses in Banda Florida, La Rioja, Argentina, with what Maarten van Hoek (2011) describes as a "comet" glyph (fig. 2.25) may provide reinforcement for a worldwide catastrophe linking the enveloped cross symbol, comets, and catastrophe. Note the same combination of glyphs at Pohnpaid: an enveloped cross and circle with a dot in the center (fig. 2.24).

Such cosmic collisions were mentioned in legends shared with the author about nearby Takaieu Mountain, indicating an older time frame than might be suspected.

These oral accounts describe "rocks flying through and falling from the sky," suggesting a quite literal bombardment of meteoric debris, a comet, or even an asteroid. Or they could be alluding to the catastrophic origin of the Taurid streams from the Pleiades constellation and the return of Encke's Comet circa 2700–2100 BCE—all of which transpired well before the construction of the newer portions of Nan Madol site.

Based on the antiquity of other megalithic global sites, meteoric showers, and related oceanic migrations, possible time frames for

Fig. 2.24. Enveloped cross with sun above, phallic monolith, Pohnpaid. Photo by Carole Nervig, 1992.

Fig. 2.25. Enveloped cross and comet, Banda Florida, La Rioja, Argentina. Photo by Maarten van Hoek, 2018.

Fig. 2.26. Enveloped cross and sun/comet, Johnson Canyon Ute Reservation, Colorado. Photo by Peter Faris, 1993.

Fig. 2.27. Venus star cross with serpent-like tail, Phoenix, Arizona. Photo by Wes Holden, 1976.

the various phases or cultural settlements of Pohnpaid activities are minimally:

Pohnpaid megalithic site, phase I: 8000–7600 BCE
Pohnpaid megalithic site, phase II: 4200–3000 BCE

According to a December 14, 1997, article by Rajeev Syal in *The Sunday Times*, "Meteor showers have immense power and destructive capability. One that exploded in 1908 over Siberia was 60 meters in diameter and yielded the energy of 2,000 Hiroshima nuclear bombs." More than one theory has associated Encke's Comet with impacts of cometary material on Earth, and with cultural significance. The Tunguska event of 1908, probably caused by the impact of a comet, has also been postulated by Czechoslovakian astronomer Ľubor Kresák to be a fragment of Encke's Comet.

Although Paul Rainbird attributes "migrations from outsiders" as the cause of deviant oral histories of Pohnpaid, his "ruptures in community historical consciousness" could also be the result of comet impact such as the Taurid streams from the Pleiades:

[These were] formed chiefly by a violent ejection of material from Encke's Comet some 4,700 years ago, but also by another ejection some 1,500 years ago, from a body moving in an orbit of similar shape and longitude of perihelion but somewhat greater aphelion distance . . . [It] was suggested that this unknown body had separated from Encke some time in the past. (Whipple and Hamid 1950)

These apocalyptic Taurid meteor bombardments affected not only Pohnpei but other locations around the world as well. Could this be one of the reasons that representations and symbols of the Pleiades, located in the constellation Taurus, are so significant in the Pacific and elsewhere?

VIEWS OVER MADOLENIHMW

And what about these out-of-place petroglyphs, circles, megaliths, and pyramid mountains, sites about which little is known, including their possible creators?

We have surmised that Pohnpaid, at least some parts of it, predates present-day Nan Madol. If the two sites were contemporary, some kind of resemblance of architectural technique or style would be expected. Not only is this not the case, there is a total absence of art or inscriptions at Nan Madol. Information about Nan Madol's construction and ruling lineage is remembered and recorded with relative detail, while Pohnpaid's legends are vague and clearly inconsistent. As well, Pohnpaid and Nan Madol share no common story lines.

That said, Takaieu Peak, in existence prior to Nan Madol, was a fixture in Nan Madol's oral histories. Ohlsipha and Ohlsopha climbed it and saw Kahnihmueiso and Namket. Duly impressed, they built or at least expanded Nan Madol to honor these submerged cities.

However, the geometric and geophysical grid positioning of Pohnpaid relative to Takaieu and Nan Madol speaks volumes. The pivotal question being: Was the original alignment between the pyramid mountain and the rock art site to Nan Madol per se as we now know it, or to the now submerged "heavenly cities of the ancients" known as Namkhet and Kanihmueiso?

If you read between the lines of the oral histories of these sites and observe their actual line-of-sight alignments, it is obvious that Pohnpaid and Takaieu are connected. To go a step further, it is probable that a more minimal "proto-Nan Madol," and/or the *cities of the ancients,* Kahnihmueiso and Namket, were initially part of this same *complex* created by the Pali navigator-priests or other similarly advanced people, possibly giants or little people, long before Sahu Deleurs entered the Pohnpei arena. Their astronomic, esoteric, and geodesic knowledge of the planetary grid system compelled these ancient architect-astronomers to align these sites, record events in stone, and amplify and/or "ground" energy into the structure of the stone altars of Pohnpaid. Kahnihmueiso and Namket were inundated, but their inland inscriptions and stone circles remain.

3

Dreams, Takaieu, and Little People

DIRECTIVE FROM A DREAM

My expat friends warned me not to go by myself. But I couldn't ignore the directive of my recurring dream: "Climb Takaieu. *Alone.*"

This was certainly not the first time I had been compelled to follow my gut rather than my cautious left brain.

For a few years I had been spending money I didn't have on ten-hour flights to Pohnpei and indulging in extravagant scuba trips—not only to Pohnpei, but also to Chuuk and Belau. At least it was a business write-off, for both Pohnpei State and the national government of the Federated States of Micronesia had contracted me to produce a brochure on Nan Madol, as well as other miscellaneous promotional projects. Nevertheless, my addiction took its financial toll.

I ignored logic and embraced the fiscal peril of selling my design business and moving to Pohnpei with no guaranteed income or a place to live. My only hopes of survival were via fundraising from the nascent Nan Madol Foundation, which might eventually offer a salaried position after a year or two. All more serious risks compared to those my 1990 pilgrimage to Takaieu Peak entailed.

CAUTION TO THE WIND

So what could be so dangerous about this remote Pohnpeian "mountain" of only 164 feet of height? Sure, I was a single, unaccompanied female.

So what? I spoke the language and knew that the only time the soft-spoken, gentle Pohnpeian, or any Micronesian for that matter, could be threatening is when they were falling down drunk. Since no alcohol was allowed outside Kolonia Town at the time, there was no reason for concern.

And for once I had the perk of a borrowed pickup, although sadly sans air-conditioning. This was a much more significant consideration as the drive was roughly a couple of hours, part of which was on isolated back roads. I use the term *road* loosely.

Back in my Peace Corps days there had been no roads at all, only muddy, unmarked footpaths around the island that had to be negotiated in a modest knee-length skirt and zories, which always added technical difficulty to what should have been easy hikes. At that time the only reasonable route was via the lagoon, *if* you negotiated a boat ride and *if* it even showed up.

Frequent ridiculously low tides often required going outside the reef. More often than not, terrifying breakers could easily drench, if not overturn, the typically small dinghy, overloaded with people and supplies. If you were lucky, its usually functional Johnson thirty-horsepower outboard motor pushed through. If not, you were stranded on the coral reef until the high tide came again. (Now, a couple of decades later, outboards remain but for the most part have been replaced by the automobile. Except for fishing. Outboards are still used to enable the addiction to which most Pohnpeian men have fallen prey.)

Demand had produced a potholed and muddy gravel road around a portion of the island.* With Pohnpei's interior producing almost four hundred inches of rain per year, the distinction between mud and gravel is routinely negligible; potholes are ever-present. Since only about a third of the island has asphalt roads, any trip undertaken that's not on these roads has the potential to be a great adventure. The farther from town, the more likely surprises await.

To tell the truth, I was kind of looking forward to some surprises on this trip. When following instructions from a recurring dream is your motivation, you must expect some surprises.

Although I don't remember many colorful details of my dream, its

---

*The road I took is paved today.

message was succinct; its purpose was not. Just why was this outing so crucial?

"You must go to Takaieu." Well, easier said than done.

TAKAIEU ALIGNMENTS

Since my days in the Peace Corps I had been aware of the line of sight from the Pohnpaid petroglyph site to Takaieu Peak, having seen it numerous times. However, I only *assumed* that it continued on toward Nan Madol (figs. 3.1, 3.2, and 3.3; plates 20 and 22).

Validation of my triple site (Pohnpaid, Takaieu, *and* Nan Madol/Kahnihmueiso) alignment theory came many years later while rereading a 1980 mapping report on Greater Nan Madol. Archaeologist Arthur Saxe articulated the significance of a direct line of sight between Nakapw Island (of Greater Nan Madol) and Takaieu. As the petroglyph site had not yet been "discovered," it would have been impossible for him to "connect the dots" from the first two locations by extending this line to the third site, Pohnpaid . . . but I did (fig. 3.4, p. 78).

Fig. 3.1. Line of sight from Pohnpaid outcrop (foreground) to Takaieu Peak.
Photo by Carole Nervig, 1990.

Fig. 3.2. Line of sight from Pahndien Point (foreground) to
Takaieu Peak to Pohnpaid (behind the clouds).
Photo by Carole Nervig, 1992.

Fig. 3.3. Line of sight from Nan Madol (foreground) to
Pahndien Point to Takaieu Peak to Pohnpaid (behind Takaieu Peak).
(Peiniot Islet to the extreme right of Nan Madol is not shown.)
Photo by Lee Arkhie Perez, 2021.

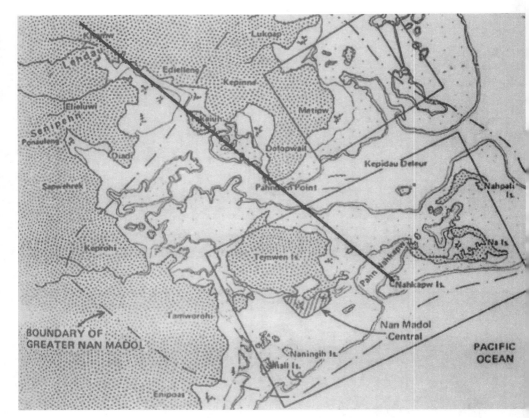

Fig. 3.4. Madolenihmw area with line of sight from Nahkapw Island to
Peiniot to Pahndien Point to Takaieu to Pohnpaid petroglyphs
in Kitamw kousapw, north of the Lehdau River.
Map by Arthur A. Saxe, 1980; black line addition by Carole Nervig, 2020.

And then there was the psychic reading that piqued my interest in
Takaieu prior to my dream . . . or even influenced its directive to climb
to the peak. When I asked about this pyramidal peak during the transmission, I was told it was a "transducer" of extremely powerful energies
given off by a pyramid on the ocean's floor beyond Nan Madol's reef.
Direct exposure would be harmful to current human consciousness, so
Takaieu provided a buffer to diffuse these energies. This information
has always resonated with me as it confirms that the triple site ley line
continued even further than Nahkapw, perhaps ending at a pyramid in
Kahnihmueiso, the drowned city of Mu.

Was this why legends state that Takaieu had been created in a magical contest to alter nature between the giant Lapoange and the little people of Mu (Muantik/Muanlap), or during ancient battles of giants, with rocks flying through the sky?

Another decade passed before I serendipitously came across archaeoastronomical significance given to this island of Nahkapw by César Esteban. He determined that Nahkapw marks both sunrise at the equinoxes and midpoints between solstices, as viewed from Nan Douwas, the focal point of Nan Madol. (Part of chapter 4 is devoted to detailing these archaeoastronomical and geometrical alignments.)

Had I known all of this at the time of my trek to the peak, I would have taken my camera so I could capture the exact alignment from Takaieu to Nahkapw Island. Hindsight. Luckily Google Earth now shows it better than others who captured the area in recent years (figs. 3.5 and 3.6; plates 21 and 22).

I was not familiar with the road to this legendary pyramid mountain, or more precisely, a conical island about 164 feet high, surrounded by mangroves, but my dream propelled me . . . as well as my curiosity.

Legend states that Takaieu was originally only the top of a mountain that was broken into pieces by a magician, the one and only Lapoange discussed previously.

I contemplated the inevitable trudge in flip-flops through foot-sucking mud sometimes up to my lower shins. *Ugh. Where is that*

Fig. 3.5. Madolenihmw Bay from inland Pohnpaid vicinity to Takaieu Peak
to Pahndien Point to Peiniot (extreme right, not included)
to Nahkapw Islet (extreme right, not included) to horizon.
Photo by Lee Arkhie Perez, 2020.

Fig. 3.6. Map showing Madolenihmw Bay with line of sight from
Nahkapw Islet (dotted area) and Peiniot Islet to Pahndien Point to Takaieu to Pohnpaid.
Map from Google Earth; solid and dotted line additions by Carole Nervig, 2021.

magician now? I thought as I bumped along the potholed road in the truck. *I'd rather levitate than deal with the inevitable route through the mangrove swamps that surrounded Takaieu.*

OFF-ROAD

First things first. I had to, of course, find the unmarked turnoff for the hopefully drivable road to Takaieu. Road signs of any sort were virtually nonexistent in rural Pohnpei. There were only a handful of street signs, even in Kolonia Town.

Finally stopping in Sapwalap, I asked the whereabouts of the turn to Takaieu. The village consisted of a tin-roofed, concrete-block, open-air elementary school, a similarly designed "dispensary," and occasional houses. Some were cinder block, others impromptu plywood boxes with the inevitable corrugated tin roof. A few were traditional *nahs,* U-shaped ceremonial platforms to which thatched roofs added the proper note of island charm. Pigs, chickens, dogs, and toddlers coexisted above, inside, and under these structures.

Hoping I could drive the majority of the distance to, well,

the vicinity, I was pleased to hear that the Takaieu area was inhabited. But I had to backtrack almost to Pilen Semwei for the turnoff, which I had unwittingly passed a few miles before.

Once on the reasonably negotiable side road I realized I had not asked how *far* it was to the family's house near this pyramid mountain. Once there, I was hoping to get directions for a path to the peak. And no one had bothered to mention the two forks in the road before the house—but luck or whatever was with me. Or so I thought . . .

I felt swallowed up by this endless jungle of monkeypod, eucalyptus, and banyan trees, but at least it was more cheerful than the mangroves. Just about the time I started calculating how I could turn my car around on a one-lane radius, a nahs appeared in a clearing ahead. Bingo.

LITTLE PEOPLE

Although no one spoke English, the shy, diminutive family was welcoming, as was typical of Pohnpeians in those days, especially for white people, as we were still somewhat of a novelty in the jungle. Not only did this family offer their two young sons to lead me to Takaieu, they provided me with a bit of the site's local lore. My Pohnpeian language skills were just not as good as they'd been when I was in the Peace Corps, so my translation of what they related to me is quite vague. What was significant was that the family itself claimed ancestry from those who had created Takaieu. They told me: "There were battles in the sky in the old times. Stones were flying and dropping everywhere. Some fell to Madolenihmw and made places like Takaieu. The people in the sky were giants. Those on Earth were our ancestors, and they hid because of the warfare and the noise."

Hearing this legend from the Takaieu family piqued memories of what Serge Kahili King, a trained shaman who holds a doctorate in psychology, had shared in *Kahuna Healing* about the Hawaiian pygmies known as Menehunes:

At some point in time long before the rise of Atlantis [that would be Mu], a group of men came from a group of stars known as the Pleiades . . . Most of the star men settled on a continent in the Pacific known today as MU. They called themselves the People of

Mu. But others called them Manahuna or Menehune, "the people of the secret power," because of their advanced technology and psychic power. Their knowledge was Huna, a fundamental philosophy for successful living . . . they began to teach this knowledge to the men on Earth. (King 1983)

There are also accounts of small but powerful little people of Tinian in the Mariana Islands. Called the *duendes,* they were healers with blue eyes, offspring of the Taga princess who married a giant.

It also occurred to me that these "stones falling from the sky" could be an account of the meteoric bombardment accompanying the second passage of Encke's Comet in 2100 BCE, or perhaps earlier catastrophes related the Younger Dryas, circa 12,900–11,700 BCE. Again, all of these references to the little people, rocks falling from the sky, pyramidal transducers, and the inevitable extraterrestrial indicators only inflamed my curiosity. I had to not only see this place, I had to *feel* it.

At last I was off on the fairly dry footpath with the two brothers. Hmmm. Once again "two brothers" reminded me of all the Takaieu and petroglyphs legends. Never mind. Two brothers is hardly an unusual phenomenon.

In less than an hour we were at the base of the mountain, and as luck would have it, the mangrove stretch was only a brief section. More often it was an endless morass of muck speckled with a maze of sizable aerial roots and sometimes evidence of not-too-serious attempts to put down stepping-stones—neither the roots nor the stones were close enough together to avoid direct contact with the swamp. Thank god there were no snakes on Pohnpei!

Amidst some small talk during a short break, I appraised the difficulty of the ascent. In reality it was only a very steep hill, but in a skirt and zories it became formidable.

As much as possible, I tried to keep both the boys ahead of me. After all, I *was* wearing a skirt.

It may seem strange that I was hiking in a skirt but it was the best way to keep cool, which was an endless motivation given Pohnpei's 110 percent humidity. Nevertheless, sweat was something you learned to live with, often by having two or three showers a day. Somehow Pohnpeians always managed to look and smell cool, fresh, and collected.

Not so with mehn wai, who were often identified among locals for their odors.

But the heat was not the only reason for being in a knee-length skirt. Culturally it was considered obscene for a woman to show her thighs or *even the shape of her thighs* in public. Going topless: no problem; wearing shorts or jeans: scandalous. In fact, locals would often steal and hide bras belonging to Peace Corps volunteers so they would be more "local"!

On an inclined trail my skirt only added to the difficult negotiation of keeping flip-flops underfoot. So after about an hour my pace slowed to a crawl, literally. The extreme, vertical terrain became laden with strangling, immense vines, fallen and mildewed trees, and larger rocks to circumnavigate. My view to our destination became obscured physically and emotionally.

The boys said we were only about halfway to the top. *Only halfway?*

One of the many reasons I was determined to reach the peak was to see the line of sight to both Nan Madol and the Pohnpaid petroglyph site. From Pohnpaid you can see Takaieu's pyramidal apex breaking the horizon over the jungle, but you cannot see Nan Madol from the

Fig. 3.7. Takaieu Peak, Madolenihmw Bay.
Photo by Carole Nervig, 1992.

petroglyph site. I wanted to get a sense of any alignments that might be at play. Mapping would have to come later—much later.

I was fairly attached to reaching my goal, but this was becoming impossible! Maybe if I had been wearing hiking boots and jeans . . .

I collapsed on a large chunk of unforgiving basalt. The boys tried to make jokes to cheer me up while I was trying to figure out why this was happening. What about my dream?

The boys asked mundane questions; I answered.

Then our chat became a bit suggestive, as often happens in Pohnpei but only *with adults*. Much of their humor centers around sexual escapades. Although family values were sacrosanct to Pohnpeian culture at that time, sex was not one of them. It was more for entertainment. "Just be sure you don't get caught" was their caveat.

Changing the subject, I questioned them about school. I had guessed they were maybe eight and twelve years old. What? They had finished already? So how old were they? *Eighteen and twenty-six?* And here I was, alone with them in the middle of the jungle! This was not good. In their culture, a woman on her own anywhere remote is suspect, if not implying consent.

Although they were polite and friendly and *small* . . . this *was* Pohnpei and I had willingly accompanied them into the wild. What kind of message did that send?

In the midst of my mounting emotional discomfort, I got it. "Are you guys some of the aramas tikitik (little people or pygmies) of the legends?"

Yes. Their ancestors had occupied this land since the original battle in the sky when all the "stones" were falling from above. Only a few of their descendants had survived due to massacre by the giants, possibly the Sahu Deleurs, who came later. While hidden in the forests, they eventually interbred with other inhabitants to produce the current "hybrids" who were residing adjacent to Takaieu.

Once again my tactic of changing the subject, this time to their diminutive ancestors, not only rendered validation of my dream's directive, but also diffused any sexual agendas that might have been lurking within the recesses of their libidos. No way my dream would have sent me into harm's way.

What a relief. I then knew that meeting some descendants of aramas tikitik was as important, if not more so, as reaching the peak. Perhaps it was even the sole purpose behind my dream.

Lesson learned: No more preconceptions about dream interpretations—just trust the guidance.

This was not what I'd been expecting. No summit. No high-intensity vibes or altered states. I was too distracted by physical discomfort and potential peril. But the exhilaration I felt in having my beliefs of prehistorical little people (and why not giants?) validated was unmatched. Progeny of the mythical sokolei or pygmies of Pohnpei were alive and well.

This was flesh-and-blood proof that oral history must be taken seriously.

Unanticipated mission accomplished.

4

Madolenihmw's Ley Lines of Antiquity

Although Nan Madol per se has become a world-class archaeological site as well as being identified as a node or sacred point in numerous global energetic or electromagnetic grid systems, its relationship to its sister sites in the Madolenihmw vicinity has not yet been identified. Both Takaieu pyramidal mountain and the Pohnpaid petroglyphs and monoliths form a straight line with Nahkapw Islet of Nan Madol and likely beyond to Kahnihmueiso, the submerged city of the "shining ones." These geodesic and geometrical relationships are not so much intentionally ignored as they are overlooked. Their function was never discovered or understood as a systematic geodetic alignment of sacred sites.

FIRST IDENTIFICATION

Dr. Arthur A. Saxe of the Ohio University Department of Anthropology, in his 1980 report on the boundaries of Greater Nan Madol, not only created a map of Nan Madol's sacred golden mean geometries but touched upon four *segments* of this relationship in noting the alignment from Nan Madol's Nahkapw reef islet to Peiniot to Pahndien Point to Takaieu Peak. However, he did not continue this line to the Pohnpaid petroglyphs. He stated:

> The southwest wall (of Nahkapw), which is oriented approximately 45–50° + to the west of grid north, when extended would cross Pahn Nahkapw channel, just miss the northeastern edges of Peniot Island

and Temwen Island, nip the edge of Pahn Dien Point, and go on to Takaiuh Peak in the harbor. This aligns four points visually. (Saxe 1980)

Noting Saxe's observation, I extended this very same line, from Nahkapw to Takaieu, until it intersected the petroglyphs and stone circles of Pohnpaid. Not only did this add another site to the alignment, but by doing so, it attached more significance to each of its three or four components. That the stone circles and rock art encompassed by this relationship are uncommon in the Micronesian Islands lends even more credence to the antiquity of these lineups and to those who created them.

Astronomy is always linked to surveying.
JOHN MICHELE, PROMINENT AUTHOR AND ICON OF
THE EARTH MYSTERIES MOVEMENT

To date, the archaeoastronomical relationships between the megaliths in and outside of Pohnpaid's stone circles located above the Lehdau River have not been investigated nor surveyed. (It is of interest that the sizable Lehdau kousap in central Madolenihmw "existed as an independent political entity prior to the rise of Nan Madol" [Hanlon 1988], suggesting older, perhaps more sophisticed cultural legacies.) Considering that most surveyed megalithic circles worldwide are constructed in relationship to the movement of heavenly bodies, it would be foolish not to expect such alignments in a site built by traditional navigators in the middle of the Pacific Ocean, if not by those of antiquity who likely had skills more advanced than just astronomy.

More important, with Pohnpaid *predating* today's Nan Madol, its alignment with Nahkapw could be a *key in locating the submerged cities of Kahnihmueiso and Namket.* Nahkapw is believed to have been manmade and linked to the two mythical stone cities, according to some archaeologists and local oral historians. In Pohnpeian language, the word *Nahkapw* translates into "new Na," hinting of a new construction.

It should also be noted that this alignment crossing Peiniot Islet lends even more credence to the antiquity of this ley line, because Peiniot Islet was used as a *surveying stone* when Greater Nan Madol was constructed to determine the cardinal directions. As legends state, Nan Madol was erected to mark the spot of the submerged city (or cities) of the ancients beneath it. In fact, further extension of this line into the ocean depths past Nahkapw could even pinpoint the location of Kahnihmueiso.

On its way to the underwater city, this very ley line could also intersect Pweliko (Pwelko), the legendary area between Nahkapw Island and Na Island, or some say south of Na Island; its precise location is unclear. According to Pohnpeian oral history, Pweliko is "hell," and is to be avoided by the proper use of "sound" (vibration, frequency), thus hinting of portals or other dimensions. Pahsed, a "heavenly place below the ocean," is also connected to this vicinity; its reef, Sounalahng, is a "reef of heaven." After all, Nan Madol, whose name means "spaces in between," was purposely located on this reef, the space between the underwater heaven and the celestial one.

Souls then descended to Pahsed, a heavenly place below the ocean. Only another brief stay in Pahsed and the soul ascended to Lahng Apap, the second or lower heaven located just above the earth. Here

Fig. 4.1. Nan Madol.
Photo by Dmitry Malov.

the soul was required to cross Kehnkepir, a spinning bridge located at the juncture of the lower heaven and earth. Below was Pwelko, a large pit where souls that fell off the spinning bridge were doomed to reside for eternity. The secret to success was singing a "song" well before attempting to cross. [This "song" could be a possible reference to vibration or the resonance of the person being of an elevated nature.] A successful walk gave the soul complete freedom to wander through all three spheres of heaven. Enilap (God) resided in the highest Lahng while eni (spirits) made their home in the lower Lahgn. (Nervig [Jencks, pseud.] 1970)

Nahkapw Island is the site of a considerable amount of stonework, and may well be completely artificial. Its placement at the mouth of

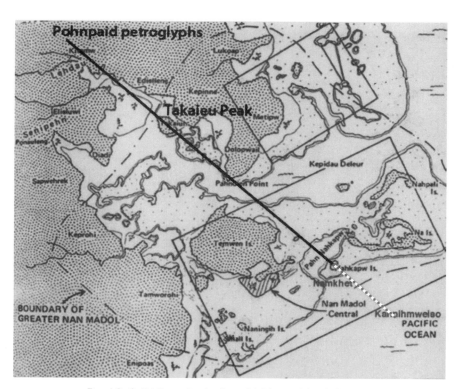

Fig. 4.2. Solid line of sight from Nahkapw Island, Peiniot,
Pahndien Point, and Takaieu to Pohnpaid petroglyphs.
Dotted line of sight from Nahkapw Islet to Kahnihmueiso vicinity.
Map by Arthur A. Saxe, 1980; line additions by Carole Nervig, 2020.

the channel (Kepidau en Nahkapw) plus the orientations of its walls indicate ties to Nan Madol Central and hold the promise of contributing to the understanding of its layout geometry. (Saxe 1980)

When viewed from the petroglyph site toward Nan Madol, Takaieu Peak is the predominate feature of the horizon and an obvious component of various archaeoastronomical and geometrical sightings and calculations (see plate 18). Confirming the author's suspicions, Paul Rainbird calculated decades later in his book *The Archaeology of Micronesia* that the rectangle of the cupules' long axis (on top of the Pohnpaid outcrop) aligns directly with Takaieu Peak (fig. 4.3; plate 23).

At the summit of the outcrop is a small pile of stones [never seen by this author*] forming a flat surface and positioned in the center

Fig. 4.3. Cupules, Pohnpaid outcrop.
Photo by Carole Nervig, 1970.

---

*The small pile of stones referred to by Rainbird is a later addition to this flat surface. The author first visited this outcrop in 1970 and many times subsequently. There was never a small pile of stones, posts, or any reference in oral histories to the possibility of their use as postholes.

a rectangle formed by four holes ground into the rock. These holes may be interpreted as post-holes and the orientation of the long-axis aligns directly with the summit of a prominent isolated hill, Takaiu [Takaieu]. (Rainbird 2002a)

Rainbird's calculated alignment of the outcrop cupules to Takaieu may not be the only one evident in stone. The channel of the "hind end" or "buttocks" rock at Pohnpaid (fig. 4.4; plate 24) may have originally functioned as a line of sight or archaeoastronomical alignment mechanism, despite local lore that states it was a body part strewn among the stone vaginas.

However, just as Saxe did not include the Pohnpaid petroglyph site in his calculations (Nahkapw to Takaieu), Rainbird did not extend his alignment (Pohnpaid to Takaieu) far enough to intercept Nahkapw of Nan Madol. Both identified only two of the three or four locations, never to completion.

Fig. 4.4. Hind end rock, Pohnpaid.
Photo by John Amato, 2010.

Local oral histories make reference to the creation of a channel that approximates the same alignment mentioned previously. It is of note that this one specific channel is mentioned in such legends, as Pohnpei Island has many "natural" channels within its shores. The aforementioned Lehdau River lies adjacent to the Pohnpaid petroglyph site. Recall that the sorcerer Lapoange was responsible for digging the channel through the mangrove swamp leading to the vicinity of the petroglyph outcrop from the waters of Madolenihmw Bay.

Additionally, Hambruch explains:

In some versions work on the island was completed when giants used their bodies to create the reef, shore, and island. (Hambruch 1936, 163)

And regarding the peak of Takaieu, recall that the two boys of Mu (Sarapwahu and Mwohnmwur) are directly connected with the creation or perhaps geoforming of this pyramidal peak:

Legend has it that the playing of two brothers, Sarapwau and Mwohnmur (Muantik and Muanlap), resulted in the rock. (Panholzer and Mauricio 2003)

ARCHAEOASTRONOMICAL DOCUMENTATION

Again, no mention of the *complete* alignment from Nahkapw to Takaieu to Pohnpaid, nor archaeoastronomer César Esteban, demonstrates that one intersection of this alignment, Nahkapw Islet, was the focus of various archaeoastronomical phenomena. In his publication Esteban determined that "the sunrise at the equinoxes or the temporal midpoint between the solstices occurs at the north tip of Nahkapw," as viewed from the focal point of Nan Douwas, the dominant islet of the Nan Madol site.

The mean orientation of the north and south external walls of Nan Douwas aligns almost perfectly with the northernmost tip of Nahkapw. (Esteban 2014)

The continuous-line arrow indicates the point where the sunrise at the equinoxes takes place. The dashed-line arrows indicate the south and north extreme of the possible positions of the sunrise at the temporal mid-point between the solstices (TMPS). Those extremes depend on the equinox considered and the solstice taken as starting point. The sun symbol indicates the size of the solar disk. (Esteban 2014, referring to fig. 4.5)

Not only did the various creators of the petroglyphs, Nan Madol, and most likely the two other submerged cities adjacent to Nan Madol accomplish feats of sheer physical construction, but their sophisticated knowledge allowed them to recognize, calculate, and align components of astronomy, geophysics, and geometry, *and* to select specific locations that articulated and amplified natural, geodesic, and resonant energies connected to the entire planet. No small feat for these "savages" of old.

The megalithic structures and rock art of the tiny island of Pohnpei clearly demonstrate that Pohnpaid was once home to an advanced

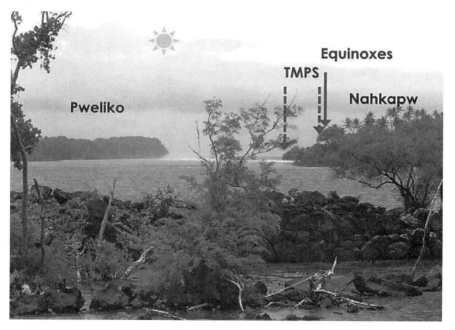

Fig. 4.5. Nahkapw Islet from Nan Douwas.
Photo by César Esteban, 2014.

civilization of the Pacific. This legacy is remembered in local myth and embodied by megalithic sites and present-day Micronesian traditional navigators who sail from one end of the Pacific to the other with only stars, currents, wave patterns, birds, clouds, and their intuition to guide them.

These original creators knew who they were, where they were located upon this planet, and exactly what they were doing by building such structures and alignments.

5

Publish, or Procrastinate and Perish

It should be stated that when the dimension of the Transcendental is added to anyone's teachings, he or she is to an extent automatically eliminated from credibility by the modern sensibility. It is inconceivable to the materialist that a peer can somehow sense the Unseen when others of reasonable education, wealth, fame, or power cannot.

ROSS HAMILTON,
THE MYSTERY OF THE SERPENT MOUND

IN NO MOOD
FOR PERSECUTION

I had been in no mood for persecution for years—rather decades, even lifetimes. Speaking my spiritual, esoteric truth had been my demise in many a past life and often left me open for ridicule here and now. Still vivid was the "bleed through" from a lifetime when my hands were cut off by the patriarchy to prevent their continued use for healing. Been there; done that. No thank you.

As a result, I procrastinated much too long before sticking my neck out with my theories regarding the virtually unknown petroglyphs and stone circles at Pohnpaid. Feeling frustrated, I picked up a pen and vented my angry reflection:

. . . Time is of the essence. Not a day goes by that I don't see one of my pet theories or findings on the Internet or in a book. Each bit of new information eats away at the originality of what has come to my attention for decades. My years of research and documentation slipping through my hands. My ultimate fear is the accusation of plagiarism. I was way ahead of the game, but now these pages make me a copycat. My fear is that after all my years of work and sacrifice, no room for credit is left for me. Who will believe me?

Nan Madol was no such problem. It was an already recognized world-class archaeological site, and I had already gained credibility by publishing its oral history and creating the Nan Madol Foundation in the early 1990s. My efforts to educate and preserve on its behalf were not only acceptable but very grounded in third-dimensional reality . . . or they had been so far.

Even my probing into what at the time was the eyebrow-raising discipline of archaeoastronomy and sacred geometry—for clues of Nan Madol's origins and functions—was emerging as politically correct. Heavyweights from the fields of anthropology, astronomy, and indigenous science were progressing down the road to legitimization and acceptance of such cutting-edge evidence. It is no longer disputed that the bulk of major and minor prehistoric archaeological sites are archaeoastronomical timepieces that often incorporate geometric and/or geodesic alignments and mechanisms relative to the Earth in their designs. Not so twenty-some years ago.

So what was my problem?

I was already published. Leila Castle, editor of an anthology titled *Earthwalking Sky Dancers: Women's Pilgrimages to Sacred Places,* had asked me to contribute a chapter, which I did: "Journey to Mu" was about my adventures on Pohnpei. In this case, by using the nom de plume Caroline Hadley Nervig, I sidestepped my lingering pattern of reluctance to expose my esoteric experiences. (Since my first and middle names are Carole Lynn, I replaced them with the name of the islands of which I wrote and used Hadley, my great-grandmother's maiden name on the Nervig side, as my middle name. Plus, Hadley is the name of respected royal lineage on Pohnpei Island.) What a coward! And ridiculously ineffective as there has only been one Nervig *ever* on Pohnpei.

Fig. 5.1. (a) original Nan Madol booklet by Carole Nervig (under the pseudonym Jencks) for the Trust Territory of the Pacific, 1970; (b) revised Nan Madol brochure for Pohnpei State Tourism, 1989; (c) *Earthwalking Sky Dancers: Women's Pilgrimages to Sacred Places*, 1996; (d) revised Nan Madol brochure for Pohnpei State Tourism, 1989.

I also had two brochures about Nan Madol under my belt. One had been handwritten during my Peace Corps days under my then married name, Carole Jencks; the other was produced by my design company based on the text of my original. Neither was copyrighted due to my youthful naivete, but my text, which I was rarely given credit for, was copied relentlessly.

These earlier writings of mine were one thing, but writing about the megalithic site of Pohnpaid near Nan Madol would be quite a different matter. One could readily prove the very existence of the petroglyphs, as they are undeniably etched in stone. However, verifying that a stone circle had once existed there would be problematic. Adding to this challenge is the reality that Pohnpaid is still for the most part unheard of and the identity of its builders unknown. With no obvious similarity to Nan Madol's architectural style or use of columnar basalt, the petroglyph site is predictably older. Nan Madol's ruling lineage and oral histories are remembered in great *detail*; Pohnpaid's are not.

Trying to figure out why both the glyphs and the stone circles were erected at this specific locale, what they meant, and who made them, all coupled with my personal obstacles of a more emotional nature, rendered me freeze-dried in chronic writer's block. I had my retrocognition* skills, but where was my *proof*? What I had to say was extremely unconventional for general consumption and clearly too unorthodox for academic appetites.

> *I never made any of my discoveries through the process of rational thinking.*
>
> ALBERT EINSTEIN

Would I ever be able to actually substantiate that Pohnpaid once housed a double stone circle? The stones are no longer in perfect alignment, plus the vegetation camouflages all but the largest megaliths. Chances of funding such a mapping project were nil, as no one was even aware there was so much more to be found.

I had to let go of the notion that I had to *prove* my theories by conventional means. My job was to just put the evidence out there, whether it be physical or metaphysical. Readers open to more alternative paradigms of Gaia's history would appreciate and recognize the kernel of truth in the theories and information I had pulled together, *proof or no proof.*

PREMATURE DISCLOSURE?

Justified or not, personal hesitations and self-doubt fueled enormous amounts of procrastination and writer's block. Some fears were rational, others less so.

---

*Retrocognition or postcognition is not easy to prove or verify. As the opposite of precognition, it refers to the ability to obtain information not usually available about past events in your own lifetime or sometime in the distant past. (The APA *Dictionary of Psychology* defines it as, in parapsychology, the experiencing of a past event as if it were occurring in the present, or knowledge of a past event that includes details that could not be learned, inferred, or verified through normal means.)

Now privy to these rediscovered petroglyphs and stone circles, I had become their self-appointed "protectress" of sorts. I had a deep inner need to cloak this still energetically active sacred site; it was not to be interfered with, publicized, or exploited. Not yet, anyway.

Pohnpaid was just too important. Its story had to be told, but *not only* with a conventional archaeological approach. Even an archaeo-astronomical survey of the site, although essential, would probably not explain the true nature of what had taken place within its perimeters. I was setting myself up for this job . . . at some point.

Was I just "going native," being too Pohnpeian by wanting to keep this secret to myself? Or was the psychic's message right: I helped create the site thousands of years ago? That would certainly explain my eccentric, if not addictive, connection to Pohnpaid as well as Nan Madol. It might also explain why I felt overly protective and reluctant to share the news. Whatever my past-life connection to Pohnpaid, I still pondered the disclosure of the new petroglyphs, as it might be considered culturally insensitive. The words of researchers Strong and Strong, referring to sites in Australia, rang a warning bell for me:

We also agreed that the sites' location and identity of the present owners will be kept secret, and that no one must even consider approaching this site unless given proper ceremony; it would be both offensive and dangerous to do otherwise. (Strong and Strong 2015)

Similarly, my decades in Micronesia and Hawai'i taught me about the mana and sacredness of these places. I did not want to violate Pohnpaid by disrespecting its secrets, nor did I wish to suffer negative repercussions of its premature disclosure. This justification was only valid *temporarily,* as after a few years a handful of archaeologists and a number of tourists would no doubt roam and probe *some* of its parts and pieces. That local Pohnpeians did not try to protect Pohnpaid with more gusto points to an absence of their direct linkage to its creation and subsequent dearth of appreciation for its significance. For the most part, the only local motivation to do so would eventually be generated by its three-dollar entrance fee to view the petroglyphs.

The second and perhaps more rational justification was that I lacked the proper "academic credentials" to say squat about petroglyphs.

Except, that is, in reference to my "hands-on" knowledge of Pohnpeian culture and the sites' oral history, their aesthetic value or design qualities based on my degree in fine art, and my years of being a professional graphic designer of symbols. Grants for epigraphic research that a relevantly titled academic would elicit would not be forthcoming.

Yes, I did possess a Pohnpeian honorific title bestowed upon me during Peace Corps days, but this did not constitute the kind of prerequisite I felt was required to broadcast the existence of this newly rediscovered site. Although Pohnpei was always my second home and Nan Madol and the Pacific grid and its sites my passion, I was void of any indigenous blood or entitled credentials that precluded permission to share my findings.

Although basically true, both the protection of the site and my low self-esteem related to my lack of credentials were probably fear-driven procrastinations rather than legitimate explanations for delay.

That said, another more concrete excuse for my writing block reared its ugly head. The only publication on Pohnpaid beat me to the petroglyph race. The only saving grace was that the majority of the petroglyphs I had photographed *were not in the report!*

Nevertheless, I gave up writing for eating sour grapes.

INTEGRITY OR EGO?

Leaving Pohnpei had not stopped my investigation of the Pohnpaid rock art. Googling websites on Pacific petroglyphs led me to numerous academic archaeological papers, the most thorough of which had been authored by Paul Rainbird and Meredith Wilson in 1999. To my astonishment, it documented some, but *not all,* of the site's petroglyphs.

I was devastated again. The report on Pohnpaid, sponsored by the Pohnpei State Historic Preservation Office (PHPO), was not a case of my words stolen, but a failure to acknowledge my role in rediscovering and creating awareness of the glyphed boulder field and its stone circles. Authors Rainbird and Wilson were likely never aware of my role. Clearly the PHPO had not shared this information as Rainbird and Wilson would surely have contacted me. Years prior to this report, I had generated a proposal via the Nan Madol Foundation that was designed to elicit funding to undertake a professional investigation of the site and document the findings. Had I not done so, this extensive new area near the known outcrop might have slipped into the oblivion of the jungle's choking vegetation, never documented. Only a repeat of the rare drought coupled with a wildfire through the rain forest would have revealed them again, if ever.

Had I not stumbled across these petroglyphs in 1992, and subsequently informed Emensio Eperiam, the historic preservation officer, of their whereabouts and taken him to the site, would this new documentation by Rainbird and Wilson have happened? Emensio was dumbfounded when he saw the grassy meadow portion of the site. He had never been there before, nor had he heard of this place.

The only others I brought to the site were deceased Pohnpei Community College archaeologist Russell Brulotte, who left Pohnpei shortly after our visit, and Dan Perin, economic developer consultant to Pohnpei State, also no longer on island.

In 1992, I brought more official attention to this site by preparing a memorandum of agreement signed by all the land owners for Pohnpaid's investigation and mapping that was presented to Pohnpei State Historic Preservation. The plan was that funding would be provided by the Nan Madol Foundation as resources became available.

My role in bringing this site to light was ignored by officials and professionals alike.

In any case, the petroglyph documentation project was eventually given to Paul Rainbird and Meredith Wilson. What caught my attention in their preliminary report was the subject of the cover photo.

Sitting on the top of the Pohnpaid rock outcrop was a traditional Pohnpeian sakau stone. Like a large, irregular, but fat basalt pancake, it was recognizable by its shape. It featured grooves that had been created by years of pounding Pohnpeian pepper root, and smaller, stabilizing stones underneath. This petroglyph site had been significant enough to merit a sakau pounding and drinking ritual, but this sakau stone was *a new addition to this site*. I knew this in a flash. I had been there many times in the late sixties while in the Peace Corps. There had been no trace of this sakau stone then.

Plus, it would make no sense to hold a ceremony that could last into the wee hours of the morning, or even days, in such an exposed location, not to mention sitting on the unforgiving basalt in the relentless tropical showers. Yes, it was certainly a hallowed spot, but to whom? Not so much present-day Pohnpeians, as their connection with its creation was ambivalent.

But the tourists would love it! And Pohnpeians, as previously mentioned, love to pull a fast one . . . *especially* on foreigners. Perhaps the idea that Pohnpeians were committing an archaeological no-no never occurred to them.

Sensing this, I wanted to alert Rainbird to the fact that his cover photo (circa 1990s) and certain text references to it were *later additions* to the outcrop, so I promptly sent him one of my Pohnpaid photos from 1969 documenting the exact spot on the outcrop showing no sakau stone. In exchange Rainbird was kind enough to send me a copy of his work, and subsequently his much appreciated permission to use his maps and findings in this very publication.

TIMING

The last of my more rational procrastinations was timing. Not only mine but the rest of the world's.

It's about humanity. For my research to find an audience, they had to be *receptive* to the idea of a highly advanced civilization's very existence and in locations where people my age were taught that only "savages" lived. Humanity, and in particular academia, had to be ready to accept that paradigm-altering archaeological evidence—which doesn't fit inside conventional boxes—can be duly ascertained and accepted, not just discarded as unscientific bunk.

The messages left with the megalithic stones and energetic grid systems remind us of our responsibility to Mother Earth along with reminding us to embrace our personal potential to attain a similarly enlightened state. This epic evolutionary process still looks very unpredictable, but it is now or never. We become spiritual stewards of our planet or self-destruct . . . or she does it for us.

Without a readership of minds now exposed to the profusion of new evidence that has jettisoned the advent of our civilized past back tens of thousands of years earlier than suspected, I would have been spinning my wheels trying to make my case for a prediluvian civilization in the Pacific. With my procrastination came new archaeological finds whose sophistication and dating have forced the rethinking of prehistorical paradigms and generated a supposition that highly skilled astronomers and architects and hunter-gatherer peoples were actually contemporaries.

In light of recent finds and their subsequent dating, I would be less likely considered a crazy woman when spouting my theories of the lost Motherland of Mu. Some of those recent finds are as follows:

40,800-year-old cave paintings in El Castillo, Spain;
40,000-year-old hand stencils in Sulawesi, Indonesia;
50,000-year-old DNA from Aboriginal Australians;
14,000–20,000 BCE dating of the sophisticated architectural/ astronomical site of Göbekli Tepe, Turkey;
20,000-year-old (plus or minus) megalithic site Gunung Padang in Java, Indonesia.

With its location in Indonesia, the Gunung Padang site is both a proven remnant of the now partially submerged Sundaland continent and a likely cultural, if not physical, component of Mu. Most importantly and unlike any other currently known sites, Gunung Padang is constructed of columnar basalt, *as is Nan Madol,* and is located within a voyaging canoe's reach of Pohnpei. I consider this to be another significant piece in the Lemuria puzzle.

Given this paradigm shift involving the antiquity of humanity, I wouldn't have to reinvent the "time line" wheel on my own. Nor, more importantly, would I have to prove it.

Humanity's state of readiness is not the only timing factor involved. The timing of cycles and seasons and stars is another factor, although considered less rational to academia. After all, this petroglyph site is linked to the stars and to voyages and to that ancient race that navigated *time* through the stars as well as the waters. The petroglyphs have given me their story and their trust—earned by my patience—over *time.*

MORE THAN MAGIC

During years of working at Nan Madol I had been exposed to its mwanamwan and synchronicities on innumerable occasions. Magic led us to this extraordinary, monumental rock art find. I was driven to tell Pohnpaid's story, but I would need more than magic.

I switched to a more conventional approach to my book. Wanting to be taken seriously rather than as a new age bliss ninny, I began researching other Pacific petroglyphs, similar artistic or content styles, advanced civilizations, indigenous shamanic symbolism, and megalithic art worldwide. I read a plethora of conventional and alternative archaeology publications and looked for clues in language and migrations.

Discoveries, synchronicities, and bits and pieces of evidence from books, magazines, and websites would tease me, rekindling my passion for answers to this lost race of the Pacific, these petroglyph makers. The search was never complete. I kept finding more connections, more possible explanations of the whos, whys, whens, and hows of this mystifying site.

Clearly the hundreds of petroglyphs at Pohnpeid wouldn't totally disappear but could deteriorate or be defaced if I didn't get on it.

But I didn't, at least the writing part. Although the exhilaration of discovering new connections between Pohnpei and other allegedly unrelated cultures fueled my research addiction, there was still no publication.

My copartner in discovery, Ronald, sent me all his photos and negatives, having neither the time nor the inclination to participate in my mega-quest of documenting the stone circle and glyphs. I'd have to go it alone.

What was I waiting for? Someone else to waltz in and steal my thunder . . . *again*?

HAWAI'I

After leaving Pohnpei to settle on the Big Island of Hawai'i, I decided it *was* time to write. I knew this intellectually, but then a full recycling of doubts, disguised as rationales, cropped up . . . *again*.

Though I doubted it was my place to spill the beans, who, if not me, had the right to proclaim the existence of these newly rediscovered petroglyphs? They had come out of hiding for Ronald and me and posed for our photos. And when would this ever happen again? Serendipitously, they revealed themselves to us in a brief window of time and space, during a time of drought on an island whose central mountains receive about four hundred inches of rain annually. Did this not constitute esoteric authority?

I had to trust my judgment now. But just in case, I checked with my Hawaiian *Kupuna* Auntie Mae for validation. Auntie Mae had been crippled by a car accident and was limited to reading and praying in her long-term-care room. I had seen her do some pretty impressive magic when she was active, but now her psychic powers had grown with her confinement. She had gone deeper.

I explained my predicament and asked for her advice on whether to disclose the existence of the stone circle of megaliths and their petro-glyphs on Pohnpei. I was not surprised when she had me open to a page in her Bible. I had seen other Hawaiians do this before, using the book as a divination tool rather than a scriptural source. The paragraph I was drawn to read did not make sense at first, especially in light of my question.

As I continued to read, though, its counsel jumped off the prover-bial page. Something about the "priesthood holding back information from the masses." Wow. How arrogant of me to think I was to make the decision of whether to share my findings or not in the first place.

All I had to do was write the book and be guided as to when its message should be shared. If it was too soon, it would be blocked. Clearly, it *had* been blocked all these years . . . by *me*.

Truth may be simple, but writing is not—especially when its expression is fused with the evil twins: fear of failure versus fear of success.

Just to ensure that all my doubts were duly dispersed, I was actually led to seek verbal permission from my "teacher" Hale Makua, native Hawaiian kahuna, renowned shaman of the Big Island and beyond. He was respected worldwide, and his presence spoke for itself. Although not Pohnpeian or even Micronesian, his spiritual status with all Pacific Islanders was a given.

I had the honor of enjoying his friendship after he became aware of my writings on Nan Madol and the Pacific energy grid. However, I very much wanted his feedback or approval on exposing these basi-cally unknown, sacred petroglyphs at Pohnpaid as well as the energy grid lines I had mapped throughout the Pacific. I didn't want to be that Westerner who spilled cultural secrets. Not only did he give me his blessing to go forward, he was adamant that I finish my book, probing as to its progress every time I saw him.

Now I had another authority figure's directive to finish the job.

Not only that, Native Hawaiians had taught me that without knowing your ancestors, you do not know yourself. I learned this very personally during a shamanic journey led by Hale Makua while I was living on the Big Island. My deceased grandfather showed up in spirit and took me to a shaman circle in Norway. There I experienced powerful visions of my past lives and relationships to the "book of records" and Norse culture.

Standing in awe of their vibration and light, I was humbled and awed by the vision of my ancestors as shamans, keepers of knowledge and wisdom. No one spoke, but I was told many things telepathically about our tradition and my lineage. My ancestors communicated that every seventh generation of a particular lineage must make amends for any commissions of foul deeds or omissions of responsibilities within the preceding seven generations. Amends could take many forms, sometimes without conscious knowledge of why they were being done. A seventh-generation descendant would just find themselves motivated toward a particular act or mission during their lifetime. Those of us ignorant of our ancestors find ourselves inexplicably drawn to certain deeds or obsessions, oblivious to what might be motivating us while continually questioning our sanity—as was the case for me.

Nothing was said, mind pictures being the communication mode, as they took me back in time. Way back. I watched in my mind's eye the migrations from the Pacific. Many races, different directions, various time frames. The early migrations were to establish outpost colonies; latter ones under duress of inundation.

Then I saw a woman with a sizable, important-looking book. I watched her navigate groups of boats all the way from the Pacific area through the Aleutian Islands to the Nordic region. All knew the way because they knew the stars.

This fair-skinned blonde woman was rescuing the book of records from the Deluge for safekeeping. Her destination was what is now Norway, and she was indeed my ancestor.

This was long ago, long before the Vikings with which we are familiar. (Or rather before the ancient culture deteriorated to what we now know as Vikings.)

As I pondered how many generations might have transpired since then, I was shown forty-nine generations. Makua had also spoken of the significance of the seventh of seven generations, who would have immense responsibilities compounded by their "seven times seven" status. Depending on average life spans, and assuming it had always been fifty to one hundred years rather than the biblical giants who lived much longer, these forty-nine generations could span from 2,500 to 5,000 years ago.

Did this explain my out-of-control passion to research Pacific sites, migrations, and what happened to the white indigenous race of the Pacific?

A feeling of dread and delight churned in my gut. Were they showing me it was my job to tell this story? To track my ancestors' history?

I tried to deny my role in this by holding my ego responsible for inventing such preposterous trip. New age lore gone wild. Yeah right. I am the forty-ninth generation from this woman and I am supposed to tell the story of her migration, her descendants, and her book. No way. Impossible.

How could anyone write about this unless they were there?

Oh no. Oh yes. The realization dawned.

It was me.

My emotional reaction was so strong, I knew in my soul it was true. I was back after seven of seven generations because this story must be told at this time. The task was formidable, but what was more difficult to swallow was the arrogance inherent in claiming my birthright.

Cultural sensitivity kicked in: Can't we allow races of color the right to their own origins in some ancient land of the Pacific?

Then they showed me the migrations again. Yes, I was there crossing the ocean with my book in my boat, but this time I saw the others. Each of the races had its seventh of seven generations counterpart; each woman carried her book of records to the four corners of the world. Black, brown, red, yellow, white, and blue. (Yes, blue. They were the ones to go underneath the mountains, and to Antarctica, to wait.)

I felt better knowing I must tell the story of my own ancestors and that my counterparts of color will also come forth to tell theirs.

How many times had I told my friends that I will feel like my life was a failure if I didn't get my writing and research completed and published? I would not rest in peace until I had finished. I was driven by some inexplicable force, which even managed to defeat my procrastinations occasionally.

Perhaps sensing my disbelief of my identity and self-doubt about my "assignment," these magnificent ancestors of mine bestowed the only gift that could actually make me believe I was up for the task.

Ancient and worn, bound with leather and inscribed in gold, and heavy with knowledge, the book of records I had carried in the boat was placed into my hands. I did not open it. No need. It cannot be "read" in the conventional manner anyway; it can only be "known"—or remembered in bits and pieces over an unpredictable time frame.

The shamans retreated into their realities and the book disappeared with them, leaving me with a sense of humility and gratitude. It is with this "permission" that I have the audacity to tell my ancestors' stories of the stones, the sites, the navigators, and energy grids of the Pacific past, known to some as Mu.

Now full circle, with my past lives and my ancestors behind me, I could revisit the mysteries of Pohnpei again and make my own case for their origins.

Yet the weight of this responsibility turned into emotional overload, not to mention the economic downturn that rendered me jobless.

Maybe a change of scenery would be the ticket. So in 2008, after two decades of living in Hawai'i, I packed it up and moved to the Pacific Northwest.

PORT TOWNSEND, WRITERS' HAVEN

The writers' haven of Port Townsend, Washington, was my next stop. I lived in a sweet yellow cottage overlooking the convergence of Puget Sound and the Straits of Juan de Fuca. All of the ships coming in and out of Seattle could be seen from my living room. What could be more inspiring?

Many, stimulated by the beauty of Port Townsend's natural setting of pines, straits, and sounds, are drawn to this charming Victorian waterfront town to attend its renowned writers' workshop or to actually write, heaven forbid. Not me. In fact, I felt rather adrift after arriving in Port Townsend. Around this time I continued to beat myself up about the writing I had not done:

. . . But what happened to the joy of writing? I keep telling everyone that I am a writer, who is writing a book. Lies. I have not touched this computer for months. So far, the narratives I have composed read boring. Who cares about what I did, or thought, or felt? How egotistical of me to think anyone would want to read such narcissistic babble?

I managed to eke out a few pages but hardly a book. What I did accomplish in the Pacific Northwest was to connect with my ancestry, an action easily achieved in this hotbed of Scandinavian culture fanatics.

Once in Port Townsend, I followed up in getting to know my ancestors—thinking this would be the ticket to light a fire under my keyboard—and indulged in tracking my conventional genealogy with a visit to my relatives in Nervika, Norway. All manifested in perfection but not so much the writing.

As time marched on, more archaeological discoveries continued to break old paradigms of anthropology and history, begging the question of a unified source or a precursor civilization.

The stage was being set. Momentum was building, creating the courage in me to bring the stone circle site out of the archaeological closet. Pieces on the alternative archaeological time line were falling into place. It became obvious that Pohnpaid and Nan Madol could bridge certain gaps in these scenarios.

And then I was blown away.

Yonaguni. Finally physical evidence of a submerged sophisticated civilization emerged. And in Oceania no less. I knew in my bones it was somehow linked to whomever had built both Pohnpei Island sites. An underwater city, like Kahnihmueiso and Namkhet under Nan Madol, Yonaguni was a tangible legacy of Mu. A handful of other cities off the east and west coast of India had also been confirmed: Dwarka, Mahabalipuram, and Poompuhur, to mention a few, and there were the pyramids off the coast of western Cuba that had been located at depths of at least two thousand feet, not all that far from the enveloped cross rock art in nearby caves. (Years prior I had first detected—I say first because no one else had yet laid eyes on the Pohnpaid enveloped cross glyphs to be able to make any comparison—that Canadian author and coastal marine engineer Pauline Zalitski's photos of "enveloped cross" rock art from a western Cuban cave were perfect matches to Pohnpaid's crosses. Little did I know then that pyramids lay underwater in relatively close proximity to those very same Cuban caves.)

This was a huge leap for me, triggering my realization that these sites around the world had to be discovered before *I* would be taken seriously about the Pohnpei petroglyphs and Nan Madol, rather Kahnihmueiso, being vestiges of Mu. These other discoveries meant my disclosures would be more noteworthy than a mere cataloging of rock art, with the kind of attention that a missing link generates. After five years in Port Townsend my healing process had slowly allowed an occasional chapter or two to escape from captivity. Eventually I even came to accept the perfection of timing and the necessity of delay. The proverbial silver lining: emotional and spiritual growth.

ECUADOR?

The United States had not fulfilled my material needs, not to mention the ravages of its culture and lifestyle on my soul. And Port Townsend was apparently not the ticket to my writing career. Retirement was looming large. So with the assistance of Google I picked my next locale out of the blue. Or did it pick me? Ecuador certainly qualified. It was home to major sacred spaces and imposing megalithic structures, which were always the criteria for my moves. Often these locations constituted a new "assignment" for my earth grid energy work. Ecuador was right on the equator and so would add a geodesic boost.

Over the years, the burden of proving my self-worth had on one hand triggered my creativity and writing, and on the other manifested various forms of self-punishment for not producing my life's work. But that is certainly another story, now transformed into a happier ending.

Would Ecuador finally provoke the completion of my book? Even being in the midst of the Andes, with their palpable spiritual energies and ample time on my hands, did not take those hands to my keyboard. After a year, nada.

EGYPT, THE COSMIC KICK IN THE BUTT

The ultimate demise of my writer's block happened in Giza. To this day, my Egyptian pilgrimage of 2014 remains unknown to family and many friends, avoiding judgment on what would be perceived as reckless both financially and physically—after all, it was the time of the Arab Spring uprising in Cairo. I had had intense emotional experiences and memories at both Stonehenge and Machu Picchu, but neither equaled with those of Egypt.

As clichéd as it might be, my experience of being inside the Great Pyramid during a private visitation, lying inside the so-called "sarcophagus," was life changing. No more doubts about what I knew I had to write; no more reasons why not. I felt and saw with my inner sight the grid lines emanating from this energetic focal point right in the pyramid. I experienced the reality of the myriad of sacred sites on Mother Earth all connected by a geodesic web, the nervous system of our mother. Egypt provided me the ultimate confirmation of why and how to tell this story. Now, nothing would keep me from it. I was fueled with the joy of having my life mission validated and from the self-confidence stemming from my acknowledged inner knowingness. Screw the credentials, the debunkers, finding publishers, the outcome.

The writing commenced and continued to completion. I returned to Ecuador as a woman on a mission. My phoenix was finally rising.

ECUADOR TO POHNPEI?

Mission accomplished. My writing was indeed finished, but I needed more photos of the petroglyphs I had found in 1992 after the drought to make my case. When Ronald and I had first come across the previously undocumented glyphs back in 1992, we were in a state of shock; documentation was secondary and required a bit more focus, for clicks on a cell phone were not yet reality.

But how on earth was I going to get from Ecuador to Pohnpei? My Social Security income would not even come close to covering that expense, and I had no benefactors—or so I thought.

Thanks to my niece Kelly, who suggested crowdfunding for my trip. It worked! To this day I am forever grateful to my donors, but even more astounded as to how thousands of dollars appeared like magic. Instant manifestation.

Okay, Pohnpei, here I come . . . again!

FAMILY MATTERS

Once on the island, my challenge was to motivate historic preservation officials and local archaeologists to accompany me to the site. I thought that showing them my amazing anachronistic petroglyph photos would do the trick. Silly girl. (And yes, being a "girl" was always part of the problem when trying to accomplish such tasks on Pohnpei.)

After a few meetings with historic preservation officials, I had still not been offered the warm bodies with machetes that I needed to clear my path to the hidden megaliths smothered with petroglyphs. I just had to let go of what I thought my schedule should be. After all, I was on Pohnpei time.

As soon as I regained my patience, my Thomas family from Lohd Pah (of Peace Corps days) called to see if I wanted to drive to the Pohnpaid site to find the long-lost petroglyphs. *Bingo!* It would be much more fun with them (although they had no idea what they were getting into).

We drove as far as we could on the barely navigable dirt road. Morleen, my "niece," wouldn't get out of the car; she was spooked by the idea of spirits at the site. Her excuse was that she would be present to move the car if another car came along, which was about as likely as a snowstorm.

Tall weeds and grass were all we could see. I was pretty sure I could spot the location of what I thought was the gigantic core of the monoliths in the distance, but between us stood a nightmare of overgrowth.

I questioned my sanity. Again. What the hell was I doing in this overgrown inferno with no discernable path in sight? A trail to nowhere?

Morleen's husband, Papiano, and *Pahsang* Madolenihmw, their friend who lived nearby, did not appear enthusiastic about our venture either, but when I started out on my own, they had no choice but to join me. Male pride is still formidable on Pohnpei.

The network of thick, prickly foliage was shoulder-high and obscured any sense of the terrain. We walked some distance to what I had identified from the car as the inner megalith group of stones. The sun was relentless; I was sure I was roasting alive. Even the two Pohnpeian men were sweating up a storm. Was it global warming making the difference, or was I was just feeling my age?

Fig. 5.2. Papiano Tihpen, midmeadow, Pohnpaid.
Photo by Carole Nervig, 2018.

Fig. 5.3. *Left:* Pahsu megalith entangled in roots.
Right: Pahsu megalith, "vagina" detail, Pohnpaid meadow.
Photos by Carole Nervig, 2018.

The closer we got, the more I recognized the site. My confidence returned as we forged painstakingly ahead. Fortunately my companions did not give up on me.

VAGINAS MATERIALIZE

Once we finally got next to the gigantic Takai en Pahsu I recognized from 1992, when the meadow site had been burned off (not the more famous, smaller one that was just off the road), the magnitude of the task at hand hit me hard. Vegetation had once again taken over the site, and I knew that clearing enough of the roots, bushes, and trees strangling these boulders would be next to impossible. It certainly would not happen by the time I left the island in ten days. It would take a team of who knows how many men and how many hours, not to mention how they would be paid. Plus, there were other petroglyphed boulders strewn over the entire meadow. The only realistic way to clear this was to burn it, which is how I'd been able to find the site in 1992 during the drought. The problem was that burning damages the surface of the petroglyphs, obviously an unacceptable strategy.

The two men who accompanied me cleared a bit around the megalith, but only enough to photograph a portion of the rock and a nondescript portion of the "vagina" area. I should have taken a lot more photos on that earlier visit in 1992, but I'd been so distracted by the experience, stumbling around the roots and pits . . . *and did I mention the heat?* I only managed to get a couple of photos, all the time incorrectly assuming I would be back in a few days for more.

Back in the thank-god air-conditioned car, we joked incessantly about the huge "vagina" stone we'd exposed. I told Morleen that she should have come with us because now her husband Papiano had a "new girlfriend." Pohnpeians love bawdy bantering!

We had only gone a short distance when I noticed an unfamiliar stone just off the road.

"Stop the car!"

Upon close inspection, it was a clam-shaped boulder with, of all things, "scallops" chiseled into its surface. Talk about a clam/vagina stone! And just feet from the road! The vagina plot thickened.

With a huge sense of relief at having found these megaliths again

Fig. 5.4. Pahsu clam rock, with author indicating scallops.
Photo by Morleen Thomas, 2018.

and confirming their reality, my desire to publish their existence grew exponentially.

The Goddess is alive and well at Pohnpaid. No stopping me now.

Ahi soai pwoat torohr wei likin imwen. "Pass it on—from this house to people outside of your house."

6

Pacific Crossroads

Diffusion, Reverse Migration, and Mu

The artist carries the dream of the people into the future.
That dream holds the essence of their journey, the long line
of their arriving and the wisdom that opens the way to
tomorrow. In the rock art of this land there are remnants
of that deeper journey, symbols that sometimes acknowledge
origins long lost to memory.

GARY J. COOK AND THOMAS J. BROWN,
THE SECRET LAND

A PETROGLYPH IS WORTH THOUSANDS OF VOICES

The urge to compare the rock art of one particular site or culture to that of another is irresistible. Proving the significance of such links, whether obvious or far-fetched, requires a match of much more than just patterns and design. Examination of the physical settings, oral histories, religious or cultural beliefs and practices, historical data, and migration patterns must also lend validation to any theories seeking to link seemingly disparate cultures.*

---

*During the examination of any oceanic archaeological sites, we must also bear in mind that various geographical designations are Western-made and, as such, are not necessarily aligned with cultural and ethnic boundaries. Micronesia was overseen as a United Nations Trust Territory under U.S. administration before forming its own government in 1979 and becoming a sovereign independent country in 1986.

Although in-depth examination is yet to be completed, the 750 *known* Pohnpaid prehistoric engraved rock art motifs provide such striking and unlikely similarities to others worldwide that a more than cursory comparison is warranted. Although this publication includes more petroglyph photographs of Pohnpaid than any other to date, *all* of the visible glyphs are *yet to be documented* by the author or others.

A petroglyph is worth not only a thousand words but a thousand voices. During the time when Mu existed, sound and resonance were imbedded into incised glyphs to create messages, to store wisdom. It is not surprising, then, to find this *same* concept of nonliteral telepathic transmission utilized by various "star nations." Memories of and knowledge about listening to and feeling sound from rock art has survived to this day in Native American cultures. This provides another paradigm for the comprehension of the Pohnpaid petroglyphs. To quote Grandfather Leon Secatero, headman of the Canoncito band of Navajo:

> Original language was transmitted by touching a glyph and receiving all the information of an entire concept contained in a single glyph. This is the reason that these glyphs appear to be scattered all over the face of a rock and not in any linear fashion. It is not words made up of individual letters or sounds which represent something else. Later permutations of this language were carved in stone in a linear style which is interpreted starting a[t] the bottom and moving upward from right to left . . . up a line which is read left to right . . . up a line right to left. (quoted in Ryder, n.d.)

Dr. Ibrahim Karim, architect and Egyptian mystery school expert, teaches that ancient hieroglyphs were recreated with precision and frequency so that the viewer could, by resonance, *actually become one with* what the symbol represented. His concept also depicts how petroglyphs were accessed in Mu, aka Lemuria: in addition to being seen, they were touched to "hear" their vibrational meanings.

Literal "translations" of rock art are speculations much colored by Western culture's limited third-dimensional perceptions of them as only "drawings." English researcher Paul Devereaux explains that geometric forms (abstractions, dots, spirals, spheres, etc.) are projections from the minds of shamans in trance. Repetitive pounding on rock with stone tools helped them attain altered states. The resonance created by these pounding sounds would also assist the process.

Aside from the quantity and surprising accuracy of the matches between Pohnpaid's glyphs and others of the world, the other exceptional feature of Pohnpaid is that its legends provide no insights about the purpose or meaning of the actual motifs or patterns, nor the physical configuration of the site. There are only legends about its supernatural creation myth. This fact could indicate a *source much older* than previously calculated by conventional prehistory of the Pacific. Bellwood (1978) agrees. He states:

> From a comparative archaeological perspective there is little doubt that the engravings at Pohnpaid are ancient and Oceanic in origin.

With this cultural bias in mind, the visual similarities between Pohnpaid's rock art and rock art encompassing all continents are nevertheless apparent. These comparisons demonstrate global diffusion between cultures long believed to be unrelated, and executed long before it was thought possible.

> At this point in our explorations, there is hardly a concept, term, symbol, deity, or mythic theme of the classic ancient cosmologies whose meanings we cannot demonstrate broad agreement about among the various traditions we have studied. Clearly what we have been exploring are not simply elements of independent traditions that were some how incidentally similar, but rather a coherent set of related symbols that were commonly shared by the cultures. The coherence of these symbols, the concepts they represent, and the ways in which they convey their meanings strongly suggests that they were part of a single, well-defined system that was meant to convey and perpetuate specific meanings. (Scranton 2015)

It is of interest that the greater Pohnpaid site and its legends possess similar esoteric and physical components, as do other megalithic sacred sites of the world: petroglyphs, megaliths, cupules, stone circles, running water (possibly a spring?), ethno-astronomical glyph content, geophysical-astronomical grid placement, and legends of portals, extraterrestrials, fertility, giants and little people, shape-shifting, magic, and, no doubt, ritual.

So what does this mean?

In the following material Pohnpaid will be examined in terms of it being not only a physical demonstration of global cultural diffusion but also a remnant of a prediluvian advanced civilization—in a word, Mu—that left its consistent mark around our world.

These comparisons are drawn from only a few of the hundreds of petroglyphs at the site.

POHNPAID, THE FIRST STONE ALTAR?

The literal translation of the name Pohnpei is "upon a stone altar." While most interpret this to mean the entirety of the actual island or the altar made by its first migrations, it cannot be ruled out that it refers to the Pohnpaid site. Presumably, the ultimate "first" stone altar would be under the waters of Nan Madol, within the heavenly city of Kahnihmueiso. One may only imagine the magnitude of this temple. Pohnpaid might have been created as a high mountain altar concurrent with Kahnihmueiso or constructed later, after its demise.

Hints of Pohnpaid's antiquity are found in an 1837 article in the *Sailor's Magazine,* a reprint from the *Hobart Town Courier.* It reports of "far greater ruins" about eight miles inland from Nan Madol, including stones with "figures" on them. This report speaks of different social systems, in which women have more equality, another clue to an older civilization that is now "above (pointing to the heavens)" (Oug 1837).

The antiquity of the Pohnpaid site renders it forgotten in traditional island lore, unless it was in fact the actual first stone *pei* created after the loss of Kahnihmueiso, the ancient prototype that all subsequent "stone altars" imitated. That the extraordinary Pohnpaid stone circles and boulder field are not mentioned in any Pohnpeian creation legends, per se, alludes to their predating cultural memory. Because the Pohnpaid outcrop petroglyphs came later over time as intermittent additions, they are mythically documented.

Pohnpaid's architects/engineers, most likely the immigrants from Eir, were vaguely referred to as the "people of old." Linked to the Kahnihmueiso/Eir/Mu era, their earliest and most impressive "stone altar" was erected near the Lehdau River in Madolenihmw. Its alignments to the pyramidal peak of Takaieu, Nan Madol, and especially Kahnihmueiso suggest that Pohnpaid predates the ancient site of Salapwuk in Kitti if it was not its contemporary.

If Pohnpaid were erected circa 7500 BCE or earlier, *and after* the original catastrophe that sank Kahnihmueiso, *and before* sea levels rose to Salapwuk's current height, Pohnpaid was low enough to be underwater when voyagers reached Salapwuk. Waters receded, resulting in Pohnpaid's currrent location at twenty feet above sea level. Pohnpaid's purpose was the same as all stone altars of Pohnpei Island's creation myths: to mark a sacred location.

In the end, the whereabouts of the original "stone altar" likely depend on when and where any given "canoe" landed, whether celestial or historic. The possibility of any number of sites increases by taking into consideration the antiquity of lost civilizations whose survivors or descendants returned generations later using remembered lore and navigational chants . . . or supernatural powers. It is well known that history is often rewritten by the conquerors, or in this case, the survivors.

MEGALITHIC MARKERS

It is commonplace for the megalithic sites that span the globe to have similar characteristics or components, as mentioned previously. Pohnpaid is no exception. A sacred place must initially exhibit or emanate enhanced earth energies of one kind or another—a mandatory component and the raison d'etre for building structures upon it.

Documentation of how a megalithic structure conducts and amplifies earth energy fields at sacred locations is found in the electrophotography technique developed by Gilbert Le Cossec. He captured nonvisible sections of the electromagnetic spectrum emissions of megalith pulsations that reached into the atmosphere as high as the magnetosphere.

> These granite Menhirs with high silicon content are good conductors and act as enormous capacitors of resonant energy from the Earth Energy currents into which they are embedded . . .
>
> Le Cossec photographed early Christian sites which were known to be built on top of megalithic sites. These Christian stones

continue to demonstrate the same pulsations of energy as the original megalithic sacred stone sites. . . .

There is a clear interplay between the electromagnetic currents generated by the Earth's magnetic field, creating telluric currents within the surface of the Earth and there [sic] transmission of the same energy into space by the carefully sculpted and precisely located megalithic stones . . .

They also help create a more stable environment by dampening the effect of sudden fluctuations in electromagnetic activity between the surface of the Earth and magnetosphere and ionosphere. (Olcott 2013)

The megaliths of Pohnpaid are basalt, reported to have a high dielectric content* (the property of transmitting electric force without conduction).

Fig. 6.1. Phallic monolith, Pohnpaid meadow.
Photo by Carole Nervig, 1992.

---

*About basalt rock, Ahmad and Zihlif (1990) state, "Some magnetic properties and electrical characteristics at low and high (microwave) frequency of basaltic rocks are reported. The magnetic measurements show that basalt rocks are ordered ferromagnetically in particle size form. The low-frequency results indicate that basalt samples have relatively high dielectric constant."

Was the phallic monolith of Pohnpaid once erect and vertical? Was its surface originally covered by hundreds of petroglyphs, or were they inscribed over time? Due to its antiquity, these questions will probably remain unanswered.

Megalithic sites around the world—particularly vertical menhirs—suggest what Pohnpaid may have looked like in its prime. The monolith of Ko'a Heiau Holomoana at Mahukona, Hawai'i provides an example (fig. 6.2).

Initially these sites were often only spots of natural beauty, identified by the energies they emitted. Placing structures upon these energetically potent sites to amplify their resonance demonstrates advanced technical knowledge. The power of such sacred places was later usurped by subsequent cultures, and eventually by organized religion. However, as Le Cossec again demonstrates with his electro-photography, the original emanations continue even after Christian churches are placed upon them.

Fig. 6.2. Ko'a Heiau Holomoana monolith, Mahukona, Hawai'i. Photo by Carole Nervig, 2005.

STONE CIRCLES

Although it's tempting to focus only on the astounding petroglyphs, it is imperative to comprehend this place of power as a complex. As is typical of any sacred site, Pohnpaid has various components: a natural basalt outcrop blanketed with rock art; an adjacent meadow to the northeast, where remnants of a double megalithic stone circle lie scattered from their original positions (fig. 6.3); running water in proximity; and at least two dozen solitary glyphed boulders and megaliths. Even more intriguing is what may lie *under* the complex or on unexposed, buried surfaces underneath the inscribed stones.

Unfortunately, there are no aerial photographs or Google Earth maps showing these circles or any megaliths in the meadow. Aerial photographs and Google Earth maps depict the outcrop only as a brown mass. That the area is cloaked in unrelenting tropical foliage is a continual barrier to documentation. Not even drones or a small plane, if they could fly low or slow enough, can permeate Pohnpaid's long-lasting anonymity. This precludes the ability to comprehensively map the archaeoastronomical relationships that stone circles typically exhibit. On-site calculations are long overdue and await the clearing of this meadow.

Fig. 6.3. Inner stone circle, Pohnpaid.
Photo by Carole Nervig, 1992.

Stones composing the inner circle are in close proximity to each other and enormous, as indicated by the six-foot adult male dwarfed by massive basalt hulks (plate 15). The "elephant" rock, found and photographed by the author, is also within this inner circle and will be discussed later in this chapter. (See fig. 6.3; plate 25.)

The majority of stones within the *outer* circle tend to be smaller and quite scattered, making it more difficult to recognize their once circular formation. They include the "bird stone," "basin stone," "scallop stone," "star stone," and colossal "phallic stone," as well as the more distant but most well-known Takai en Pahsu "vagina stone" and others yet to be identified and documented.

What appears to be another stone circle or configuration in the Madolenihmw District was shown to the author in 1991 in a forest clearing while en route to a waterfall inland from Wapar. The Pohnpeian guide acknowledged the spot, called Wuk Kutoahr (fig. 6.4 and 6.5), as possessing mwanamwan and historical importance but would not elaborate on why, nor share relevant legends. The existence of other such circles on Pohnpei Island is likely, whether completely hidden in upland volcanic forest or unnoticed because their original components are no

Fig. 6.4. Proposed stone circle in the vicinity of Wapar-Pohnlangas, Madolenihmw.
Photo by Carole Nervig, 1992.

Fig. 6.5. Proposed Wuk Kutoahr stone circle, Pohnlangas, Madolenihmw.
Photo by Carole Nervig, 1992.

longer in a circular configuration. Sapwtakai and Salapwuk in the Kitti District are distinct possibilities for investigation.

The proliferation of stone circles in Europe and North America is common knowledge. In fact, geophysical subsurface imaging has revealed "Superhenge," larger man-made circular structures near Stonehenge, possibly constructed eleven thousand years ago. More recently, at least one hundred thousand stone circles have been identified in Africa. The site known as Adam's Calendar (fig. 6.7) is calculated to be the oldest, from 75,000 to 160,000 years old. Most shocking was the 176,000-year-old date of four hundred hewn stalagmites used to intentionally construct rings a thousand feet from the entrance of Bruniquel Cave in southern France. Of these, Chris Stringer, paleoanthropologist of the Natural History Museum in London, said, "These must have been made by early Neanderthals, the only known human inhabitants of Europe at this time" (BBC News 2016). The circular stones at Göbekli Tepe (fig. 6.6) are well-known to those with a background in the subject.

Fig. 6.6. Göbekli Tepe, 20,000–12,000 BCE, Turkey.
Photo by Ilkay Dede.

Fig. 6.7. Adam's Calendar, 158,000–73,000 BCE, South Africa.
Photo by Adwo.

Fig. 6.8. Badrulchau, Belau, Micronesia.
Photo by Suzuki Kaku, 2018.

While abundant in Europe and North America, and to some extent in South America and Asia, stone circles are not, to date, as plentiful in Oceania, but they do exist (fig. 6.8).

Certainly any number of Pacific islands other than Pohnpei have held their share of stone circles, evidence of which no doubt may have been removed as mankind continues to develop natural landscapes at an alarming rate. In 1928 a stone circle was "discovered" on Tongareva, Cook Islands, by Sir Peter Buck, noted New Zealand medical doctor, anthropologist, and museum director. He intimated it was created *before* the island's Polynesian marae (stone temple) building culture. Buck said:

> My discovery in 1928 of circular arrangements of stones on the islands of Atutahi and Naue . . . one of these circles is on the island of Naue, on the lagoon side of the Mahue marae. Ten pillars of medium size are arranged roughly in a circle about 37 feet in diameter. The other structure is on the lagoon side of Atutahi about 120 yards from the Rupe-tangi-rekareka marae. It consists of eight limestone

pillars with long spaces between some of them. Other pillars have probably been removed. The enclosed space is more elliptical than circular. If an extinct people built the circles, they must have built them before the marae builders arrived. (P. H. Buck 1932)

Did people in Australia erect a megalithic circle prior to people in Africa having done so? According to the wealth of archaeological evidence found on-site and tribal elders' confirmations, Frederic Slater, Egyptologist and president of the Australian Archaeological Research and Education Society, claims this stone arrangement on Tongareva is potentially the most sacred archaeological site in Australia. "The mound is one of the oldest; I should say *the* oldest, forms of temples in the world, and dates back to the . . . advent of first man."

Fig. 6.9. Stone circles in Mullumbimby, Australia.
Computer-generated image by Richard Patterson, 2013.

Fig. 6.10. Waitapu, pre-Polynesian solar observatory, New Zealand.
Photo by Martin Doutré.

Again, though less known than those of Western civilization, stone circles with archaeoastronomic alignments are now documented in China, India, Japan, Korea, and South America. According to Laird Scranton's *Point of Origin,* megaliths, stone circles, and the placement of upright monoliths represented the ancestors and in India were the earliest forms of the Sakti goddess tradition, often taking the form of standing stone pedestals.

Megalithic sites in India are dated from 7000 BCE in North India, around the Ganges Valley, to 2500 BCE in South India, in Karnataka and 1000 BCE in Tamil Nadu. (Rajagopalan 2010)

This time frame from India not only encompasses Pohnpaid's construction phases from at least circa 7600 BCE, from the earlier boulder field to the rock outcropping, but also falls in the midst of the Jōmon period, which lasted from about 14,000–500 BCE and represents the beginning of "civilization" in Japan. (The date of 3117 BCE, fixed by

Megaliths.net as the era of the "Megalithic Survey of the Earth," is within these parameters as well but perhaps *is* skewed by the proliferation of more recently discovered European sites.)

Hundreds of stone circles have cropped up all over Japan. Of particular note is the four-thousand-year-old Oyu site, another "double stone circle" configuration within the Pacific Rim, like the one found on Pohnpaid. Ceremonial stone circles first appeared in Japan at the onset of the Jōmon era. The fact that Oyu is of Jōmon origin strengthens its probable connection with descendants of Mu.

Chinese archaeologists discovered an ancient observatory, dating back to some 4,100 years ago, in north China's Shanxi Province. The Taosis site is at least three thousand years older than the thousand-year-old observatory built by the Mayans, claimed He Nu, a research fellow with the Institute of Archaeology of the Chinese Academy of Social Sciences (according to *China Daily* 2005).

It may also come as a surprise that Korea still has more standing megaliths than any other country to date. "The president of the World Megalithic Association (WMA) in Korea, Yoo In-hak, claimed in 1999 that 25,000 dolmens still existed in Korea as opposed to 80,000 dolmens and standing stones thirty years previous. Most have been destroyed by land development, construction and ignorance" (Megaliths.net, n.d.).

Because it is part of both the Pacific and Atlantic Rims, one would expect to find cultural continuity of stone circle observatories across South America. Such is the case. The megalithic astronomical observatory of Calçoene, Brazil, consists of 127 blocks of granite, each up to four meters tall, standing upright in a circle measuring more than thirty meters in diameter. Near Puno and Lake Titicaca, the thirteen-thousand-foot Sillustani complex (fig. 6.11) contains both stone circles and two chullpas (megalithic stone towers). Time will no doubt continue to reveal others camouflaged by overgrown Amazon jungles or located on remote Andean peaks.

The erection of stone circles on the island of Pohnpei is significant for two reasons. First, their presence reinforces the status of both Pohnpaid and the whole of Pohnpei Island as *sacred space*. Ibrahim Karim explains in biogeometric terms the energetic essence of the circle and how it embodies sacred space.

Fig. 6.11. Sillustani stone circle, Puno (near Lake Titicaca), Peru.
Photo by Nicola Messana.

We refer to the quality produced by the wisdom of the universe as the "Centering Quality," which takes the qualities inherent in the balancing role of the center and spreads them into the whole shape giving it all the same energy quality as the center.

The actual center of the central point has no time or space attributes, and therefore connects to a different dimension than the geometrical figure it balances. This transcendental connection of the center to another dimension is a doorway through which the primordial timeless moment manifests in the duality of motion and shape. The shape actually becomes multidimensional through the "Centering Quality." (Karim 2010)

The second reason that the erection of stone circles on the island of Pohnpei is significant is because it establishes the Pohnpaid complex as a case in point for cultural diffusion. These circles and the advanced astronomical knowledge required to build them are found on *all* continents, with the exception of Antarctica—unless her melting glaciers expose their megalithic secrets and provide even more clues to the connection. Exactly which culture(s) or race(s) created Pohnpaid, and during which time frame, remains to be seen. Possibilities include ancient navigators, sun worshippers, technologically advanced progeny of Mu, extraterrestrial or interdimensional intelligence, or, sequentially, all of the above.

STAR REFLECTOR BASINS

Of the three documented basin stones at Pohnpaid, one was likely utilized for stargazing or astronomical calculations; the other two are linked to fertility and birthing. The single "star reflector" basin boulder has a distinctly dissimilar look from the two more sensual "vagina" basin megaliths (known to Pohnpeians as Takai en Pahsu). None of these three known basin stones are in particular proximity to each other within the site.

Observation is in order to determine if water is continually present in this shallow basin, as is shown in the photograph taken during a drought, which is not common for Pohnpei. Although rainfall is frequent, water caught in this boulder could evaporate quickly. It could be questioned whether or not a metaphysical factor keeps it full of water in the baking sun.

The petroglyphed basin stone probably used for stargazing is located in the outer stone circle. Its interpretation as an archaeoastronomical device is based on its resemblance to similar megalithic water basin mechanisms found across a variety of cultures. Accurate prediction of celestial events was crucial to all ancient peoples, especially any culture of navigators, and was essential for establishing their religious and political authority.

The geometric style patterns that intersect the water depression on its surface indicate this particular water basin stone was used to track celestial movement. As the reflections of the night sky moved across the water's surface, the etched markings indicate how a specific heavenly body changed its position. Without these glyphs it would be easier to assign a different function to the water in the basin. Perhaps it was used for purification or fertility rituals, for instance. Until scientific archaeoastronomical calculations are measured, one can only guess as to what celestial alignments the stone articulated: solstices/equinoxes, solar/lunar, stellar/constellational, or planetary.

The most convincing evidence of utilization of the basin stone for archaeoastronomical calculations is the petroglyph adjacent to it (figs. 6.12 and 6.13). It bears a strong resemblance to the Carolinian star compass used by Pacific seafarers (fig. 6.14).

Fig. 6.12. Star reflector basin stone with geometric inscriptions, Pohnpaid meadow.
Photo by Carole Nervig, 1992.

Fig. 6.13. Star reflector
basin stone with
geometric inscriptions,
Pohnpaid meadow.
Photo by Carole Nervig, 1992.

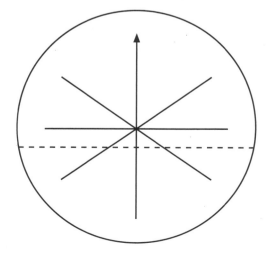

Fig. 6.14. Carolinian sidereal
(star) compass.
Illustration by Alexandra Edwards
after Ward H. Goodenough, 1953.

The basin stone petroglyphs are not the only motifs found at Pohnpaid that indicate an astronomical function. The phallic rock has a glyph that also relates to navigation or stargazing, perhaps specifically a star compass (figs. 6.15 and 6.16; plates 26 and 27). Alexandra Edwards explains that the "wheel in a circle" petroglyph demonstrates knowledge of the stars in relationship to each other by their unequal positioning to each other and the cardinal directions. This is more evidence that one of Pohnpaid's functions was celestial observation and calculation.

> But as it is, it resembles the Carolinian star compass even more, since the stars lie in unequal positions in relation to each other and the different cardinal points. In this case it would be marking Cassiopeia-Scorpius, and as it is crossing from the East to the West, it would probably be indicating a SW direction. (Edwards 2017)

Fig. 6.15. Wheel compass petroglyph, among other petroglyphs
on the phallic monolith, Pohnpaid.
Photo by Alexandra Edwards, 2017.

Fig. 6.16. Detail of wheel compass on the phallic monolith, Pohnpaid.
Photo by Lynn Danaher, 2017.

As components of sacred megalithic sites, ancient stones with basins or pits aligned for astronomical observation are not unique to Pohnpaid or Oceania. More are being identified as investigations expand to more remote areas of the world. The water mirror stone at Machu Picchu (fig. 6.17) utilized during Inti Raymi summer solstice rituals is an excellent example. On Facebook, Juan Pablo Francolini, of the Centro de investigación de la Nueva Conciencia y Culturas Madres, explains:

> The astronomers / as called "Laramas" were the ones who should witness these events, using the astronomical water mirrors "Nayra Samka" and the "intiwatana" stone markers, recording these events in the Kipus, ring records, calculating and predicting through the yupanas or Andean calculators.

Star reflector mirrors are not always circular. At Cochasqui, a site of fifteen pyramids in Ecuador, two circular platforms are found on the top of one of these pyramids. Upon each of these platforms are two small holes surrounded by trenches in which conical stones were placed.

Fig. 6.17. Mirror stones, solstice sun, Machu Picchu, Peru.
Photo by Xxxyyy123, 2014.

Fig. 6.18. Friday stone, Konezerye Luga, Russia. Legend has it that the water in this stone never dries.
Photographer unknown.

Fig. 6.19. Male (upright) and female (basin) stones, Mo'okini, first heiau, Hawai'i, dated to 490 CE.
Photo by Carole Nervig, 1996.

Fig. 6.20. Basin stone, Basemah culture, Indonesia.
Photo from the Jambi Cultural Conservation Center.

Fig. 6.21. *Left:* Bullaun bowl, Ireland. *Right:* Bullaun bowl, New Zealand.
Photos by Martin Doutré.

Fig. 6.22. Possibly originally a basin stone, later repurposed as a lusong (grinding stone). Pågat Guam, Micronesia.
Photo by Michael Bevacqua, 2010.

Some researchers believe these channels, when filled with water, acted as mirrors to observe the stars. Other examples of mirrors from around the world are shown on the previous pages.

Another universal function associated with water basin mirrors is divination. Gazing at the water opened "vision," or the unconscious, to "see" the unseen or nonphysical dimensions. In fact, Masao Hadley, noted Pohnpeian oral historian and author of *Nan Madol: Spaces on the Reef of Heaven,* told me in personal communication that this is exactly how the pool Namweias at Nan Madol was used. As I wrote in my booklet on Nan Madol, published in the 1970s, "It was in the reflection of this pool [Namweias] that [folk hero] Isokelekel discovered his old age and committed suicide. Smaller than Nanweias, Peirot was the pool in which any part of the world could be seen."

FERTILITY RULES

At Pohnpaid, only one overarching legendary and metamorphic theme is apparent to date: fertility. Whether related to fecundity or birthing, Pohnpaid's sexy boulders all allude to procreation in one form or another. These boulders number five to date: one gigantic "vagina" stone, or Takai en Pahsu, within the inner stone circle; one smaller Takai en Pahsu near the access road; a "hind end" stone; a clam-shaped boulder also near the road; and one phallic monolith.

It's anyone guess how many more fertility megaliths may be found in the future when the entire site is cleared, or just how vast an area the site actually encompasses. (Beyond the Pohnpaid site, a Takai en Pahsu has also been reported by *Soulik en Lohd* within Lohd kousap, Madolenihmw.)

Female (vagina) stones dominate Pohnpaid in both number and traditional lore. That said, the single known male (phallic) representation is clearly no minor element and is quite impressive, both in size and in the rock art that covers it.

Monolith or Phallus?
The male stone, the distinctive and gigantic phallic monolith in Pohnpaid's meadow, has no legends associated with it. Its importance is indicated by the profusion of all manner of petroglyphs that cover its

exposed surfaces. And what of its now-buried surfaces? Any number of glyphs could be present *if* this stone once stood erect in the earth. With no hint of its *function* from Pohnpeian oral accounts—whether as upright monolith for archaeoastronomical alignments or for fertility practices—comparisons to physically matching stones that actually *do* have legends attached to them may provide the only clues to its function.

As with most petroglyph sites, there is the distinct possibility that inscriptions of such a vast amount necessarily took place over an enormous time span, layer upon layer. It would be most helpful to utilize technologies such as lichenometry (the study of lichen growth on a rock surface) to obtain approximate ages of the hundreds of petroglyphs at Pohnpaid.

Fig. 6.23. Phallic monolith, Pohnpaid.
Photo by Carole Nervig, 1992.

Fig. 6.24. Petroglyphs on phallic monolith, Pohnpaid.
Photo by Carole Nervig, 1992.

Fig. 6.25. Kauleonanahoa phallic rock, Molokai, Hawai'i.
Photo by Walter Stiedenroth.

Fig. 6.26. Muisca El Infiernito phallic rock, Colombia.
Photo by James Wagstaff.

Fig. 6.27. Phallic rocks, Metsamor, Armenia.
Photo by Andrew Selkirk, 2013.

Pohnpaid's phallic stone might serve a similar purpose as the prominent Kauleonanahoa phallic stone of Molokai: to help women conceive. Upright phallus stones of Chucuito, Peru, were part of ancient religious rites to cure women of infertility—not unlike Pohnpeian lore attached to Pohnpaid's vagina stones.

> Pohaku also factored into the conception of children. On Moloka'i, the famous phallic stone, Kauleonanahoa at Pala'au, Moloka'i has the power to help women conceive. According to tradition, if a woman goes to Kauleonanahoa with offerings and spends the night there, she will return home pregnant. (Aluli and McGregor, n.d.)

There is no rule that such a monolith, especially Pohnpaid's, served only one role. Over vast periods of time and any number of cultures, the phallic menhirs entertain many interpretations, particularly when found within sacred megalithic space. After all, many ancient cultures associated sex with supernatural forces, especially the magic of fertility.

One interpretation of significance from the Egyptian mystery school teachings, *and most other esoteric traditions,* uses the erect penis image to symbolize the transmission of spiritual energy and enlightenment. The phallus represents the spinal column, the conduit for kundalini energy to rise from the base chakra to the higher centers of the pineal, pituitary, and thalamus glands during the enlightenment experience.

If other elements of Pohnpaid indicate esoteric or spiritual influences (for instance, pyramids, winged sun disks, and the seven-headed serpent, which also signifies the chakras and enlightenment), it is not out of the question that its phallic monolith would also be a representation of a universal esoteric process or belief.

Pohnpaid's Vagina Stones

Just off the road between Pohnpaid's outcrop and its bouldered meadow lies the smaller, well-known Takai en Pahsu, with its pronounced female "basin." Whether it was once part of the outer or secondary stone circle is unclear. If so, its current location might indicate that it was a) moved, b) aligned with other megalithic components, or c) aligned between unknown points even outside of Pohnpaid proper.

As we have established, oral history relates that the Takai en Pahsu is the vagina of a mythical woman who broke into pieces, and it's said to this very day that touching it induces pregnancy. Its potency derives from it being the only physical remnant of a goddess from the skies who "broke into pieces" or was "eaten by a group of men," depending on which version was recalled. Alleged stone "buttocks" of this same woman lie nearby on the other side of the path.

Although significantly different in size, both of the two vagina or birthing basin stones at Pohnpaid have a sensual, more feminine look than the stargazing basin. Their smoother surface would allow a more comfortable seat if, in fact, they were utilized in a birthing process.

The other gargantuan basin megalith is in the inner stone circle core. Unlike the roadside Takai en Pahsu, no traditional lore accompanies this enormous vagina megalith because, until this publication, Pohnpeians were not even aware of its existence. Nor are there legends that account for the small and geometric style incisions in its vaginal area (not visible in the photograph) . . . all of which indicate its antiquity.

Fig. 6.28. Smaller Takai en Pahsu (vagina stone), roadside, Pohnpaid. Photo by Carole Nervig, 1992.

Fig. 6.29. Takai en Pahsu with incised genitalia, inner circle, Pohnpaid.
Photo by Carole Nervig, 1992.

Fig. 6.30. Hind end rock, Pohnpaid.
Photo by John Amato, 2010.

Plate 1. Takai en Pahsu "fertility" stone with burned meadow and megaliths in background, 1992.

Plate 2. Takai en Pahsu with author, Pohnpaid meadow, near the road, 1992.

Plate 3. Portion of burned boulder field, Pohnpaid meadow, 1992.

Plate 4. Phallic monolith, Pohnpaid meadow, 1992.

Plate 5. Double-enveloped cross on phallic monolith, Pohnpaid meadow, 1992.

Plate 6. Triple-enveloped cross and sun on phallic monolith, Pohnpaid meadow, 1992.

Plate 7. Grid motif on phallic monolith, Pohnpaid meadow, 1992.

Plate 8. Grid motifs and small enveloped cross (*top*) on phallic monolith, Pohnpaid meadow, 1992.

Plate 9. Pyramid or runway motif on phallic monolith, Pohnpaid meadow.

Plate 10. Boat or canoe glyph on phallic monolith, Pohnpaid meadow, 1992.

Plate 11. "Star mirror" basin surrounded by inscribed astronomical motifs, Pohnpaid meadow, 1992.

Plate 12. Detail of astronomical inscriptions on basin stone, Pohnpaid meadow, 1992.

Plate 13. Winged sun disk stone, Pohnpaid meadow, 1992.

Plate 14. Bird, star, or Pleiades motif on stone,
Pohnpaid meadow, 1992.

Plate 15. Inner circle of megaliths (note adult on right),
Pohnpaid meadow, 1992.

Plate 16. Gigantic
Takai en Pahsu
stone, inner
megalithic circle,
Pohnpaid meadow,
1992.

Plate 17. "Elephant" stone, inner megalithic circle, Pohnpaid meadow, 1992.

Plate 18. Panorama from top of Pohnpaid outcrop, with Takaieu Peak on the left side of the horizon, 1992.

Plate 19. "Clam" boulder with author pointing to "scallops," Pohnpaid meadow, near the road, 2018.
Photo by Morleen Thomas.

Inset: Detail of "scallops" on "clam" boulder, Pohnpaid meadow.

Plate 20. Line of sight from Pohnpaid outcrop (foreground) to Takaieu Peak, 1990.

Plate 21. Madolenihmw Bay from inland Pohnpaid vicinity to Takaieu Peak to Pahndien Point to Peiniot (extreme right, not included) to Nahkapw Islet (extreme right, not included) to horizon.
Photo by Lee Arkhie Perez, 2021.

Plate 22. Line of sight from Nahkapw Islet (far right of Nan Madol but not shown) to Peiniot Islet (right) to Pahndien Point to Takaieu Peak to Pohnpaid.
Photo by the Micronesia Seminar.

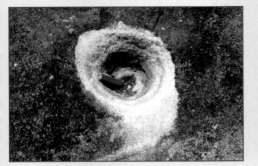

Plate 23. *Top:* Two of four cupules on top of the Pohnpaid outcrop in alignment with Takaieu Peak. *Bottom:* Detail of a cupule, 1992.

Plate 24. "Hind end" rock with possible alignment groove, Pohnpaid meadow.
Photo by John Amato, 2010.

Plate 25. Inner megalith circle, Pohnpaid meadow, 1992.

Plate 26. Astronomical wheel compass with enveloped cross and fish or turtle motifs on phallic monolith, Pohnpaid meadow.
Photo by Alexandra Edwards, 2017.

Plate 27. Detail of astronomical wheel compass on phallic monolith, Pohnpaid meadow.
Photo by Lynn Danaher, 2017.

Plate 28. Layers of petroglyphs on phallic monolith, Pohnpaid meadow, 1992.

Plate 29. Detail of Takai en Pahsu, Pohnpaid meadow, near the road, 1992.

Plate 30. Core circle of winged sun disk stone, Pohnpaid, 1992.

Plate 31. Triple-outline enveloped cross on phallic monolith, Pohnpaid meadow, 1992.

Plate 32. Detail on phallic monolith, Pohnpaid meadow, 1992.

Plate 33. Detail on phallic monolith with circled cross and geometric motifs, Pohnpaid meadow, 1992.

Plate 34. Serpent head and sun petroglyphs, Pohnpaid outcrop, 1992.

Plate 35. Humanoid petroglyph, Pohnpaid outcrop, 1970.

These geometrical carvings or genital incisions on Pohnpaid's largest vagina stone recall those found on a basalt boulder in Gunung Padang and dated to between 8000 and 5000 BCE. To refresh, Gunung Padang is a megalithic site in Indonesia constructed primarily of columnar basalt, as is Nan Madol. There is no association of fertility to the Gunung Padang rock currently, nor are the incisions positioned upon a vagina shape as at Pohnpaid. Of added significance is the correspondence between the 8000–7000 BCE time frame estimated for the first phase of Pohnpaid and Gunung Padang.

Although the popular description of the "hind end" stone of Pohnpaid characterizes it as part of a sky goddess broken into pieces, the stone is not particularly reminiscent of buttocks. It could have served an entirely different function. Perhaps its channel or groove was used for aligning archaeoastronomical movements, or for providing a line of sight to other sacred locations or stones.

The fertility function attached to these stones known as Takai en Pahsu is primarily based on Pohnpei legends, current beliefs, and physical similarities to other Pacific "birthing" stones. That they could also be star reflectors cannot be discounted, especially when other sites also possesses both star basins and birthing basins. No traditions suggest that these Pohnpeian vagina stones were specifically used for the birth process, but such similarities with Hawaiian birthing sites beg the question.

The undeniable resemblance of Pohnpaid Takai en Pahsu to certain *pohaku* (birthing stones) at the complex of Kukaniloko, Oahu (fig. 6.32, p. 144), strongly suggests that both were used in a similar manner. In the midst of a pineapple field near Wahiewa, the entire site emanates potent spiritual energies, or mana, as does Pohnpaid's boulder-strewn meadow, in the author's experience. Kukaniloko is one of the most powerful sacred sites of Oahu. As mentioned earlier, it was at this site the Hawaiian ali'i (royal) children were birthed.

Because early Hawaiians believed the geographic piko (navel) of Oahu was Kukaniloko, the monument was symbolically the most powerful birth site for the island' [sic] most famous high chiefs. The Ho'olonopahu Heiau (temple) associated with Kukaniloko was subsequently destroyed, as were many others in the area, for pineapple and sugar cane plantations.

Fig. 6.31. Seven-foot basin, Michigan.
Photo from *Ancient American* magazine.

Fig. 6.32. Stone basin, Kukaniloko, Oahu, Hawai'i.
Photo by the Institute of Astronomy, University of Hawai'i, 2000.

Fig. 6.33. Stone basin, Solomon Islands, Oceania.
Photo courtesy of the Harold Scheffler Papers, Special Collections and Archives, UC San Diego, 1969.

Select places and resources were recognized to have special powers of healing. Structures for healing were also constructed to focus healing life forces at these sites. We discuss the more prominent places and sites below and note that there are many more healing places and sites which are known only to local communities and 'ohana. Pohaku or stones are believed to hold mana or spiritual power. Pohaku are featured in shrines as manifestations of 'aumakua or family guardians and akua or deities and 'uhane or spirits. Throughout the islands are famous and named pohaku, which figure prominently in healing and health. A row of 18 stones, credited with the power to absorb pain, was laid down on both the right side and the left side of the central birthing stone, Kukaniloko, a large stone that supported the mother in a semi-sitting position. A chief stood at each of the 36 stones to witness the birth. (Aluli and McGregor, n.d.)

Archaeoastronomical functions have also been assigned to the Kukaniloko site, as discussed previously, providing more than just a physical likeness to Pohnpaid.

One of the basin stones at Kukaniloko was believed to be a reflecting pool for watching the zenith passage of celestial objects, not unlike the stargazing basin at Pohnpaid. Some of the stones were also used to map stars and mark seasonal changes, combining fertility with the stars and seasons. Lately, because of the wide view of the skies

Fig. 6.34. *Left:* Kane-Lono, detail with sun dagger, Kukaniloko, Wahiawa, Oahu, Hawai'i.
Photo by the Institute of Astronomy, University of Hawai'i, 2000.
Right: Compare the image of the sun dagger with this core
circle of winged sun disk stone, Pohnpaid.
Photo by Carole Nervig, 1992.

from Kukaniloko, the site is also believed to be a sort of Hawaiian Stonehenge. Designs and shapes on its stones could have been used by early Hawaiians to track the movements of celestial objects, reports a team from the University of Hawai'i Institute for Astronomy after their April 2000 investigation.

Pohnpeian traditions do not cite a birthing use per se, for Pohnpaid, only the fecundity aspect of creating pregnancy by a mere touch—an "immaculate conception." If this site was used *initially* for birthing by peoples earlier than the remembered Pohnpeian lineages, the lack of its legendary records regarding its birthing function is no surprise. One must question how this Pohnpaid basin became connected to fertility. The answer may lie in the entire site's utilization by long-forgotten civilizations and its relationships with the celestial—those women "coming from the sky" and hidden in clam "rocks." So it is that legendary legacies indicate that their creation or original source was from those very stars.

BASINS AS RITUAL FONTS

In some cultures (not necessarily prehistoric), basins may serve as receptacles of "holy water" used for blessings, curses, prayers, and ritual washing. Although there are no oral traditions of rituals performed at Pohnpaid, it is a plausible concept, considering its three stone basins. The universal practice of baptism might well have originated with star map basins, whose water was "holy" to astronomer-priests. This water, in time, was recycled for purification or healing ceremonies. In Egypt, not only were newborn children baptized to purify them of blemishes acquired in the womb, a ritual bath preceded initiation into the cult of Isis. A pagan baptism ritual preceded the Christian sacrament.

CUPULES

Aside from water basins, cupules demonstrate yet another way stones are utilized as star maps and other as of yet undetermined functions.

Cupules are considered rock art and occur worldwide and in almost every prehistoric and historic period. Normally they are shallow bowl- or cup-shaped indentations carved, pecked, or pounded into a rock surface for cultural purposes. They rarely occur singly, usually forming groups.

Cupules appear also in numerous Holocene contexts in China, for instance on dolmen, but there is a universal trend, in all continents, for the oldest petroglyphs being primarily cupules. (Bednarik 2008)

Cupules are never formed completely naturally. Either they are hewn entirely from stone or a natural depression has been embellished. Neither are they to be confused with abrasion-formed grinding hollows of natural or cultural origin, used for processing food, dye, or other material.

I cannot think that these cup-marked stones and cups and rings are only coincidentally identical the world over and it may be that they once did have a common origin and common symbolism. We are a long way from determining what those are though. What we do know is those cup marks, or cupules, have been dated to at least 100,000 years ago and some as far back as 700,000 years. (Varner 2012)

The meaning and function of cupules are often nebulous, intangible, and diverse. No surprise is the connection with shamans and their rituals. It is of note that the Pohnpaid cupules are also linked with oral histories of journeys to other worlds, again reinforcing the idea that the site may have been used as a portal by shamans or other interdimensional travelers.

A cup-marked stone located in Roseville, California at an ancient Maidu village site is said to have been an entryway by shamans to the other world. After they had reached a state of trance they would fly through the cup mark to the nearby stream where they would then journey to the spirit world to learn new healing techniques. When they returned they would have learned those new ways and applied them to their people. (Varner 2012; see also fig. 6.40, p. 150)

Some researchers assert that cup marks *with rings* depict resonance or the radiation of waves, perhaps from infrasound antennas, a kind of prehistoric global signal system. Although sound is an observable component of the Pohnpaid outcrop, only four cupules or mortars have been found to date and they have no encircling rings around them to indicate resonance.

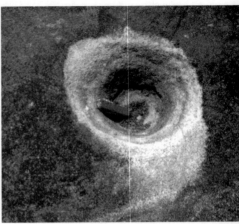

Fig. 6.35. Two of four cupules on the Pohnpaid outcrop, in alignment with Takaieu. Photo by Carole Nervig, 1992.

Fig. 6.36. One of four cupules, Pohnpaid. Photo by Carole Nervig, 1992.

The previous director of tourism for the Federated States of Micronesia proposed to the author that the cupules/mortars were used to house ink for traditional tattooing, with the recipient lying in the center of the inkwells. Perhaps this was a more recent historical *recycling* of the cup marks, but considering the geodesic alignments inherent in their positions, it is not necessarily their original function. This recycling phenomenon is likely to have occurred at innumerable cupule sites for the mundane purposes of grinding, collecting "sacred" water, and other such tasks.

With inherent obscurity as the rule, one exception is noteworthy: a common and documentable function of cupules is as star maps in which stars or constellations are represented by cup marks. Additional markings may accompany cupule configurations and include solstice and equinox points, comets, the Milky Way, the ecliptic, the celestial equator, the circle of precession, and ecliptic poles and pole stars. The indigenous Cañari of Ecuador created a lunar calendar with cupules in certain positions and angles to catch the reflections of the moon in water for each moon month of the year (see Holloway 2015).

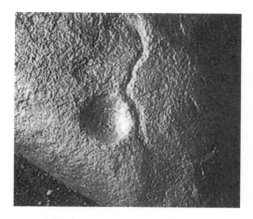

Fig. 6.37. Bhimbetka cupule, dated to the Lower Paleolithic, Madhya Pradesh, India.
Photo by Robert Bednarik, 2001.

Fig. 6.38. Cañari lunar calendar, Ingapirca, Ecuador.
Photo by Angela Perryman.

For the lunar calendar of the Cañari, "the stones were carved in certain positions and angles to catch the reflections of the moon in water for each moon-month of the year" (Holloway 2015).

Most probable is that Pohnpaid's cupules were also used in an archaeoastronomical or geometrical grid alignment for sightings and calculations, particularly with Takaieu, the pyramidal mountain nearby, which in turn aligns with Nakapw of Nan Madol, then with the sunken city of Kahnihmueiso.

Examples of similar celestial calculation functions abound, with cupules in Oceania (including Samoa), Indonesia, India, Australia, New Zealand, South and North America, the British Isles, Scandinavia, Europe, and Russia, with many dated in the time range of Pohnpaid. The oldest known Stone Age art was a cupule found in the 1990s on a boulder in Auditorium Cave, Madhya Pradesh, India. Dates ranging from circa 700,000–290,000 BCE have been established for the Indian boulder by researchers. Some theorize the "meander" adjacent to the cupule may represent a comet.

Found near special vantage points or a significant *ahu* (altar or shrine) on Rapa Nui (Easter Island) are cupules or "'solar ranging devices' or 'sunstones' thought to be aligned with setting solstices and equinoxes," states archaeologist William Mulloy (1975). William Liller, author of *The Ancient Solar Observatories of Rapanui: The Archaeoastronomy of Easter Island,* identified another Rapa Nui stone as a "star stone" due to fact that the formation of its cupules matched the Pleiades.

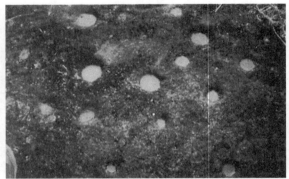

Fig. 6.39. *Left:* Rapa Nui solar ranging device.
Right: Star map of the Pleiades embedded in rock, Rapa Nui.
Photos by William Liller, 1993.

Fig. 6.40. Entry to the Maidu spirit world, Roseville, California.
Photo by Gary R. Varner, 2012.

Fig. 6.41. Cupules, Samoa.
Photo by Martin Doutré.

Archaeologists and Native Americans believe the "Skystone" located in Bonney Lake, Washington, is an ancient observatory, possibly used by more than one extinct culture. Archaeoastronomer Dennis Regan calls it an incredibly accurate scientific tool used by extraordinarily knowledgeable ancient astronomers.

Fig. 6.42. Skystone, Bonney Lake, Washington.
Photo from *Ancient American* magazine, 2003.

Skystone's level top is punctuated by numerous man-made holes. It measures four and a half feet high by twelve feet across, with carved stone steps to the top. The holes form a near perfect parallelogram alignment, indicating the summer and winter solstice sunrise and sunset to within less than 1 percent error. (The Skystone parallelogram resembles the oldest part of Stonehenge, which is marked by four postholes in the exact same manner.) Also indicated are the major and minor lunar standstills. Other pits point directly to Mt. Rainier, Mt. St. Helens, and Mt. Adams and could have been used as baselines. According to Regan, the markings on the Skystone are so precise they could be used today with extreme accuracy.

In addition to grid alignment sightings, the four cupules on the Pohnpaid outcrop may also have been used to track celestial phenomena in a similar manner to those of Skystone. Comprehensive archaeoastronomical mapping would confirm this potential by determining if the cupules did actually form parallelograms.

The mere presence of cupules at Pohnpaid further validates its designation as a sacred site similar to hundreds around the world. It joins the plethora of evidence pointing to massive cultural diffusion of a commonly held religious or astronomical purpose.

Knowledge of celestial movement is crucial for traditional navigators. Literal depictions of their vessels at Pohnpaid are minimal but present.

CANOES OR BOATS?

Whether connected to the varying entities known as the "Sea People" of old or not, there is no disputing the people of Pohnpei's radical need for navigation skills and voyaging craft due to the island's isolation in the vast Pacific.

Considering Micronesia's culture of the sea and the Pohnpaid site's proximity to the ocean, and probable archaeoastronomic alignments, it would be predictable that a petroglyph resembling a boat motif is inscribed on the phallic boulder of the outer stone circle. Logical conjecture would see it as a traditional outrigger, but a reed boat design from South America or Rapa Nui (Easter Island) is not entirely out of the question.

The earliest discovered remains from a reed boat are 7000 years old, found in Kuwait. (Lawler 2002)

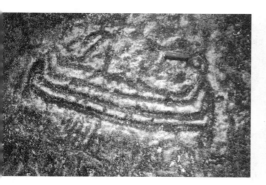

Fig. 6.43. *Left:* Boat or canoe petroglyph, Pohnpaid.
Photo by Carole Nervig, 1992.
Right: Compare the Pohnpaid petroglyph with this totora reed boat, Lake Titicaca, Peru.
Photo by Checco.

Reed boats were also constructed from early times in Peru and Bolivia. In South America, totora reed boats were used by pre-Incan civilizations and are still in use on Lake Titicaca today. They were also used on Rapa Nui, where, according to the Easter Island Foundation, totora reed has been growing for at least thirty thousand years. These reed boats can range up to almost one hundred feet in length, sufficient for ocean voyaging, as the famous Norwegian explorer and adventurer Thor Heyerdahl proved. And Rapa Nui is considerably closer to Micronesia than it is to South America.

If the canoe or boat petroglyph were inverted, it might represent a headdress or plethora of items not in the repertoire of Western thinking or images.

Until the entirety of the petroglyphs on the huge phallic rock at Pohnpaid is carefully mapped, pondering the nature of each of that rock's glyphs and its relationship to others is implausible (see plate 28). However, what is not questionable is the predominate presence of defined "enveloped crosses" on this same phallic rock.

THE ENVELOPED CROSS

To date, the most frequent and distinct symbol at the Pohnpaid site is the equilateral enveloped cross, yet no oral traditions mention its presence or meaning.

Several of these equidistant crosses are found in the boulder field and appear exclusively on one particular phallic monolith, which may demonstrate the significance of the rock or the outer stone circle that houses it (see plate 31). More of these crosses may exist on other gigantic stones yet to be investigated, especially the buried or underground portions of them.

Theories abound on the meaning of the simple *center cross* portion of this symbol and its derivatives. From primordial times to modern, this equilateral cross of a simple angular design was embedded in cultures spanning the four corners of the world. Its use was usually esoteric or spiritual, but not originally "religious." Its presence conveys numerous possible representations: a simple heaven/earth; the four architects of creation cosmologies; polarity themes (positive/negative, yin/yang, male/female); the four elements (earth, air, fire, water); or the four directions (east, west, north, south).

Crosses executed with oval-shaped arms encompassing the center angles are more unique. The incorporation of an "envelope" to the crossed lines gives added, if not quite divergent, meaning(s) to that of the angular center portion alone.

The Pohnpaid crosses are outlined in repetitious lines curving around the crosses' arms, creating a distinct design rhythm that is elegant and sophisticated. Some have one outline; others have two or three. Aside from, or in addition to, execution of artistic style, what was the meaning of this repetitious motif of the single, double, and triple outlines? One assumption would be that each incremental outline acts as a counting system, perhaps measuring time, distance, frequency, or strength. In certain American indigenous traditions, the outlines indicate the phases of Venus and would be consistent with other evidence of stargazing at Pohnpaid.

Archaeologist Edmundo Edwards and his daughter Alexandra Edmonds, authors of *When the Universe Was an Island: Exploring the Cultural and Spritual Cosmos of Ancient Rapa Nui*, as well as numerous related archaeoastronomical publications, propose that the cross envelopes might signify a cultural astronomical measurement of guiding stars or *etak*, utilized in Carolinian navigation systems, that defines distances as celestial "sections." This cross—representing a guiding star, namely Venus—would be consistent with cultures worldwide, not just Carolinian or Austronesian.

Fig. 6.44. Single-outline enveloped cross
on phallic monolith, Pohnpaid.
Photo by Carole Nervig, 1992.

Fig. 6.45. Double-outline enveloped cross
on phallic monolith, Pohnpaid.
Photo by Carole Nervig, 1992.

Fig. 6.46. Triple-outline enveloped cross
on phallic monolith, Pohnpaid.
Photo by Carole Nervig, 1992.

Fig. 6.47. Truncated enveloped cross
on phallic monolith, Pohnpaid.
Photo by Carole Nervig, 1992.

It may be possible to consider that the envelope cross design represents a guiding star as described in the Carolinian etak system of
navigation, where each island lies at a distance of etaks—a term used
interchangeably to refer to the "sections" or the stars—these originally being the "envelopes" outside of the cross that also became an
art style. (Edwards 2017)

Many indigenous North American cultures have a different conception about such petroglyphs; crosses represent places in the rock where shamans "enter" the spirit world. This could well be the case at Pohnpaid, given that various oral histories mention a "doorway" in the rock outcrop.

However, the scarce legends that exist only refer to the creation of the overall Pohnpaid site and the "writing" upon its rocks, *never the meaning of the glyphs themselves.* This absence of knowledge or memory of the petroglyphs' meaning indicates that they may well have been generated by prehistoric cultures absent from the locale for millennia.

Crosses of Oceania

Is this pattern of the enveloped cross found or interpreted elsewhere in Micronesia, or in the Pacific?

Yes, but as with Pohnpaid, no specific references to, or definitions of, this symbol appear in their oral histories, and so the meaning behind the symbol remains elusive.

Enveloped crosses are tracked and their distribution noted by anthropologists as they attempt to create a time line and migratory path from Southeast Asia and the west Pacific to the central Pacific islands. Voyaging Austronesian and Lapita cultures spanned the Pacific Ocean for millennia before the epoch of the Polynesians. Not unexpectedly, in light of the sophisticated navigational knowledge and skill of the ancients, the enveloped cross motif has been documented at Vanuatu, New Caledonia, Papua New Guinea, Manus, New Hanover, the Solomon Islands of Melanesia, and more recently Pohnpaid and Australia. Spriggs (1997) proposed dates between 2000 and 1100 BCE for Melanesian crosses, often engraved upon boulders. According to archaeologist Roger Green, from the University of Auckland, and David Roe, from the Australian National University, this motif is thought to have appeared alongside Lapita pottery decoration that began between 3500 and 3300 BCE (cited in Rainbird and Wilson 2002). Although not an exact match, a more elaborately styled outlined cross appears on Belau, Micronesia, on pottery from a cave burial.

Astoundingly, Aboriginal rock art dating to forty-nine thousand years ago was discovered in a remote area of southern Australia in November 2016. According to reporter Lucy Pasha-Robinson (2016),

Giles Hamm, a consultant archaeologist and doctoral student at La Trobe University, was shown the site by Adnyamathanha elder Cliff Coulthard, who "came across the arid site, known as Warratyi, which showed Aboriginal Australians settled there 49,000 years ago, 10,000 years earlier than previously thought." This pushes the Aboriginal culture back an additional ten thousand years (see Hamm et al. 2016) and supposes that enveloped cross motifs used at Warratyi could have been used at Pohnpaid and other sites considerably earlier than suspected.

Fig. 6.48. Enveloped cross on a menhir, Goodenough Bay, Milne Bay Province, Papua New Guinea. Photo attributed to F. E. Williams, circa 1920s–1930s.

Fig. 6.49. Enveloped cross engraving, Melanesia. Illustration by Peter Bellwood, 1978.

Fig. 6.50. Enveloped cross engraving, Melanesia. Illustration by Peter Bellwood, 1978.

Fig. 6.51. Pottery, 2500 BCE, Belau, Micronesia. Illustration by Felicia Beardsley and Umai Basilius, 2002.

Fig. 6.52. Sacred four symbol of the Uighur people in Asia. Illustration by James Churchward, 1933.

One must question the true origin of the Lapita culture given the prolific use of the "American or Venus cross" and other recognizable motifs. *Ancient Celtic New Zealand* author Martin Doutré denotes a pot so identified that shows a Lapita face encompassed by an Egyptian ankh cross and two "Venus" cross variations. "The face is long, with wide eyes, small mouth clench, and a leptorrhine nose, beneath which is a moustache . . . all European or Caucasoid features" (Doutré 2018a).

Although numerous Melanesian cross examples exist, no explanations of *what* they signify have been published to date (to the author's knowledge). It is reasonable to consider that Austronesians or Lapitas merely enhanced existing rock art sites by adding a new "layer" of petroglyphs to what was already inscribed.

Archaeologists Paul Rainbird and Meredith Wilson stated in a 1999 unpublished report to the Pohnpei State Historic Preservation Office: "This form (enveloped cross) has a restricted distribution in the western Pacific." That this motif is in fact found beyond the western Pacific speaks of more distant and divergent origins that include not only the entire Pacific and the Americas, but examples from the Middle East.

Meaning from the Americas

The enveloped cross is found throughout the Americas, where it is known as the "American cross" or the "Quetzal cross." Contrary to the absence of meaning in Oceanic lore, in the Americas its symbolism is consistently defined by a variety of indigenous cultures as representing Venus (or Quetzal), the morning/evening star.

> Maya and some of North America, where there (are) mythological elements that point to the identification of the symbol with the planet Venus. (Sánchez 2006b, translated by the author)

When a serpent glyph is found in proximity to an enveloped cross pattern (both symbols for Quetzalcoatl), they become "Quetzal crosses" to archaeologists. The Aztec Quetzalcoatl is denoted by Venus alone or is shown as a serpent becoming Venus by its proximity to her. Similarly, the Maya linked Venus with Kukulcan, the feathered serpent. Some connect this serpent/Venus combination with comets or other cosmic deities (perhaps one and the same), such as the Incan Viracocha and A Mu Ra Ca of present-day Colombia.

In the early sixteenth century, when they first walked ashore at what is now Colombia, the Spaniards were informed by their Indian hosts that they had appeared in "the Land of A-*Mu*-Ra-Ca" (Więcej 2019).

In Maya culture, Venus was not only observed, as is the case for many of the ethnic groups all over the Americas and the Caribbean, it was studied in all its orbital movements across the sky (Sanchéz 2006a).

Note that *all* versions of the Pohnpaid enveloped crosses, consisting of one, two, or three outlines, are found in the Americas.

Aside from the fact that Venus was one of few planets discernable with the naked eye, something significant occurred with it that compelled its continual observation and frequent appearance in both North and South American rock art and especially with the serpent "comet" companion. The cataclysmic impact of a comet associated with Venus would certainly give rise to obsessive tracking of its whereabouts.

Yet another explanation of the prevalence of these various forms of the enveloped cross, in addition to the Venusian ones, stems from its more universal meaning as "map of the cosmos," also relevant outside the Americas. As mentioned earlier, the four circular elements are symbolic of the four directions or the four builders/architects: the sacred forces of creation. This very concept and imagery originated in the Motherland of Mu, according to James Churchward.

Fig. 6.53. Single-outline enveloped cross, Tularosa Creek, New Mexico.
Illustration by Elizabeth Welsh, 1995.

Fig. 6.54. Inscription on rock 2,300 feet underwater, Punta del Este, Isla de la Juventud, Cuba.
Photo by Paulina Zelitsky, 2001.

Fig.6.55. Hinkiori petroglyphs, Peru.
Photo by Father José Álvarez, 1942.

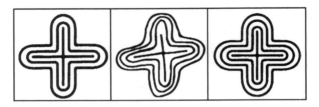

Fig. 6.56. Petroglyphs, Rio Orinoco, Venezuela.
Illustration by John Greer, 1997.

Fig. 6.57. Triple-outlined enveloped cross, Ometepe Island, Nicaragua.
Photo by Suzanne Baker.

Like most other ancient Mesoamericans, the cross was in reality a mental map of the cosmos. It Symbolized the five sacred directions: the four cardinal points and the center. Each direction was associated with certain gods, colors, and sacred realms, as well as one of the four trees which formed the tamoanchan [kingdoms]. The idea of the four-cornered universe is still present among [native Mexicans] today, and is symbolized by crosses, diamonds and other similar forms. (Lawhorn 2010)

Fig. 6.58. Quetzal Venus and serpent photographed near Phoenix, Arizona. Photo by Wes Holden, 1976.

Fig. 6.59. Shoshone enveloped cross with serpent (notice the outer border), central western United States. Illustrator unknown.

Fig. 6.60. Hohokam enveloped cross with serpent, Arizona. Photo by Sand Carved Designs, 2004.

Fig. 6.61. Rock art, Melanesia. Illustration by Peter Bellwood, 1978.

Fig. 6.62. Mound Builder culture's symbol of Mu. Illustration by James Churchward, 1933.

Fig. 6.63. Babylonia, from a seal impression, fourteenth century BCE. Illustration by A. T. Clay, 1910.

Fig. 6.64. Enveloped cross of the Uighur culture of Asia. Photo by Haluk Berkmen.

Providing more credence to the possibility of this linkage between the Americas and Oceania, Amerindian and Melanesian enveloped cross motifs are plentiful exact counterparts (with the single, double, and triple outline patterns); Melanesia and the Americas have *perfect* duplications.

In addition, widespread matches of yet another type of outlined cross are found at Pohnpaid as well as in the Americas.

Enveloped Crosses as Verticals

Articulation of the Pohnpaid double cross "stick" is less than identical to American and Melanesian vertical cross "sticks"; nevertheless their connection is still viable. The vertical version of the Pohnpaid enveloped cross is classified as a "swaddle" by Paul Rainbird and Meredith Wilson in their catalogue of Pohnpaid petroglyphs for the Federated States of Micronesia and Pohnpei historic preservation offices. However, Native American lore also links this double cross with Venus, depicting its twin aspects: morning star and evening star.

> The name Quetzalcoatl has been interpreted to mean "Precious twin," indicating that the Morning Star and Evening Star are one and the same. (de Borhegyi 2012)

Director of Boston University's Institute of the Study of the Origins of Civilization and Yale-trained geologist/geophysicist Robert Schoch proposes another interpretation of the universal vertical double or triple cross motif.

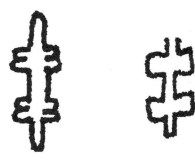

Fig. 6.65. Vertical crosses, Pohnpaid, on the outcrop.
Illustration by Paul Rainbird and Meredith Wilson, 2002.

Fig. 6.66. Vertical cross, Melanesia.
Illustration by Peter Bellwood, 1978.

Fig. 6.67. Quetzalcoatl, El Ticomate, Mexico.
This symbol is shown in Patterson (1992) and can also be seen in Sanchéz (2006b), where J. Soustelle (1967) is credited.

Fig. 6.68. Petroglyph, New Caledonia in the South Pacific.
Illustration by Jean Monin and Christophe Sand, 2012.

Consider the concept of the fourth state of matter—plasma. Plasma consists of electrically charged particles. Familiar plasma phenomena on Earth today include lightning and auroras, the northern and southern lights, and upper atmospheric phenomena known as sprites (Schoch, n.d.)

Schoch theorizes that a cataclysmic plasma event thousands of years ago was triggered by "solar outbursts and coronal mass ejections (CMEs) from the sun, or possibly emissions from other celestial objects." Stronger and more prevalent violent atmospheric plasma discharge(s) might cause intense electrical discharges whose impact could result in incineration of the Earth's surface, followed by abrupt climate change and the end of the last Ice Age. Schoch continues:

Los Alamos plasma physicist Dr. Anthony L. Peratt and his associates have established that petroglyphs found worldwide record an intense plasma event (or events) in prehistory . . .

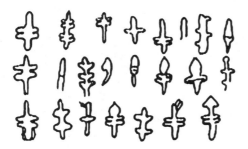

Fig. 6.69. Petroglyphs, Pohnpaid.
Illustration by Paul Rainbird and Meredith Wilson, 2002.

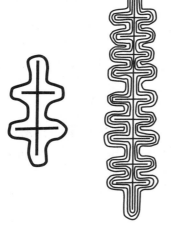

Fig. 6.71. Vertical cross, Hinkiori Pillcopata, Peru.
Photo by William Farfan-Rios, 2017. Reprinted with permission from C. Levis, *Science* (March 3, 2017): 925–31.

Fig. 6.70. Petroglyphs, New Caledonia in the South Pacific.
Illustration by Christophe Sand, 2012.

Fig. 6.72. Rock art, Dripping Springs, Arizona.
Photo by Wes Holden, 1976.

[They] determined that powerful plasma phenomena observed in the skies would take on characteristic shapes resembling humanoid figures, humans with bird heads, sets of rings or donut shapes, and writhing snakes or serpents—*shapes reflected in countless ancient petroglyphs.* (Schoch, n.d., emphasis added; see also Peratt 2003)

Such events generated by our electrical universe likely etched memories that inspired universal indigenous symbols—especially when such devastation followed. Whether this was the inspiration for Pohnpaid rock art is but one theory; perhaps sound depictions are another.

The stone at Nayarit, Mexico (similar to New Caledonia's), provides another unconventional translation of this double cross stick motif. Alex Putney translates this glyph (fig. 6.73) to mean "roaring 30 resonances," which identifies a function of transducing planetary resonance. (It has been noted previously that the Pohnpaid basalt outcrop has a natural sound component that is also referenced in its legends.)

Fig. 6.73. Equilateral cross stick, Nayarit, Altavista, Mexico.
Photo by William Farfan-Rios, 2017.
Reprinted with permission from C. Levis, *Science* (March 3, 2017): 925–31.

Fig. 6.74. Equilateral cross stick, New Caledonia in the South Pacific.
Photo by Jean Monin and Christophe Sand, 2004.

Another iconic example of petroglyph phrases at the Altavista complex (Nayarit, Mexico) is a large sign that further conveys the resonant purpose of the sacred stone for transducing planetary resonance. The central linear figure is outlined twice to form a triplicate design that gives a sense of reverberation and denotes the *raua* glyph for "roaring," composed of three lines. Altogether the ligature reads: *raua Tridasa,* meaning "roaring 30 resonances." Indeed, scientific analyses confirm the stones themselves still reverberate with the more than 30 inaudible frequencies of infrasound resonance that comprise the planetary symphony. (Putney 2014; emphasis in original)

Thus the question of *why* the enveloped cross motif is so prevalent in the Americas (not to mention worldwide) has feasible explanations, whether or not they're related to the planet Venus, Lemurian/Mu legacies, depictions of planetary resonance, the comet-related winged serpent deities, or solar-induced plasma phenomena, for example . . . or perhaps all of the above, given the vast time span involved.

MU LEGACIES VIA SEA PEOPLE

Descendants of the survivors of Mu, called the Sea People by some, are diffuse and have been absorbed into various prehistoric cultures that account for such shared motifs. One possibility is that the Sea People spread, not necessarily created, the enveloped crosses. Not a single culture, the Sea People have diverse origins, of which only a few are specifically identified as Etruscans, Trojans, Sardinians, Anatolians, and untold others that may be even more ancient. Sea People are often considered "sun worshippers," a hint of their Muvian descent.

One of many examples from the Americas is the similarity between the Pohnpaid crosses and the one found in a cave off Guanahacabibes Peninsula, western Cuba, the matching features of which are quite pronounced. Paulina Zelitsky, the ocean engineer who found them, noted that similar "American crosses" are found in numerous Cuban caves and probably date to thousands of years before Columbus. She attributed them to the Sea People in an interview with Linda Moulton Howe (2001b):

The image is from the Cuban Isle of Youth and restored by archeologists. But there are a number of similar (Cuban) caves: one in Matanzas and one in Quanacabibe that were not restored. The age of these nobody knows. But the scientific community believes they belong to the "Sea People."

Interestingly, she later found underwater structures, possibly pyramids, off the coast of western Cuba. This is quite feasible given that Cuba has been submerged three times.

Sea People are associated with hieroglyphic Luwian glyphs in which Lu translates into "star," possibly Venus. In Mayan the same symbol that stands for Lu in Luwian is used in the Ek and Lamat glyphs, which are used both separately and together to represent the Mayan word *Ek,* also meaning "star/Venus."

Fig. 6.75. Luwian hieroglyph Lu (star).
Illustration by Fred Woudhuizen, 1992.

Fig. 6.76. Mayan glyph Ek (star),
Swift Creek style from Georgia.
Illustrator unknown; as shown by
Williams and Elliot (2009) and Daniels (2012).

Fig. 6.77. Mayan glyph Lamat
(Venus/Quetzalcoatl), Swift Creek style,
Florida.
Illustration by J. Eric S. Thompson, 1962
(see also Daniels 2019).

Fig. 6.78. Petroglyph, New Caledonia in
the South Pacific.
Illustration by Christophe Sand, 2012.

The fact that the Swift Creek potters placed both symbols in a cartouche shows they believed these two symbols conveyed closely related or identical concepts. In Mayan, both of these symbols, the diamond and cross, are closely associated and used both separately and sometimes together to represent the Mayan word ek, "star/Venus." (Daniels 2012)

If in fact the "Sea People" or "Star People" were one group who scattered the enveloped crosses, and if the planet/glyph Venus is a universal symbol for the Goddess—or threatening comet(s) and other anomalous phenomena—examples should be found outside of the Americas and Oceania, even if their graphic execution is not identical. What is *not* extraordinary is that this "Star of Venus" motif is found throughout Phoenicia and Mesopotamia. *Quite remarkable, however,* is that this motif is utilized throughout the entire world, even in Pacific cultures.

The Rest of the World

The eight-pointed symbol representing Venus as the morning or evening star, or the "Star of Ishtar," was used as early as 3000 BCE on clay tablets from Sumeria to represent the Assyrian and Babylonian goddess known as Innana or Ishtar/Astarte.

Central to this diffusion concept is the name of the Pohnpeian mother goddess, Ines or Inaz, a cognate to Innana, aka Inez. And the Egyptian word or hieroglyph for *star* means both "star" and "doorway," thus star door or time door. This recalls Pohnpaid legends of the petroglyph outcrop being a "doorway" to other worlds used by the two boy magicians.

The Encyclopedia Britannica online explains:

The Akkadian Ishtar is also, to a greater extent, an astral deity, associated with the planet Venus: with Shamash, sun god, and Sin, moon god, she forms a secondary astral triad. In this manifestation her symbol is a star with 6, 8, or 16 rays within a circle.

For an interesting visual metamorphosis between cymatics and the Venus star, see the video posted to Youtube by Revelation Watcher (2012).

Fig. 6.79. Jade ornament featuring sacred emblem, Peking, China.
Illustration by James Churchward, 1933.

Fig. 6.80. Venus star, Tablet of Shamash, Babylon.
Illustrator unknown.

Fig. 6.81. Naacal-Mu symbol, 10,000 BCE, Mexico.
Based on a record by William Niven; drawn by James Churchward.

Fig. 6.82. Cymatic pattern, 3835 hertz.
Photo by Stephen W. Morris, University of Toronto.

Fig. 6.83. The Great Ruler—Empire of the Sun, Nevada tribe.
Illustration by James Churchward, 1933.

Fig. 6.84. Author's drawing of earring and three-feather headdress from Unakoti, Tripura, India.

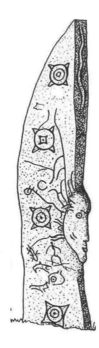

Fig. 6.85. Stele, 200 BCE,
Okunev, Siberia.
Illustration by Project Avalon.

Although it might be a stretch to compare the design configuration of the Mesopotamian Venus star symbol to the enveloped cross per se, there are *intermediary* motifs that provide a link between all versions. These intermediary symbols are found in the Americas, Oceania, Japan, India, and Hawai'i, to name a few . . . and perhaps Pohnpaid!

Fig. 6.86. Star bird stone, Pohnpaid, with bird outlined for clarity.
Photo by Carole Nervig, 1992.

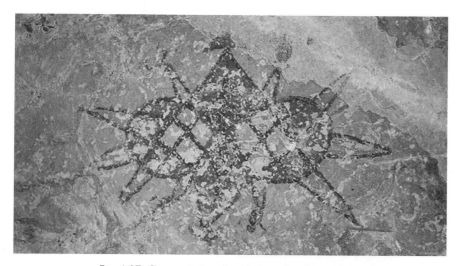

Fig. 6.87. Cave painting, East Timor, Southeast Asia.
Photo by David Palazón.

Fig. 6.88. Mayan Venus.
This symbol is shown in Sanchéz (2006b), where
Patterson (1992) is credited.

Fig. 6.89. Swift Creek design from Georgia.
Illustration by Frankie Snow, 1998.

Fig. 6.90. Mayan Venus glyph.
This symbol is shown in Sanchéz (2006b), where
Patterson (1992) is credited.

Fig. 6.91. Venus Lamat glyph on Olmec potsherd.
Illustrator unknown. As shown by Daniels (2012).

The connections between the Venus symbols in the Americas and Mesopotamia are not news. What is newsworthy is finding these symbols in Oceania and other surprising locations. Rock art up to twelve thousand years old has been found in caves in East Timor, including some of the oldest pieces of art in the Indonesian region.

Fig. 6.92. Dance mask (note the blonde hair), Latangi, Papua New Guinea.
Photo courtesy of Museum of New Zealand Te Papa Tongarewa.

Fig. 6.93. Magic protective embroidered sleeve worn by an Ainu woman, Japan.
Photo by Lars Krutak.

Fig. 6.94. Rinconada star being, Petroglyph National Monument, Albuquerque, New Mexico.
Photo by Biolifepics.

Fig. 6.95. Kimono pattern detail from an Ainu garment, Hokkaido, Japan.
Photo by Carole Nervig, 2018.

A DIFFERENT ORBIT FOR VENUS?

In his book *The Many Faces of Venus,* researcher of comparative mythology and archaeoastronomy Ev Cochrane hypothesizes that Venus could have had an entirely different orbit during the Neolithic era, or that it was somehow equal to or enjoyed even more status than the visible sun. Vedic, Chaldean, and Judaic cultures all speak of the planet Venus's appearance with horns, tails, or a beard of fire. It could be speculated that this ancient obsession for tracking Venus was motivated from a time when it once was a super comet, and the associated fear of its returning to wreak havoc as such.

Another more extraordinary explanation for the repetition of the "Venus stars" and other universal symbols of antiquity is David Talbot's "Saturn theory." Author of *The Saturn Myth* and coauthor (with Wallace Thornhill) of *The Electric Universe,* Talbot not only suggests a different orbit for Venus but posits that all then-known planets were in straight alignment and much closer to the Earth, not scattered erratically and distantly as they are today. Because Jupiter was "behind Saturn" and not visible, Saturn dominated Earth's sky. It thus represented the sun in most mythologies, for in actuality it appeared physically much larger than our visible sun. So aligned, the planets would produce a visual layout exactly matching worldwide Venus symbols from antiquity. These symbols depict the Saturn "sun" creating a circular background, Venus with comet-like "arms" extended out, and smaller Mars as the dot in the center. The shadow created on Saturn is the source of the crescent symbol. Talbot goes into detail about universal prehistoric doomsday myths (meteor crashes, months of no sun, floods, and so on) that validate these catastrophic events on Earth, which were recorded in the form of this consistent and accurate symbol.

Fig. 6.96. "Star" petroglyph, Pohnpaid. Note how this motif resembles previous star images.
Photo by Carole Nervig, 1992.

Fig. 6.97. Representation of Saturn overshadowed by Venus and Mars.
Image by the Thunderbolts Project.

Fig. 6.98. Representation of Saturn overshadowed by Venus and Mars.
Image by the Thunderbolts Project.

Fig. 6.99. Cross circle with crescent moon and sun on phallic monolith, Pohnpaid.
Photo by Lynn Danaher, 2017.

Fig. 6.100. Mesopotamian symbol showing combined aspects of 6.97 and 6.98.
Image by the Thunderbolts Project.

The Thunderbolts Project's diagrams show Saturn as the background sphere with crescent shadow; Venus is white with "arms"; and Mars is the center sphere.

Of note is the presence in these diagrams of *both* the enveloped cross and the circled cross glyphs—two of Talbot's universal doomsday symbols—at Pohnpaid.

Esoterically, all of these extremely universal cross versions might embody much less literal concepts: stages of creation, paths to enlightenment, theoretical quantum schematics, or other shamanic and multidimensional phenomena. And as such, they would have no geographical or

Fig. 6.101. Petroglyph,
Vanuatu, Oceania.
Illustration by Jean Monin and
Christophe Sand, 2015.

Fig. 6.102. Canoe prow,
Solomon Islands, Oceania.
Photographer unknown.

cultural boundaries, nor be subject to quantitative or third-dimensional analysis paradigms. The plethora of metaphysical considerations, too extensive to explore in the scope of this publication, should nevertheless be considered when analyzing any rock art from sacred sites.

Regardless of the *interpretations* of the enveloped crosses, migrations that we now know are possible could render diffusion of the Venus archetypal enveloped cross a reality. Or did the crosses *originate* with Mu, with the Venusian Kumaras of the Lemurian Pandyan kingdom referred to in the Ramayana and other mythical texts? Was this cultural Venus "fixation" from the submerged lands of the Pacific and Indian Oceans then exported outward, like spokes on a wheel, to colonies of advanced culture (Peru, Mayax, Atlantis, Egypt, Mesopotamia, Japan, Tibet, China, India, etc.) before and after Mu's inundation? And was the

Quetzalcoatl archetype a surviving sage from the devastation of Mu?

One of the "Naacal/Maya" glyphs present on stone tablets discovered north of Mexico City by mineralogist William Niven has been deemed to be at least twelve thousand years old based on its geological depth. James Churchward's writings noted Niven's tablets as physical, or at least cultural, artifacts of Mu. Such an origin would clearly provide a rationale for the matching cross symbols from Mesopotamia, the Americas, China, Japan, Scandinavia, and Oceania.

According to James Churchward, the Uighur civilization, which covered an extensive area of Asia, was the first and primary colonization destination of Mu migrations to the west. One of their symbols is a version of the enveloped cross plus four dots. With a Lemurian origin, this glyph symbolized the creative process of Deity plus the four creative forces of nature rather than Venus.

One undeniable factor that, regardless of their source, links all iterations of these crosses across the world is their design of either a) an enveloped cross of four or eight arms and multiple outlines, spokes, or rays or b) a modified diamond shape.

Whether due to a common origin that predates known migrations and cultures, such as Mu; a planetary catastrophe triggered by Venus or her comets; a worship of extraterrestrial or ancient planetary deities or demigods; or their manifestation as symbols of universal collective consciousness, the enveloped cross and its variations bear witness to another definitive case of cultural diffusion . . . even if we are not *yet* certain of exact routes and time frames.

THE CIRCLED CROSS

Although not as rare as the distinctive enveloped version, another universal cross motif is found at Pohnpaid: the circled cross (sometimes called the solar, sun, wheel, quartered, or cosmic cross, among many other names). Only two petroglyphs of this simple but powerful cross have been located in the stone circle at the Pohnpaid meadow *to date*, in contrast to the many enveloped crosses found there.

Since the dawn of time the proliferation of the simple circled cross across different continents and cultures renders it so generic that it approaches the archetypal. It is frequently found in the symbolism of prehistoric cultures, particularly those of the Neolithic and Bronze Age (presumably 7000–3000 BCE), and continues to relatively recent historical times.

Its presence communicates a plethora of concepts that range from the abstract, often spiritual rendering of a solar or other deity, and unity or wholeness (as represented by the circle specifically). More concise depictions of the union of polarity (with cross added) include, to mention a few, heaven/earth; the four architects of creation cosmologies; positive/negative themes (yin/yang, male/female); the four elements (earth, air, fire, water); the cycle of life/death; and the four directions (east, west, north, south).

When the circled cross is referred to as a representation of the sun, meaning our sun, what is usually overlooked is that its representation as such does not necessarily refer to our *galactic* sun. The concept of "sun worshippers" is often misunderstood when taken literally, for it assumes that our sun was their actual deity rather than *a symbol for their deity*—and as such, a representation of power, energy, and light. The Ra glyph from Australia is believed by some to represent the sun of our ancestral extraterrestrial origins. The cross in a circle may also refer to the esoteric "great central sun" of creation, or to the universe as Deity, or another dominant planet/star of bygone times, or even Venus . . . again.

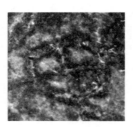

Fig. 6.103. Petroglyph on phallic monolith, Pohnpaid.
Photo by Carole Nervig, 1992.

Fig. 6.104. Dhaymoole rock art, Somaliland, Africa.
Photographer unknown.

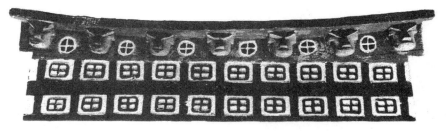

Fig. 6.105. Bai (men's house) detail, Belau, Micronesia.
Photo by Carole Nervig, 1991.

Fig. 6.106. Ra glyph, Gosford, Kariong, NSW Australia.
Photo by Valérie Barrow, 2018.

Fig. 6.107. Petroglyph, Puu Loa, Hawai'i Volcanoes National Park.
Photo by Carole Nervig, 1999.

Fig. 6.108. Bowl, Papua New Guinea, Oceania.
Photo from the Wartburg Theological Seminary.

No such definitive evidence is yet apparent for a Venus or solar interpretation of the circled cross at Pohnpaid or in Oceania. Only its use and matching design found across the entire Pacific suggest possible links . . . as does the parallel path of the enveloped cross from the Americas.

Fig. 6.109. Woodcarving, Honiara, Solomon Islands, Oceania.
Photo by Eddy Degrout.

Fig. 6.110. Viracocha, Tiwanaku, Bolivia.
Photographer unknown.

Fig. 6.111. Ancestral female of Yap State, Micronesia.
Photographer unknown.

Fig. 6.112. Mask or effigy, Vanuatu.
Photo from the Musée d'Aquitaine collection.

Fig. 6.113. Shell gorget (pendant),
Cox Mound, Tennessee, 1250–1450 CE.
Photo by Herb Roe.

More common in North America than Central and South America, the circled cross design is near universal among Amerindian cultures, and central to California's Chumash tribe as well as the cultures of the Mound Builders. A specific example of its Venus/feathered serpent connection is the petroglyph at Three Rivers, New Mexico, which is defined as a Venus-Quetzalcoatl or lightning god representation.

Fig. 6.114. Venus-Quetzalcoatl lightning god, Three Rivers, New Mexico.
Photo by Melanie Hobson.

Fig. 6.115. Chumash Painted Cave rock art, California.
Photo from the collaboration between CyArk, California State Parks, and Santa Ynez Valley High School 2021.

Fig. 6.116. Norrkoping rock carving, Himmelstalund, Sweden, outlined for clarity.
Photo by Antony Macauley.

Fig. 6.117. Mississippian shell pendant, Florida.
Courtesy of the Smithsonian National Museum of the American Indian.

Fig. 6.118. Cross earrings, Olmec head monument 4, La Venta Museum, Mexico.

Fig. 6.119. Rock art, Palmasola, Acapulco, Mexico.
Photo by Fernando Reyes Alvarez.

Furthermore, certain Mesoamerican circled crosses, often pecked, demonstrate a function and are not merely symbolic references to Deity, sun, or Venus. According to Anthony F. Aveni and Horst Härtung, this symbol of the circled cross was utilized at Teotihuacan and other Mexican sites for calculation of archaeoastronomical alignments, geodetic architectural benchmarks, and calendric purposes.

> Of all the traits of Mesoamerican cosmology perhaps none is more pronounced nor widespread than the quadripartite division of the universe. A study of the basic properties of these pecked crosses reveals that their purpose transcends the purely symbolic. The carvings appear to have functioned as architectural benchmarks, devices for determining astronomical alignments, and calendar counting devices all at the same time. (Aveni and Härtung, n.d.)

Europe is not without its circled crosses either, most particularly in Scandinavia. Old Norse runes bestow these symbols on their highest god, Odin, and his beautiful goddess, Frigga. Most powerful of the goddesses, Frigga is goddess of love and fate, the equivalent of Venus. Another clue to a possible Venus/comet connection is demonstrated in Norway. A circled cross is carved on a stool and surrounded by two dragons or serpents, a combination found time and again in the Americas as representing not only Venus, but Quetzalcoatl, Viracocha, A Mu Ra Ca, and in some cases comet symbology.

Fig. 6.120. Norse Odin cross.

Fig. 6.121. Circled cross,
9000–3000 BCE, Armenia.
Illustration by Lilit Mkhitaryan, 2016.

Fig. 6.122. Luwian hieroglyph.
Illustration by Fred Woudhuiz, 1992.

Fig. 6.123. Norse rune representing Frigga (Venus).
Photo by Asmus Koefoed.

Fig. 6.124. Circled cross, Helanshan, Ningxia Hui, China.
Photo by Robert Bednarik, 2013.

Another association to the quartered crosses found in Micronesia and elsewhere is the hieroglyphs of the Luwian Sea People, although the Luwians might be just the *transporters* of symbols that were created and utilized long before their time.

Fig. 6.125. Rock art, Belau, Micronesia.
Illustration by William N. Morgan, 2010.

Fig. 6.126. Rock art, circled cross earrings, Belau, Micronesia.
Illustration by William N. Morgan, 2010.

Fig. 6.127. Circled cross on a storyboard, Belau, Micronesia.
Illustrator unknown.

Of the Luwian glyphs, at least three are found at Pohnpaid: the circled cross, the enveloped cross, the simple equilateral cross, and possibly a fourth, the Venus or morning/evening star. The outlined circled cross and simple circled cross are central to many motifs found in Belau, Micronesia, while the enveloped cross is common in Melanesia . . . and of course the Americas.

According to the late Barry Fell, a former Harvard epigraphist, the Luwian language accompanied the Sea People on their journeys that reached as far as the U.S. Southwest.

Barry Fell was perhaps the first to suggest that Minoans, followed by the Sea Peoples, Libyans and Phoenicians, discovered the rich metals of the American Southwest after 2000 BCE and developed its first civilizations, for which the cultural earmarks were pithouses, adobe, trade centers like Snaketown, fortresses and walled cities, painted pottery and irrigation systems.

It would appear that the Pima and Papago Indians, whose ancient name was Hohokam ("Sea Peoples") long stood apart from other Indians and preserved their ancient roots until the mixing and melding of Indian populations that occurred under the Spanish.

The presence of 7–10% Greek and related DNA in Pima populations today (Yates 2015)

Like many words in the Hopi, Zuni, Pima and Azteco-Utan languages in general it [the name Hohokam] is composed of South Semitic elements. In Egyptian, it literally means "Sea Peoples" or "Foreigners." The historic Sea Peoples came from Asia Minor and once threatened to conquer the Egyptian empire. (Yates 2010)

Evidently the Sea People did not stop once they reached the U.S. Southwest and continued into the Pacific with their enveloped crosses, or . . .

Conversely, the enveloped cross, as well as the circled cross symbols, originated in the Pacific during the time of the Motherland Mu and were transported to its colonies in the Americas and then on to Atlantis, then Asia Minor, Turkey, and Greece.

Taking into consideration that Atlantis was influenced by its *predecessor*, Mu/Lemuria, commonalities between the two cultures are to be expected and passed on to subsequent cultures. Frank Joseph, editor of *Ancient American: Archaeology of the Americas before Columbus,* suggests a connection between Atlantis and the Luwian Sea People during an interview with investigative journalist and documentary filmmaker Linda Moulton Howe (2001a):

Some Luwian script has supposedly been found in Italy and they think that is an important link between the Etruscans and Asia Minor, or what is now Turkey. And the Luwians were maritime people, very proficient at sea . . . and this crossed oval symbol of theirs related to what is lettered as "lu" is also goes across all the columns in comparison to other languages where the symbol appears to mean "star" . . . But maybe. That "lu" that is repeated is like they are identifying themselves, the Luwians. They might have called themselves the "lu." It is very interesting. That whole cultural context is Atlantean because the Atlanteans were plugged into the Trojans.

The Trojans themselves had a story of Atlantis. Their founder was Dardanus who came from Atlantis.

Now the question arises, if *Lu* means "star," then wouldn't the *Luwians* be the "Star People" rather than the "Sea People"? Amerindians, like Pacific Islanders and all indigenous peoples, often relate that their ancestors came from the stars. However, some Pacific Islanders specifically add that they are offspring of the interbreeding of Star People with the people of Mu before its submergence. This suggests another indication of extraterrestrial connections to the Pohnpaid glyphs, Luwians, and their cross glyphs.

Dots continue to be connected from prehistoric/indigenous culture to prehistoric/indigenous culture by analogous accounts of extraterrestrial presence in their not-always-so-distant past. What until recently (and still by many) has not been taken seriously and dismissively labeled myth or legend are stories that tell very specific details of extraterrestrial origins or contacts. These events include the origins of certain human races or cultures through either migration or interbreeding; extensive contact of varied natures, both positive and negative; exchange of information or instruction for the advancement of our civilizations by enlightened alien leaders across such sectors as agriculture, the sciences, spirituality, and so on and so forth; and their actual residency on Earth.

Fig. 6.128. "Deity" with circled cross on heart, phallic monolith,
Pohnpaid, shown also outlined in white for clarity.
Photo by Carole Nervig, 1992.

Fig. 6.129. Circled cross.
Image captured by *Opportunity*,
Mars Exploration Rover, 2014.
Courtesy NASA/JPL-Caltech.

Fig. 6.130. Motherland symbol, from
the Egyptian Book of the Dead.
Illustration by James Churchward, 1933.

Due to a contemporary cultural/intellectual bias, these oral accounts as input for analyzing incomprehensible archaeological or sacred sites are systematically ignored, discounted, and ridiculed by academia.

In light of the now known quantum probabilities of life elsewhere in the universe . . . and especially the photographs from the *Opportunity* rover in 2014 showing what appear to be petroglyphs on Mars, serious consideration must be given to extraterrestrial influences when prehistoric, or even historic, material cultures and archaeological/sacred sites are being investigated. Ignoring smoke from oral histories is no longer acceptable and renders the fire invisible.

Another site with otherworldly circled cross symbolism is found in Sri Lanka. Sakwala Chakraya is a shallow carving on the surface of a granite rock face, most often labeled a physical "stargate" for the purposes of teleportation or interdimensional travel. Of interest is its repeated use of the circled cross in its six-foot, circular diagram. Speculation on the meaning of these crosses mimics other aforementioned explanations. Hindus and Buddhists also believe this petroglyph is some kind of map of the world; however, evidence—such as that below by Ukranian researcher Vladimir Kovalev—does not support this.

There are no other known images similar to Sakwala Chakraya in Hindu or Buddhism culture. There are no other known ancient images similar to Sakwala Chakraya in the World at all, except of some masterpieces of prehistoric art. (Kovalev 2013)

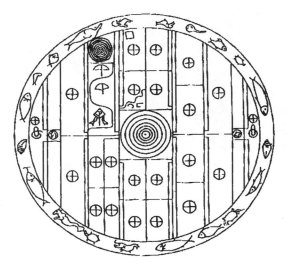

Fig. 6.131. Sakwala Chakraya,
six-foot-diameter "stargate," Sri Lanka.
Illustration by H. C. P. Bell, 1901.

According to Kovalev, this was a schematic drawing from the perspective of "Wave Theory and theoretical foundations of Radio Engineering (TRE)" for "vibroacoustic infrasound oscillators/transmitters." In this diagram, he theorizes, the seven central concentric rings likely "symbolize some kind of an oscillation process, radiation from antenna (acoustic radiation) . . . and the circled crosses denote 'antenna resonators of *domed* infrasound receivers or just simply volumetric resonators of any kinds.'"

Pohnpaid's rock art is brought into this cosmic milieu via both its circled cross and enveloped cross patterns. Each design may represent concepts of alien origin *or* primordial terrestrial inception by advanced civilizations. Alien cultures, if not lost civilizations, or both would certainly provide one explanation to global consistencies of visual images found at indigenous archaeological and sacred sites.

Whatever the source or symbolic intention of Pohnpaid's rock art, and other Pacific rock art too, the fact remains that the quartered circle symbol crossed both the Atlantic and the Pacific. However, the pertinent question is, once again, not only in which direction did it travel—as it likely did in both directions—but from which direction did it *first* travel?

And that answer would be *from Mu*. Radiating out in all directions initially, in some cases the circled cross symbol then returned to its origins via subsequent cultural migrations.

GRIDS AND GEOMETRICS OR JUST ART?

An hourglass-shaped motif, along with others on Pohnpaid's phallic stone, could be part of a larger pattern. Or it could be an undecipherable representation, with an intricate style reminiscent of Mayan, Korean, or Japanese styles. Another perspective suggested by author of *The Babel Texts* Derek Cunningham (2018) is the possibility of "a global written text (. . . one language) and a common spoken language," which in the author's opinion points to Mu. His recent discovery that this global written text, which is 5,300 to 5,600 years old and from Lingjiatan, China, is based on astronomy provides yet another contender for the identification of geometric motifs of Pohnpaid. Whatever the case, a correct interpretation of any number of motifs carved on Pohnpaid's stones remains incomprehensible because of their overlapping layers, complexity, and abstractness.

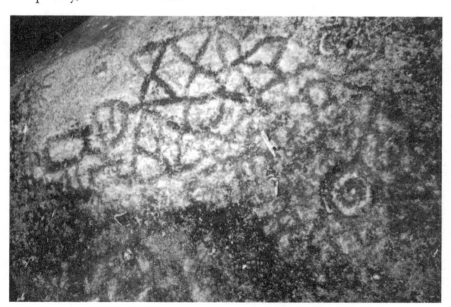

Fig. 6.132. Detail of phallic monolith's geometric pattern, Pohnpaid.
Photo by Carole Nervig, 1992.

Fig. 6.133. Petroglyphs, Pohnpaid.
Illustration by Paul Rainbird and Meredith Wilson, 2002.

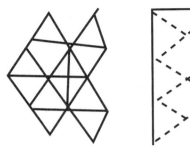

Fig. 6.134. Geometic patterns of petroglyphs, Vanuatu.
Illustration by Jean Monin and Christophe Sand, 2015.

A series of rocks from India, South Africa, and Australia with similar geometric engravings are of extreme antiquity, with patterns suggesting grids, maps, or astronomical alignments.

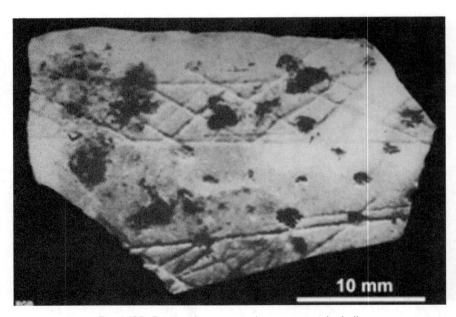

Fig. 6.135. Engraved geometric lines on ostrich shell,
23,000 BCE, Patne, India.
Photo by Robert Bednarik, 2003.

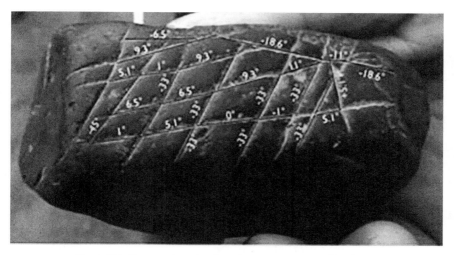

Fig. 6.136. Engraved angles found on a stone near Bambara.
Hieroglyphs of Kariong, Gosford, Australia.
Photo by Stephen and Evan Strong, with Derek Cunningham calculations.

Bearing no likeness to the other intricate gridlike or maplike patterns on the phallic stone is another rectangular design that's more like the style of the artist Mondrian than it is Mayan. Ungrounded speculation could suggest it might be a schematic plan of nearby Nan Madol, or a plan of what may lie underneath the waters off its nearby reef. Conceivably more significant is that the grid pattern on Pohnpaid's phallic stone lies adjacent to enveloped crosses. This is also seen in petroglyphs in the Dominican Republic. However, the enveloped crosses at Pohnpaid are not as closely placed to its grid patterns as those in the Dominican Republic.

Google Earth underwater images near the Madeira Islands (off the northwest coast of Africa) might hold clues to the meaning of these maplike grids on the phallic monolith. Such a comparison to the petroglyphs of Pohnpaid is not out of the question, considering the explicit description of the city of Kahnihmueiso beneath the waters near Nan Madol.

The puzzling motif at Pohnpaid is one that could be interpreted depending on its orientation. Is it a structure? Or perhaps it illustrates the portal or "doorway" used by the legendary brothers who left the outcrop to travel the world? All that's missing is the portal or doorway, such as those seen in Turkey and Peru.

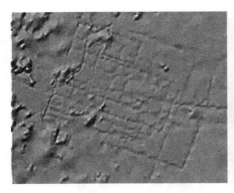

Fig.6.137. *Left:* Underwater grids in 2009 near Madeira Islands.
Google Earth reported technical issues in 2012 and published a blurrier
version of the same site. Could the blurring be intentional?
Right: Outlined by the author for clarity.

In any case, the heavy saturation of glyphs at Pohnpaid is likely the
result of layers inscribed upon layers by various peoples and cultures
over time.

Fig. 6.138. Portal doorway, 900 BCE, Mher Urartian, Turkey.
Photo by Ben Men Lyun.

Fig. 6.139. Naupa Huaca
spirit people portal, Peru.
Photo by Stuart Hoskin.

WINGED DISKS

The surface of the phallic monolith is not the only appearance of a map or grid-like glyph at Pohnpaid. Another boulder's incised pattern evokes a feeling of direction or location, perhaps beyond our planet and even the three customary dimensions.

Although it is not possible to confirm its original placement, this somewhat smaller stone with an astonishingly complex petroglyph is found in what is tentatively identified as the outer Pohnpaid stone circle. Covering the visible side of it is *half* of a "winged sun disk" motif consisting of a central double circle broken into twelve segments. This is similar to the classic houses of the zodiac, with one wing attached to the circular portion. Of note is that the zodiac is used not only by astrologers, but also by astronomers to map the heavens. Protruding from one portion of the zodiac's wheel is an outlined winged structure, bent near its center, with an infrastructure of shorter lines formed at ninety-degree angles to each other, such as the trusses of a bridge.

These ninety-degree angles in the wing may depict how ascended masters travel via their *merkaba*, or "divine light vehicle."

Similar in appearance to the winged disk motifs of antiquity, the Pohnpaid wing has an additional visual quality of a "you are here" map for interdimensional travel or space travel. The attachment area of the wing on the zodiac's wheel could illustrate the entry point into our galaxy from points beyond, with the specific *"route" of ninety-degree angles* through interdimensional space-time showing the way to the home of the "mappers." Interestingly, esoteric circles (with connections to Venus) refer to the use of the "ninety-degree phase shift" to pass into the "universe of timelessness," or to put it another way, other dimensions, as the mechanism used by ancient elders who founded this Earth. When ready to surpass matter, energy, time, and space, they utilized this method to vacate this physical planet for nonphysical realms. *This petroglyph could be a record of this process.*

> Actually, the Els were not known by that name until they achieved this Theta condition. Before this they were known as the Cyclopean Race. It was their method of leaving physical existence and conditions that gave them the name of Els. Through the secret use of the Ninety Degree Phase Shift they abandoned the Earth and the entire Galaxy and left it vacant for humanity. A ninety-degree angle forms the letter "L." Therefore, when we call them Els we are referring to a symbol of their race and not really to a name. (Williamson 1961)

Other geometric forms that appear to hang from the wing structure could be unrelated or belong to a different layer of glyphs. Accurate mapping of the stone surface is necessary before a coherent understanding of this intriguing pattern can be attempted. Also helpful would be "decoding" of its geometries by quantum physicists, mathematicians, or astronomers.

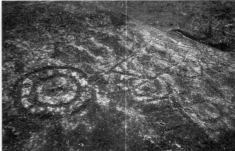

Fig. 6.140. Winged disk, boulder in meadow, Pohnpaid.
Photos by Carole Nervig, 1992.

A distinct but obscure version (fig. 6.141; one of many Mesopotamian versions of the winged disk symbol) incorporates comparable "trusses" to those of the Pohnpaid version. The positioning of the trusses is similar but the angles of Pohnpaid's wing are ninety degrees. Consequently this is not a perfect match, nor are the circular center graphic contents. Otherwise, the positioning of components—the circular center with symmetrical trussed wings—is not only remarkably similar but extraordinarily rare in prehistoric glyphs from around the world.

Fig. 6.141. Mesopotamian illustration of Nintura's flying divine storm.
Image posted online by mesopotamiangods.com.

Fig. 6.142. Winged disk bird, Belau, Micronesia.
Illustration by William N. Morgan, 2010.

Fig. 6.143. According to Churchward, the "oldest of feathered wing circles," Naacal civilization.
Illustration by James Churchward, 1933.

Fig. 6.144. Winged sun disk, Thebes, Egypt.
Illustration by Samuel Sharp, 1863.

Fig. 6.145. Butterfly from Naacal texts, Mexico.
Illustration by James Churchward, 1960.

Fig. 6.146. Mayan symbol, Guatemala.
Illustration by James Churchward, 1960.

Fig. 6.147. Yuyao Gate, Hempedu, China, circa 4800 BCE.
Photo by James Jiao.

More validation of the winged disk motif is the unmistakable match between Guatemala and China, which is of particular interest due to the antiquity of the Yuyao Gate (circa 4800 BCE).

The winged sun disk is one of the oldest esoteric symbols in human history. All continents and centuries have their variations, each with slightly different iterations and symbolism, often related to alien contact and their advanced knowledge. One website discusses a unique and fascinating yet plausible interpretation for winged disk imagery that is universally applicable:

> The symbol of a wing made of feathers joining to a star can be seen in the records of ancient cultures residing in various regions of South America as well as Australia. It represents how the Sun and its flight are powered by collecting charge. An example of this is shown by placing the Butterfly Nebula, M2-9 with its visible glow discharge, alongside the Wing of Egypt.
>
> The electric nature of birds and their anatomy explain the founding principles of electric Stars. This concept is explained in further detail by Horus. (GodElectric.org, n.d.)

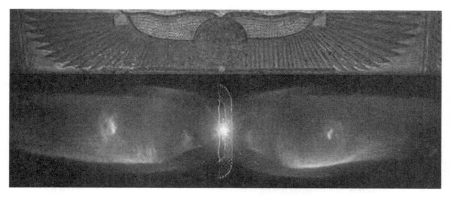

Fig. 6.148. Butterfly Nebula star system.
Photo by GodElectric.org.

Also indicating sophisticated knowledge of the heavenly bodies is the possibility that this "zodiac" circle of Pohnpaid's winged disk was utilized as an archaeoastronomical mechanism for calculating celestial alignments. Or perhaps it was used as a calendric device, similar to the rock "compass" of Hawai'i.

Returning to the site of Oahu's Kukaniloko "birthing stone," we can see a method for charting celestial alignments demonstrated on the Kane-Lono rock. In 1982, retired U.S. Army Major Harry G. Kurth discovered a connection between a diamond-shaped rock at Kukaniloko and that of Kiribati's "stone boat" formations in Micronesia that are used as star compasses. Kurth called this the "Kane-Lono" rock (cited in Selin 2000). Faint radial lines on it possibly marked the months of the year.

Fig. 6.149. Sunset shadow on Kane-Lono rock, Kukaniloko, Oahu. Compare with fig. 6.140, p. 196.
Photo by Institute of Astronomy, University of Hawai'i, 2000.

Similarities may be observed between the Kane-Lono rock "compass" and the segmented circle of the "winged sun disk" petroglyph of Pohnpaid. There is no way to determine at this point if this particular Kane-Lono boulder is in the position it was initially meant to assume for its original, intended purpose, as is the case at Pohnpaid. Along with technical measurements and calculations, the orientation factor is essential in determining archaeoastronomical functions of the "zodiac" circle in the half-winged disk glyph . . . to date, the most enigmatic glyph at Pohnpaid.

What *is* consistent about the winged disk symbols, regardless of interpretations, is their widespread presence in Micronesia, on Pohnpei, and on Belau.

PYRAMIDS

A runway? A beaker? A pyramid? A one-of-a-kind glyph (fig. 6.150) located on the phallic rock at Pohnpaid conjures all such images—assuming its truncated apex is to be viewed as its top. If the triangular shape is inverted or oriented in another direction, it becomes a complete mystery.

Considering that Pohnpaid has many of the classic components of sacred sites, the probability that its creators or their ancestors were sun worshippers, pyramid builders, and voyagers is plausible. Although not a specific pyramidal shape, per se, the megalithic monument underwater at Yonaguni, Ryukyuk Islands, Okinawa, is in closer proximity to Pohnpei than Indonesia/Sundaland. Thus, the site of Pohnpaid, with its monoliths and petrographs, may have been inspired by Kahnihmueiso, the underwater city of Nan Madol.

The Pohnpaid petroglyph, if it is that of a pyramid, could be documenting similar structures under Nan Madol or in Indonesia/Sundaland, Australia, or other pyramids across the globe. Petroglyphs found in Okinawa reinforce that the concept of pyramids was known in Oceania and the Pacific Rim and on the continent of ancient Mu.

Since 1978, the Japan Petroglyph Society, headed by the late Professor Nobubiro Yoshida, has found no less than three thousand engraved rocks throughout Japan, and fifteen inscribed tablets. The engravings depicting pyramids were excavated from areas of Okinawa inhabited by Sobata Sea People from circa 12,000–6,500 BCE. Eighty-five percent of these

Fig. 6.150. Pyramid or runway on phallic monolith, Pohnpaid. Photo by Carole Nervig, 1992.

Fig. 6.151. Engraved tablets, Okinawa.
Photo by Yamasaki Seidau, 1933, from the Museum of Okinawa.

stones were located at summits of sacred hills that have been used as places of worship since prehistoric times by Sea People who still believe in their legendary homeland, Nidai-Kanai (aka Mu). This is according to Yoshida, who identified the encircled W-like motifs as emblematic of Mu. Remarkably, the petroglyphs on these rocks could only be deciphered using the Sumerian language. Yoshida states, "If they (the Sobata) were not after all navigators from Mu itself—spreading its cultural influences to both sides of the Pacific—then they may have been the direct inheritors of a thallasocratic tradition from the Motherland after its geologic demise" (Joseph 2005).

Not only the Okinawan engravings but timelines of Sobata peoples and their sunken homeland Nidai Kanai are validated by geology.

3000 engraved rocks . . . were excavated at one of sanctuaries in Okinawa where, since prehistoric ages about 12,000 to 6,500 B.P., "Sobata sea-people" used to dwell and build peculiar Okinawan structures . . . even today Okinawa native sea people have sincere faith and pious belief in the legendary homeland, "Nidai-Kanai," which is believed to have been located in a very far place in the ocean, where their ancestors lived happy life forever. Some scholars suppose that their legendary homeland must be the lost, sunken continent of Mu . . . but according to under sea archaeology . . . geological catastrophe must have happened in 12,000 B.P. These dates correspond to legendary Okinawan stories. The stone tablets tell complete stories of the Mu's culture and religion at that time . . . provide us clues to the enigmatic origins of human letters and languages . . . 30% of them could be deciphered with Proto-Sumerian and Sumerian cuneiforms . . . could suppose is that in the late prehistoric ages, Sumerian seafaring tribes threatened by Akkadians invasions fled

Fig. 6.152. Chou Kung Tower star observatory, Gaocheng, China.
Photo by Gary Todd.

to the seas. Some tribes reached prehistoric Japan, which the scholars, who belong to The Epigraphic Society of Harvard University, used to suggest . . . Emeritus Professor Barry Fell (late President of E.S.) . . . was sure the Sumerian seafaring people reached the Far East while other groups reached the Americas B.C. (Kawagoe, n.d.)

Fig. 6.153. Mayan pyramid, Tikal, Guatemala.
Photo by Ulf Huebner.

Fig. 6.154. Pyramid of Candi Sukuh, Java, Indonesia.
Photo by Takashi Images.

Fig. 6.155. Temple pyramid, Kukulkan, Chichen Itza, Mexico.
Photo by Lunamarina.

Considerably less likely is that this triangular-shaped petroglyph is a representation of some form of "runway," as is found in the Nazca area of Peru or on the solid rock mountaintop of Fuerte de Samaipata in Bolivia. If this were the case, the perception of aerial orientation and landing maneuvers would be prerequisites for its delineation.

Fig. 6.156. El Fuerte de Samaipata "runway," Bolivia.
Photo by Pyty.

Fig. 6.157. Possible pyramid or mound at the back of a meadow,
Rasalap, Kitti, Pohnpei Island.
Photo by Carole Nervig, 1991.

It is not out of the question that a pyramid of some sort exists buried under the jungles or hidden in the mountainous rain forest of Pohnpei's interior. Such a challenging endeavor as the systematic exploration of the island's almost impenetrable upland jungles for any hidden archaeological structure has never been undertaken but would likely result in the uncovering of additional megalithic sites, if not a pyramid.

For example, the mound at the back of Rasalap meadow in Kitti District on Pohnpei Island might just hold such secrets.

When exploring the upland area of Rasalap, Kitti, the author sensed a pyramidal shape camouflaged by the vegetation at the edge of an uncharacteristicly flat, grassy meadow. When she questioned the Pohnpei State Historic Preservation officer accompanying her if it might not be a hidden pyramid or megalithic structure, his response was not denial. Rather, he cautioned, "We will keep some of these places to ourselves," either insinuating the need to preserve the mwanamwan of the place or indicating that the "discovery" and documentation be made by Pohnpeians, not by foreign archaeologists as in the past.

Along with the potential for megalithic structures or pyramids to be in the interior of Pohnpei, the oral histories of Pohnpei make a compelling case for an underwater pyramid or man-made urban complexes. Numerous accounts refer to Kahnihmueiso and Namket, the two underwater cities adjacent to Nan Madol that lie off the fringing reef's perimeter at an unknown depth. Brothers Olisipha and Olosopha were so inspired by seeing these cities from atop Takaieu Mountain that they selected the site for the current Nan Madol to "mark their spot" and to honor them. These "cities of the ancients" or "heavenly cities" may well be part of a now submerged stone complex that might contain a pyramid or two, similar to the ruins submerged off the coast of Yonaguni, Japan, or under the Bay of Cambray, India, which was inundated at the end of the last ice age.

Pyramidal structures are currently found in three Micronesian locations: Belau, Kosrae, and Pohnpei.

Figure 6.158 shows the pyramidal structure on the Belauan island of Babeldaob. It consists of both a stepped pyramid and another truncated

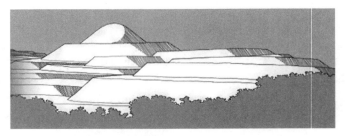

Fig. 6.158. Pyramid with dome, Babeldaob, Belau, Micronesia.
Image by William N. Morgan, 2010.

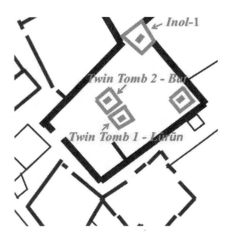

Fig. 6.159. Insaru pyramids, Leluh, Kosrae, Micronesia.
Image by William N. Morgan, 2010.

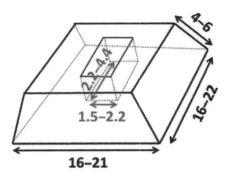

Fig. 6.160. Pyramidal tomb, Leluh, Kosrae, Micronesia.
Image by Z. Richards et al., 2015.

pyramid with a dome at its apex, set in a shallow valley surrounded by terraced hillsides.

Figures 6.159 and 6.160 show pyramidal structures on Leluh, Kosrae, which is only 348 miles from Pohnpei and connected to Nan Madol by oral history and its striking architectural resemblance. Some say these two islands were once connected by a land bridge upon which the god Nanspapwe escaped the wrath of the Sahu Deleurs. Leluh houses two truncated, crudely constructed pyramids.

The third pyramid is the stepped enclosure of Nan Douwas at Nan Madol. Despite the existence of these three sites containing pyramidal structures, the more likely location of the most significant pyramid(s) would be offshore. In fact, *underwater pyramids within the city of* Kahnihmueiso may be exactly what is represented in the pyramid glyph of the phallic monolith.

Polynesia also claims several "pyramid" sites including those of Tahiti, Samoa, and Rapa Iti. Add to this similar structures in Australia, Oceania, and the Americas, and the Pacific is bridged with the material culture of pyramidal structures . . . and the global circle of pyramid locations is complete.

ROVING GANESHA

The pyramid is not the only oceangoing cultural image bridging the Americas with Asia. Recall from chapter 1 that the sacred elephant is another formation present among the inner circle of monoliths at Pohnpaid.

Conventional Pacific migration theory might more easily accommodate the movement of elephant imagery (which is traditionally related to the elephant god Ganesha) from India or Southeast Asia through Indonesia and then eastward to Micronesia. Less acceptable would be migration from the other direction, east to west, despite the fact that the Norwegian adventurer Thor Heyerdahl proved it viable. Although not precisely centered in the Pacific islands, Pohnpei could feasibly be influenced by migrations or voyaging from either direction, as demonstrated by modern-day voyagers crisscrossing Oceania with only their indigenous navigation techniques.

Although elephants do not belong in the Americas either, there is no dearth of documentation in pre-Columbian cultures about this wisest of beasts. In these pre-Columbian cultures they appear to have had the same exalted or worshipped status as they did in Asia. They are similarly depicted throughout the Americas, and conceivably even at Pohnpei.

In light of other diffusional cultural imagery at Pohnpaid, the presence of an elephant is no more surprising than its other "out of place" global matches.

More remarkable is how the author came to find and recognize a particular "elephant" stone on her first exposure to Pohnpaid (recall fig. 1.15, p. 23). That Pohnpeian elders actually bothered to take a photo of this very stone validates its significance. Even though geologists might otherwise describe the stone as just a large formation of pahoehoe lava rather than the remnants of a megalithic Ganesha, they would be hard-pressed to give a rationale for the completely out-of-character action of a local shaman wanting to document this particular chunk of basalt with a photograph. Not to mention that the elders insisted on giving me this very same photograph years before I saw the elephant rock or knew it existed! How could my friend have known that the stone in the photograph would be part of my *future* discoveries?

Recall my astonishment from chapter 1:

Once I had seen the stone, I became fixated on what an image of an elephant was doing on Pohnpei. To my knowledge, there are clearly no accounts of elephants in Micronesia. Despite the incredible accomplishments of the ancient Pacific navigators, I could not conjure up an image of an elephant cruising on an outrigger canoe!

Perhaps Ganesha worshippers had carved an image of their cherished elephant god for this site in the distant past, prior to the arrival of current Pohnpeians. I knew of pachyderm motifs and sculptures that had been found in Mexico, another location not frequented by these enormous mammals. Did that mean the Hindus were here, as well as the Mayans? Or perhaps there was a common source to explain it all?

As one author reveals:

Actually there is no founder of Hinduism as Hinduism was not founded as a religion. It was a culture that basically flourished in India, which later took form as a great religion. (Dudhane 2021)

A common source to explain an elephant at Pohnpaid would be the culture of Mu. Perhaps shamanism (perhaps the most ancient form of spiritual work on Earth) or the animistic roots of Hinduism originated on Mu, or the Muvian postdiluvian colonies in India and the Americas brought Ganesha worship back to Pohnpei during reverse migrations after the Deluge. Hinduism is the oldest continuous spiritual or religious practice known. Among Hindus, the elephant-headed god Ganesha is one of the most worshipped.

Not only is Hinduism the oldest religion to grow out of shamanism, but its focus on nature, more so than any other religion, is another extremely significant aspect that points to origins in Mu culture. In addition to Pacific Islander oral histories, which include those of the Mo'o (Mu) and the Japanese, Naacal Hindus also report the existence of Mu as their Motherland. That their beloved Ganesha would appear on an island in the midst of the Pacific is not out of the realm of possibility,

Fig. 6.161. Kailasa temple in cave 16 of the Ellora Caves complex, Maharashtra, India. Photo by Vinayak Jagtap.

Fig. 6.162. Ganesha, East Mebon temple, Angkor Wat, Cambodia. Photo by Amineah.

regardless of the odds. As Shankara Bharadwaj Khandavalli has said in her Hindupedia entry "Concept of Motherland," "It is a uniqueness of Hindus to treat land as mother and a goddess." And if, as author Mark Amaru Pinkham explains, the migration and reverence for serpents did indeed come from Mu, why not elephants as well? He states:

> The migration of "Naga serpents" to Bharata Varsha from Mu might also be alluded to in other authoritative scriptures of India, but under a different name. For example, some texts allude to Rutas, a lost continent from which, asserts the French translater Louis Jacolliot, many of the original inhabitants of India migrated. Rutas appears to be the Hindu term for Rua, a Polynesian name for the lost Pacific continent of Mu. (Pinkham 1997)

Landmasses submerged at the end of the last ice age must also be taken into consideration when examining hypothetical Pacific spiritual-cultural migration. Multiple ancient Tamil and Sanskrit works contain legendary accounts of an entire continent—called Kumari Kandam—in the Indian Ocean that joined Madagascar, the southern tip of India, Sri Lanka, and Australia, being lost to the ocean between 30,000 and 3000 BCE.

Another such landmass is Sundaland. The shallow Sunda Shelf connects Indochina, Borneo, Java, Sumatra, and Japan and is likely the origin of the Austronesian race. The closer proximity created by these submerged areas would have allowed easier transport of Ganesha worship to and from what is now known as Micronesia and other Pacific islands.

Proximity from the Americas would likewise allow elephant imagery to reach Pacific islands from the opposite direction.

> Don't be surprised when you spot images of Lord Ganesha and various Hindu Gods at the Guatemala Museum. Or if you realize that Ganesha idols were found from a quaint temple of Mexico City's Diego Riviera. The state of Vera Cruz in Mexico and Venezuela's Quiragua also revealed the bearings of Lord Ganesha. Excavations and manuscripts from Central America prove without a doubt— Lord Ganesha was worshipped in the Aztec culture. Interestingly,

Fig. 6.163. Ganesha object found in 1975 by thirteen-year-old boy in Dogun, Australia.
As reported by the *Gympie Times* on October 30, 1975.

Fig. 6.164. Rock art, Kane Creek, Moab, Utah.
As seen on roadtripryan.com.

Lord Ganesh is shown wearing the loose garments of the Aztec civilizations in this part of the world.

Alexander Von Humbolt, a European anthropologist who lived between 1769–1859, was the first to postulate the Asiatic origin of the early American civilization. Over 150 years ago, he wrote that the Mexicans worshipped a human figure whose head resembled an elephant. A remarkable and non-accidental resemblance with the Hindu God, Lord Ganesha. (Hari and Hari, n.d.)

And to take these global Ganesha links even further, renowned author Laird Scranton, lecturer at Colgate University, connects Ganesha with the Dogon culture of Africa. Scranton's meticulous research of archaic cosmology, symbolism, and linguistics of the Dogon, Göbekli Tepe, predynastic Egypt, pre-Vedic India, and China, among other topic areas, brings their shared Ganesha ideologies full circle to the Maori of New Zealand in his 2018 publication, *Decoding Maori Cosmology*.

In this author's opinion, these associations and the migrations they imply validate the Pacific Motherland culture as progenitor of the great Mother Goddess culture. Scranton may conclude that it began in the Fertile Crescent, but the author begs to differ; all began in Oceania. With the inundation of Pacific landmasses, the *point of origin* of the archaic, matriarchal tradition that gave birth to globally consistent mythological systems *disappeared*, creating the *appearance* that sophisticated colonies (Indian, Chinese, Atlantean, Egyptian, Sumerian, Maya, Dogon, etc.) were the *source* of these traditions. Generations later, migrations turned back toward the Motherland of the Pacific, with remnants of her matriarchal cultural legacies and remembrances of her landmasses, but found only islands.

NAGAS, KUNDALINI, AND THE SEVEN-HEADED SERPENT

Serpents were "creatures" that were revered by ancient Hindus (who called them Naga), Buddhists (who called them *Mu*calinda), Jainists, Sikhs, and ancient Americans alike. The serpent (Naga/Nagi in Sanskrit) with seven heads, Narayana (Vishnu), is found in sacred texts such as the Bhagavad Gita, the Vedas, and the Puranas. Churchward (1933) states: "The seven-headed serpent originated in Mu and was there called Naga."

Halfway around the world, a seven-headed serpenthas replaced a human head on a stele from Veracruz, Mexico, and a three-thousand-year-old petroglyph of a seven-headed being was found in Siberia. The "sacred seven" is central to Mayan spiritual belief systems as serpent/kundalini/chakra power, as indicated by this stele. Numerous mythologies refer to "seven serpent kings/creators/sages, or galactic deities of this world" . . . all legacies of Mu.

Hunbatz Men, a modern Mayan daykeeper and ceremonial leader, has attempted to reconstruct the initiatory sciences of the ancient Maya in his book, *Secrets of the Mayan Science/Religion*. In analyzing etymology and surviving Mayan temples he concludes that Mayan religion was based around a system of seven centres, very similar to the Hindu chakras. In both systems the realization of the divine serpent-power is the goal . . . Men also discusses a seven-headed serpent form carved on a monolith in Aparicio, Veracruz, Mexico, and notes that Buddha was bitten by a seven-headed serpent while in the river of initiation. "This serpent is called chapat in India. Curiously, the people of the Yucatan, Mexico, have the same word and it, too, refers to the seven-headed serpent, just as in India." (Gyrus 2007)

Men (1990) says: "The number **seven** is **sacred** within **Mayan culture**. It is considered to be the number of the Divine and a **reminder of the galactic** forces" (emphasis in original).

That diffusion of this seven-headed serpent originated in Mu/Lemuria and spread worldwide is reinforced by the following definition of Narayana with its reference to "resting place" and "close association with water."

The naga, or mother serpent, was regarded as a type of deity who bestowed the benefits of fertility and healing on humanity. The naga was considered to be aquatic and symbolized a principle of primeval sanctity that was concentrated in the primordial element of water. (Scranton 2015)

The Deluge of the Motherland (Mu) clearly sent many beings to their final resting place under the ocean, thus survivors considered it a holy place.

The online Wisdom Library explains:

Narayana is the name of the Supreme God in his infinite all-pervading form . . . another meaning of Narayana is "resting place for all living entities." The close association of Narayana with water explains the frequent depiction of Narayana in Hindu art as standing or sitting on an ocean. (Wisdom Library, n.d.)

Fig. 6.165. *Top:* Serpent head, outcrop, Pohnpaid.
Photo by Carole Nervig, 1992.
Bottom: Petroglyphs, Madolenihmw, Pohnpei.
Illustration by Paul Hambruch, 1911.

Fig. 6.166. Rock art, Melanesia.
Illustration by Peter Bellwood, 1978.

Not coincidently, what approximates a seven-headed serpent is found as a petroglyph upon the Pohnpaid outcrop, just as both the sacred elephant and the seven-headed serpent are present in various forms throughout sacred sites of Asia.

Serpent motifs can also be seen in examples from the Americas.

Fig. 6.167. Rock art,
Valle del Encantado, Chile.
Photo by Auristela Aranda Quintana.

Fig. 6.168. Toltec stele,
sacrificed ballplayer, 400–700 CE,
Aparicio, Veracruz, Mexico.
Photographer unknown.

Fig. 6.169. Seven-headed serpent stool, Museo Mindalae, Ecuador.
Photo by Cynthia Lopez, 2016.

Of course, snakes and elephants are not indigenous to Pohnpei or most Pacific islands. If they were present in antiquity, a major rise in sea level or a catastrophic flood would have eliminated most species originally present on any large landmass such as Mu. So a serpent motif at the Pohnpaid site (fig. 6.165, p. 214; plate 34) would indicate only symbolic usage by migrations prior to the current Pohnpeians or ancestral memories from prediluvian civilizations, including "Serpent People," for instance—rather than a realistic illustration of historical Pohnpeian culture.

> The galactic race has been known since time immemorial as the "Serpent People." The serpent is a symbol of waveform energy, a sperm symbol representation of life. (Le Poer Trench 1960)

Unlike Pohnpeian oral histories (with the exception of the forgotten eel goddess Ilake), Melanesian mythology cites a specific serpent god. The native drawing of Agunua* or Hatuibwari contains a zigzag design in its serpentine form that could be representing a kind of waveform energy such as a sine wave, spiraling DNA, or kundalini. Although the Melanesian rock art graphic published by Peter Bellwood in 1978 is not accompanied by reference to the number seven, its actual image is strikingly comparable to the Pohnpaid serpent-head glyph.

Naga is revered in Javanese culture as a crowned giant magical serpent god with only one head—*but sometimes with wings*—thus linking this Naga serpent concept to winged disk or feathered serpent icons, or perhaps even the multicultural flying dragons.

Hawaiians also had their serpent or lizard deities, referred to as Mo'o, and in some cases as Mu. As in Melanesia, it was portrayed as a zigzag line, observed anthropologist Martha Beckwith when visiting the Pu'uloa petroglyphs in Hawai'i Volcanoes National Park.

> A jagged line was a "mo'o" (a lizard). (Beckwith 1914)

---

*According to Wikipedia, Agunua (alternate name Hatuibwari) is the cosmic serpent god of the people of San Cristoval Island of the Solomon Islands. He is the chief god, and all other gods are only an aspect of him. He is also the god of the sea.

Fig. 6.170. Hatuibwari/Agunua, cosmic serpent god with a human head, four eyes, and four breasts, Solomon Islands, Oceania. Indigenous drawing.

Fig. 6.171. Four-winged serpent, Egypt. Illustration by W. R. Cooper, 1873.

All of the above graphic and symbolic connections serve to mutually reinforce their common origin from Lemuria/Mu, but these relationships are definitely not limited to the Asia/Pacific vicinity.

This equivalent seven-headed serpent image has traveled even farther than Asia, Oceania, and the Americas—to Sumeria and Africa to be specific—or vice versa. The visual images used in Swaziland and on the Sumerian mace head may not be close matches to Narayana. However, certainly the literal concept of seven multiple heads on a serpent deity is the same, with all that its presence implies about cultural or spiritual diffusion.

The symbolism of seven *anything* may also refer to the mysterious and enlightened "seven sages" who permeate mythic lore as primordial creators and teachers of humanity. Also prevalent in legends and creation myths is the reference to seven ages or epochs that are the past and future cycles of world creation and subsequent destruction. Central to these concepts centered around the number seven are the stars of the Pleiades, the galactic travelers believed by some cultures to be their ancestors, and by others, the very progenitors of the human race.

Fig. 6.172. Naga, Anarajapoora, Ceylon (present-day Sri Lanka). Illustration by James Churchward, 1933.

Fig. 6.173. Buddha shielded by Naga.
Photo by Nikorn Pensri.

Fig. 6.174. Hero or god fighting a seven-headed monster. Shell plate, 2500–2400 BCE.
Photographer unknown.
Bible Lands Museum, Jerusalem.

Pleiades are frequently depicted as seven dots or seven stars, and identified on a mythological level with groups of seven divine beings. (Verderame 2016)

Although not a seven-headed serpent motif, a basalt boulder in the grassy meadow area of Pohnpaid displays a configuration of stars, likely seven, which could very well represent the Pleiades. (See plate 14; the photo does not capture the entire group, so this theory is based on the author's recollection.)

Perhaps a combination of all "seven" concepts can account for the mythic saturation in so many cultures: The seven serpent sages came from the seven Pleiades to teach enlightenment by opening the seven chakras and thus achieving the ability to transcend, rather than be destroyed by, the shift between the seven cycles or worlds of Earth. It is of note that the name for the Pleiades among the Aboriginal Wiradjuri of Australia is *Mu*layndynang.

Sirius and the Pleiades, both in Mesopotamia and Egypt, are often alluded to as being home to humanity's creator gods, feminine in nature, that assess humanity's evolutionary status from time to time to determine their worthiness (to be allowed to continue to develop), also referring to the Seven Hathors (Sirius, Sothis, Star of Women). Ancient Egyptian records refer to the Pleiades as "Krittikas," meaning "female judges of mankind" . . . (Pleiades) were also known to the Chinese, found in Chinese records c. 2350 BCE . . . The unique Zuni (A'shiwi) people of New Mexico knew them as "Seed Stars" . . . Subaru in the Japanese culture . . . As Oceanids, they are the "the Water Girls," the name the Aborigines knew them by. In India, they are known as Krittika, meaning the female judges of humankind, perhaps derived from Mesopotamian influence . . . in ancient Mesopotamia . . . as MUL.MUL (the Stars). (Fiorenza 2019)

Puzzling petroglyphs documented, presumably at the Pohnpaid site, by the German Sudsee scientific expedition in 1910 are possibly related tangentially to those of serpent imagery or "halo" imagery.

Drawings Paul Hambruch made for that German expedition were likely from the Pohnpaid site proper (improperly labeled Nan Madol

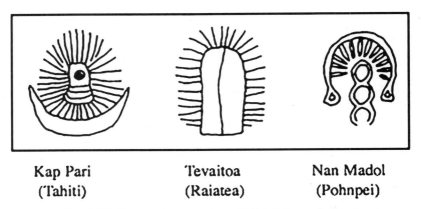

Kap Pari
(Tahiti)

Tevaitoa
(Raiatea)

Nan Madol
(Pohnpei)

Fig. 6.175. Petrogyph comparison, Tahiti, Raiatea, Pohnpei
(not Nan Madol or Pohnpaid per se).
Illustration by Paul Hambruch, 1911.

by Japanese archaeologists); no distinction between Nan Madol and Pohnpaid was made by Hambruch in 1910/1911 for whatever reason. Possibly related to the Pohnpaid seven-headed serpent glyph (fig. 6.165, p. 214; plate 34), Hambruch's renditions show more elaborate curvilinear designs with head "rays" that he called "halos." Whether he just embellished the petroglyphs or they have been weathered to the extent that they are now unrecognizable, neither of his versions were visible to this author and do not appear to match the seven-headed serpent I saw at Pohnpaid. No photographic documentation of these "haloed" petroglyphs—only Hambruch's drawings—are included in the report prepared by Paul Rainbird and Meredith Wilson for the Federated States of Micronesia in 1999. One more mystery to solve.

The origin of the classic universal symbols of the winged disk and the seven-headed or winged serpent may be indeterminable at this point in time, but their antiquity certainly is unquestionable, as is their presence at Pohnpaid. Could there be other primordial symbolism the Pohnpaid petroglyphs share with the rest of the world?

THE MOTHER GODDESS

If Pohnpaid and its glyphs are indeed as ageless as they appear, should it not possess the ultimate one? What could be more universal and primordial than the Mother Goddess, aka Venus? Found in the four corners of the world, she is also no stranger to Pohnpei Island. Her presence at Pohnpaid echoes a continuum of global matriarchal tradition, or at least the tradition of the female deity, with some examples dating back hundreds of thousands of centuries ago.

Her subtle form escapes many of those who inspect the huge basalt outcrop of Pohnpaid as hundreds of other petroglyphs compete for their attention. Nevertheless, she is undeniably a classic mother goddess motif and, not surprisingly, found within a megalithic complex known for its vagina stones.

Unlike her rivals, the Pohnpaid outcrop goddess petroglyph has not been dated with a reliable method, as is the problem throughout the site. According to the Art Encyclopedia, the majority of Venus figurines (Stone Age statuettes of women with exaggerated sexuality and no facial details) date from thirty-three thousand to twenty-two thousand years ago; a few other goddesses have an almost inconceivable antiquity.

> Most Venus figurines share similar characteristics of design and shape. Typically lozenge-shaped, with a wide fat belly tapering to the head and legs, they usually have no arms or feet, or any facial detail. Furthermore, their abdomen, hips, breasts, thighs, vulva are often deliberately exaggerated. (Art Encyclopedia, n.d.)

The Venus of Tan-Tan, dated to 500,000–200,000 BCE, is an alleged artifact found in Morocco. She and her contemporary, the Venus of Berekhat Ram, 700,000–230,000 BCE, from the Golan Heights, Israel, have been claimed as the earliest representations of the human form.

From a more recent time frame is the Dogu Venus of the mid-Jōmon era, 3000–2000 BCE, found at the Tanabatake site on Honshu Island, Japan. This time frame is comparable with that of most other Venus figures found in European locations.

Venus and mother goddess names are often interchangeable, generically assigned labels for a plethora of female fertility images, probably a result of their antiquity and the subsequent dearth of information required for specific identification. It could also be said that both names

Fig. 6.176. Mother goddess, outcrop, Pohnpaid.
Photo by Carole Nervig, 1992.

Fig. 6.177. Venus Willandorf, 25,000 BCE, Vienna.
Photo by Neil Harrison

represent the same actual *concept* in all cultures from time immemorial and that Venus in her many guises has always been one and the same with the Goddess and vice versa. Another more outrageous, but nevertheless possible, interpretation of why the multitudes of goddess or mother goddess images were labeled "Venus" (or equivalents) indicates that the goddess was literally a Venusian, *from* Venus.

The Pohnpaid goddess petroglyph has no oral history surrounding her.

She does, however, validate her archetypal identity as Mother Goddess or Venus, not only by her voluptuous goddess motif and facelessness, but by her very location. Pohnpaid's goddess petroglyph is not the sole signature or sexual reference at Pohnpaid. That fertility is undeniably a significant theme of the entire complex is affirmed by her image in the midst of at least five other megaliths with recognizable male and female anatomical elements: outer Takai en Pahsu; the female "hind end"; the inner stone circle Takai en Pahsu with genitalia incisions; the "clam with inscribed scallops"; and the phallic monolith—all described previously.

Especially compelling is that this classic goddess motif is a match to such *very ancient* Venus figurines found in locations not directly connected to Pacific cultures at such antiquity.

Nuku'uoro "Venus"

Although only tangentially related to Pohnpaid and its goddess or fertility imagery, but nevertheless quite extraordinary, is the similarity between a carved wooden likeness of the goddess Dinongaa, found on the atoll of Nukuoro in Pohnpei State, with a Venus statuette found in Russia. Other astonishing likenesses to Dinongaa are found in biological remains in Peru and in the Kurgan statue of Crimea, as well as in statues from the Naga people of northeastern India.

In spite of the fact that the Nukuoroan and Russian Venuses are less voluptuous than the other classic goddess images, the Dinongaa and Aeidu (Tino Aitu) ancestral deities from Nukuoro do make an incredible match with two small statuettes found in Zaraysk, Russia. Nukuoro, a tiny atoll 311 miles from Pohnpei Island, is geographically part of Micronesia but culturally considered to be Polynesian.

According to an article in the journal *Antiquity* in 2008, one

Fig. 6.178. Venus, 20,000 BCE, Zaraysk, Russia.
Photo from Amirkhanov Lev *Antiquity,* 2008.

Fig. 6.179. Dinongaa, female deity, and Aeidu, ancestral male deity, Nukuoro, Micronesia.
Illustration by A. Eilers, 1934.

Fig. 6.180. Sredny Stog ancestor statue, Kurgan mounds, Crimea.
Courtesy of the Dnipropetrovsk National Historical Museum.

Fig. 6.181. Angami Naga statues, northeastern India.
Photo by J. H. Hutton, 1921.

of the Russian statuettes is presumed to be finished and stands at a height of nearly 6.7 inches (17 cm); the other is clearly incomplete and about half as big. The Zaraysk carving has a feminine form reminiscent of "Venus" figurines found from Siberia to the Pyrenees. The birdlike heads on both versions are an almost identical shape, giving both a pronounced extraterrestrial appearance. The Nukuoroan deities are carved of wood in male (Dino Alige) and female (Dehine Alige) versions, as creator/ancestor God and Goddess. The one *unfinished* Russian statuette could be the male counterpart as in the Nukuoroan pair. Curiously, the Nukuoroan carvings more closely resemble the Russian ones than the more voluptuous "Venus" petroglyph from their neighboring island of Pohnpei. This does not negate a relationship. It does, however, imply a different one than our present paradigm of historical chronology and ancient navigation routes might offer up.

A rationale for such similar yet distanced motifs is, once again, connection via a Pacific Motherland.

For example, the Nagas of northeastern India are considered "spiritual adepts" who escaped Mu before it sank. They too have statues resembling the Nukuoroan Dinongaa and Russian Zaraysk statue. It is of note that the Naga culture has other links to motifs found at Pohnpaid, such as the seven-headed serpent deity mentioned previously.

Even though *these* monuments of fertility are obvious and numerous, the feminine procreative theme at Pohnpaid is not to be *confined* to fecundity or anatomical forms. Mythical archetypal aspects of the feminine divinity are also exhibited at Pohnpaid.

And what could be more so than the Seven Sisters of the Pleiades?

THE SEVEN SISTERS

We have discussed the Pleiades previously but will delve more deeply into our discussion of them here (recall fig. 6.96, p. 174). Few constellations are revered as intensely and as widespread as the Seven Sisters of the Pleiades. That this is due specifically or solely to their femininity is unlikely. Their significance stems from a plethora of reasons and the multitude of roles they play in our mythic past, in certain esoteric circles, and in their influence on our present and future. Deviating from culture to culture, their functions encompass navigational baselines, astrological seasonal markers, mythic superstar goddesses, and even ancestors in certain Pacific island cultures. For some they are seen as no less than the progenitors of the human race, or at least part of it.

> The high visibility of the star cluster Pleiades in the night sky has guaranteed it a special place in many cultures, both ancient and modern. The heliacal rising of Pleiades often marks important calendar points for ancient peoples. (Schaefer, n.d.)

Consideration will be given here solely to possible rationales for the appearance of the Pleiades as petroglyphs at Pohnpaid, how they are linked with Mu, and how such rationales are shared worldwide.

Before exploring the significance of the Pleiades further, clarification is in order regarding the seven "star" glyphs found on a boulder in Pohnpaid's outer stone circle. Although each of the seven glyphs is similar to each other, their placement may not be a precise match to the actual celestial configuration of the Pleiades. With no photograph of the entire stone with *all* its glyphs, the author is relying upon her memory of the impression that they were in the formation of the Seven Sisters. The other aspect in question is the nature of these glyphs. Are they birds? Stars? Airplanes? Seven sages? Or spacecraft?

If they are in fact depictions of the Pleiades, they offer further validation of Pohnpaid's status as a place of power, because the seven glyphs, whether they are birds or stars, demonstrate commonality with criteria of sacred sites worldwide. These criteria include mythical accounts, ethno/archaeoastronomy, geodesic grid location, interdimensional portal, and extraterrestrial contact, to name a few examples. The "bent" arm present in all seven Pohnpaid glyphs could represent "motion" of some kind, which is also inherent in these criteria.

Mythical Status

The nocturnal visibility of the star cluster Pleiades on all continents has guaranteed it a prominent place in many cultures, with its heliacal rising marking their ancient calendars.

That the Seven Sisters play an even more prominent role in Pacific lore is due not only their visibility, but also to their primary position and critical function in calendric and celestial navigation calculations. Knowledge of the stars and the flights of birds often meant life or death for ancient mariners on the high seas. Thus the Pleiades attained mythical status while dictating the beginning of their calendar year.

> To the Kanaka Maoli the stars' appearance in the night sky also signifies the beginning of the Makahiki, the most important holiday of the year. It is the traditional Hawaiian celebration of the harvest and time of personal rest and spiritual and cultural renewal. (Smith 2000)

Not as obvious as the Pleiades' technical astronomical function is the universality inherent in the etymology of its name: the Oceanic languages of voyaging cultures consistently use the root *ma* in their names for the Pleiades, as follows:

Mataliki: proto-Polynesian
Makali'i: modern Polynesian, meaning "highborn" stars
Matariki: Maori, meaning "tiny eyes"
Mata'ariki: Maori, meaning "the eyes of god"
Makara: Aboriginal Australian (this name was also connected to Orion)
Makeriker, Magarigar, Magirigir, Mariker, Makarika: Micronesian
Mapúlon, Moropóro, Molopólo: Filipino

Even the name of Nan Madol, Pohnpaid's neighbor in the Madolenihmw District, begins with *ma* and is sometimes spelled *Nan Matal,* a closer match to the proto-Polynesian *Mataliki.* Arguably, *ma/mu* is the most ancient word in the world, being the root for *mother.* The Motherland, Mu or Lemuria, is inextricably tied to the Pleiades via these Pacific names. Either the Pleiades played a significant role during the time of Mu, or the Pleiades were considered the literal Motherland of the inhabitants of Mu, or both. The Wiradjuri Aboriginal Australian name for the Pleiades is *Mu*layndynang. An even more direct relationship between Mu and the Pleiades is demonstrated in Babylonian mythology and astronomy, in which the Pleiades are called MUL.MUL or "star of stars" in their star catalogues.

> The Pleiades are known in Mesopotamia through the Sumerian name MUL.MUL—the stars. This term is known only from Assyrian and Babylonian sources, particularly from the 1st millennium BCE. In fact the later tradition in Akkadian language adopted Sumerian terms for the stars and constellation names, while we have few or no references at all to them in Sumerian sources. (Verderame 2016)

Because doves are also legendary representatives of mother and motherhood, they offer another link to the Pacific Islanders' use of *ma* in their naming of the Pleiades for Mu, for Motherland. A literal reason behind this mother-dove symbolism is that only doves/pigeons (and flamingos and certain penguins) produce their own type of milky substance for feeding their young.

Etymology provides further associations between *ma, mu, mother,* and the Pleiades. The website Constellation of Words gives the following definition:

> *Mother* of the Pleiades and Atlas' first wife. Pleione from *plein,* "to sail" making Pleione "sailing queen" and her daughters "sailing ones." (emphasis added)

A forgotten parent language could account for the universal connection between *mother* and *mu* and *ma.* Examples abound. *Mu* meant "mother" in old Egyptian (*mu, mut,* and then *maut,* the great Earth Mother in early Egypt), eventually mutating into *mou, mau,* and finally *maau* in Coptic. According to etymonline.com, *mother* in proto-Indo-European languages is *mater* (Sanskrit *matar,* Latin *mater,* Old Irish *mathir,* Old Norse *moðir*). Even more telling is the Mandarin use of *māma* or *muquīn,* the Hindi *mātā* or *ma,* Nepali and Tibetan *aama,* Finnish *emä,* Basque *ama,* and Sumerian *ama,* to mention a few.

Wings of Doves

Across millennia and cultures, few symbols have a tradition as long and as rich as the dove. Transformation, peace, and spiritual enlightenment are consistent themes inextricably linking doves and the Pleiades. A universal Motherland accounts for these widespread similarities.

A classic symbol for spiritual ascension is the bird, usually a dove. This concept is not exclusive to Christianity, as most pagan Pleiadian legends *predate* biblical ones. The majority of pagan versions involve transformation of humans into stars or doves, a process that may be interpreted as humans reaching enlightenment.

Orion pursued seven daughters of Atlas and Pleione for seven years until Zeus answered their prayers for delivery and *transformed* them into seven stars, or in some accounts, seven doves or pigeons. This escape and transformation of mythical females is found worldwide. According to etymonline.com, from Greek the word *Pleiades* means perhaps literally "constellation of the doves" and comes from a shortened form of *peleiades,* the plural form of *peleias,* "dove" (from the Proto-Indo-European root *pel,* meaning "dark-colored, gray"). Mythological transformation may connect the sisters, doves, and star motifs.

The dove is also the constant companion of both the pagan Mother Goddess and Christian Mother Mary. This nonphysical spirit (known as the Holy Spirit in Christianity), portrayed almost always as a dove, clearly demonstrates the notion of enlightened feminine spiritual energy, nurturing and peaceful. A quick search on Wikipedia relates that doves appear in the symbolism of Judaism, Christianity, and Paganism. The pagan goddesses Atargatis, Ishtar, Inanna, Astarte, and Aphrodite (and Venus), are all depicted with doves. Another reference to the dove is found in ancient Babylonia, where the goddess Astarte was transformed into a dove.

Because Pohnpaid has several fertility stones and a petroglyph of an actual mother goddess, the placing of the Seven Sisters with all of their implied symbolism on one of its stones serves to reinforce the divine feminine theme of the site. In Aboriginal Australian culture, the Pleiades played a leading role in female initiations.

> Many Indigenous peoples, including the Aboriginal Australians, share the idea that animals and stars are our greatest teachers. Of these, the birds of the Pleiades play a leading role in the initiation of young women. These shamanic practices lie at the heart of all Aboriginal women's rituals and ceremonies, especially those relating to the Dreaming of the Seven Sisters. (Andrews 2004)

At this point I must divert attention from the spiritual doves of mythology to a *seemingly* unrelated photograph taken on the Big Island of Hawai'i by the U.S. Army on November 11, 2001. It was displayed on a wall at the archaeological office in the Pohakuloa Army base located on Mauna Kea.

This 13,796-foot inactive volcano is not only the highest mountain in the world (if measured from its base at the bottom of the Pacific Ocean) but the holiest place in all of Polynesia. Originally the whole peak region of Mauna Kea, including Lake Waiau, was considered a sacred site; access was limited to priests and ali'i, native Hawaiian

Fig. 6.182. Goddess Wai'au as a red-headed dove, Lake Waiau,
Mauna Kea, Hawai'i, 2001.

royalty. Mauna-o-Wakea, aka White Mountain, is considered the home
of Wakea, Sky Father, who mated with Haumana, Mother Earth,
becoming the progenitors of the Hawaiian people. Its summit is ruled
by Poliahu, goddess of ice and snow.

The photograph of a red-headed "dove" was taken at 13,020-foot
Lake Wai'au (fig. 6.182), a heart-shaped lake just beneath the summit of
Mauna Kea, and arguably one of the highest lakes in the United States
and the Pacific basin. Its environs house funerary ashes and umbilical
cords of the Polynesian ali'i.

Its sacrosanct waters are home to a third goddess, Wai'au, shape-
shifting guardian of the lake, who bathes in it and drinks from it. As
illustrated in the photo above, this is one more example of a female
transformation into a bird. The bird in the photo begs to be recognized
as the goddess Wai'au herself. Of the four varieties of doves found in
Hawai'i, none have red heads. *Plus*, this documented bird *is not physical;*
it is transparent.

Wai'au—is the guardian of the lake, which bears her name. She bathes Poli'ahu, and refreshes her drinking gourd with sweet water, which she can fetch by using *her bird form* to fly from place to place. (ifa.hawaii.edu.hilo; emphasis added)

If islands in the Pacific, and all of Australia, are the only surviving portions of the Lemurian landmass, then Mauna Kea, its highest peak, certainly holds her own secrets, including a shape-shifting dove goddess.

That Mu or its submergence, aka the Flood, is linked to the dove and the goddess is likewise reinforced by pre-Christian sources of Babylon. Mackenzie (1915) relates, "In the Epic of Gilgamesh the dove was released to search for the end of the deluge."

Another account mentions this same association.

When the goddess was thus represented as the Dove with the olive branch, there can be no doubt that the symbol had partly reference to the story of the flood; but there was much more in the symbol than a mere memorial of that great event. (Hislop 1858)

By no means limited to legends of Pacific Islanders or classical mythology, the seven star/dove lore is shared by two dissimilar doctrines: those of the Bible and cosmic esoteric theosophy. Revelation 1:16 describes the coming on the Messiah: "In his right hand he held seven stars" (NIV). Baker (1952) explains, "In Theosophy, it is believed the Seven Stars of the Pleiades focus the spiritual energy of the Seven Rays from the Galactic Logos to the Seven Stars of the Great Bear, then to Sirius, then to the Sun, then to the god of Earth (Sanat Kumara) and finally through the seven Masters of the Seven Rays to us."

Thus the significance of seven is undisputable, whether they were birds, stars, or other spiritual entities; they are clearly at home in the Pohnpaid sacred site.

Birds, Stars, or Both?

Celestial astronomy is central to the cultures of prehistoric oceanic peoples. Against all odds, their voyages crossed thousands of miles to locate tiny specks of land in a haystack of water. In fact, in the vicinity of the Caroline Islands (Pohnpei, Chuuk, Kosrae, and Yap) less than 0.02 percent of the surface is land. It is no wonder then that the symbolic presence of stars or doves in the form of the Pleiades are found at Pohnpaid.

The connection between navigation and constellations is obvious; slightly less so is another link to birds and their innate sensing mechanisms.

> The inbuilt navigation system of birds, in particular, made them reliable companions to ancient mariners where certain species indicated the presence of landfall. (Andrews 2004, citing Elphick 1995)

Like the birds, Micronesian voyagers themselves attain an internal, self-sufficient ability they rely upon to guide them across the waters. Ancestors passed this highly technical knowledge orally from one generation to the next, from time immemorial.

> The Micronesian navigator holds all the knowledge required for the voyage in his head. Diagrams are sometimes constructed in the sand for pedagogical purposes, but these, of course, are not taken on voyages. (Hutchins 1995)

Celestial navigation works on Earth's surface waters, but these star/dove glyphs could also involve galactic or interdimensional navigation, or geodetic tracking.

Archaeoastronomy and Earth Grids

Archaeoastronomical alignments and mechanisms are frequently embedded in sacred architecture at sites that were themselves selected for their geodetic location or identified for their strong electromagnetic fields. Pohnpaid is no exception.

> The association of doves with geometric measurements is intriguing in the light of scientific research into the eyesight of pigeons [doves are members of the pigeon family] and their cognition, which suggests the birds' flight is determined by a combination of visual grids and sensitivity to the earth's magnetic field. (Cook 2001)

Doves and pigeons have an *innate ability to survey*, by seeing or sensing visual grids and alignments or strong electromagnetic fields. Could this be the rationale behind their inscription at Pohnpaid, to represent this concept? A similar detection technique, understood or "felt" by the ancients, may have allowed the site's creators to geodetically determine power spots, portals, or energy grids.

> Though little was known about these ancient forms of computation until recently, the science of geodesics shows that the celestial alignment of ancient structures involved a highly sophisticated surveyor system. (Andrews 2004)

In addition to housing petroglyphs, the Pohnpaid site is also one point of three in a straight alignment between Takaieu Peak and Nan Madol, and if this line is extended, it culminates at the underwater cities of Kahnihmueiso and/or Nahmket. Still to be determined is how exactly the stone with the seven glyphs aligns into this larger pattern emanating from cupules on the Pohnpaid outcrop. This relationship may never be established with the star stone, as there is no way to ascertain the stone's original position within the outer circle of Pohnpaid's boulders.

It must not be assumed, however, that these seven dove/star glyphs have *only* to do with earth grids, navigation, or archaeoastronomy. Their possible allusions to stellar ancestry or intervention should not be ignored.

Stellar Ancestry

More fascinating, yet more subjective than the utilitarian role of the Pleiades in traditional navigation, is the potential of its being the home cluster of planets to the progenitors of the Pacific Islanders, as well as other indigenous peoples. Smith (2000) explains:

> Na Huihui o Makali'i is a cluster of stars the English-speaking world calls the Pleiades or the Seven Sisters. The Makali'i is much revered in the Hawaiian tradition as the place from which, according to legend, the first Hawaiian people came to Earth and the star-based calendar of the ancestral Hawaiians has long placed special significance on their ties to the Makali'i.

According to the Facebook page AuthenticMaya, the Pleiades were apparently characterized the same way in Guatemala:

The early Monte Alto Culture and others in Guatemala such as Ujuxte and Takalik Abaj, made its early observatories, using the Pleiades and Eta Draconis as reference, they were called the seven sisters, and thought to be their original land.

These mythic implications, if even partially true, are extraordinary and are reason enough to be promptly dismissed by conventional academics. However, as stated previously, there is often a seed of truth in many oral histories, especially when they are consistent over distances and cultures.

Pleiadian mythology from around the world also suggests this is a commonly held belief among Indigenous peoples, who not only see themselves as caretakers of our planet but who claim to be either descended from the Pleiades, or at the very least, related to them in some way. (Andrews 2004)

Clearly, esoteric sources do not hesitate to identify the Pleiadians as humanity's ancestors, at least partially. Since certain aspects of Pohnpaid suggest it was an interdimensional portal, it could be that the Pohnpaid/Nan Madol/Kahnihmueiso vicinity was the first, or at least one of the first, entry portals for the Pleiadians, rendering it sacrosanct.

The Pleiades group is the home of a humanoid species. The Pleiadians are most similar to Earth humans. Earth humans supposedly were created by using mainly Pleiadian DNA. (Jiang and Li 2007)

The author was told very matter-of-factly, time and again, not only by practitioners of native Hawaiian and Maorian spiritual practices, but by native genealogists as well, that their ancestors came from the stars—literally—and in some cases with specific identification to the Pleiadians, with whom they procreated to produce mixed offspring.

In Polynesia, specific, named ancestors of existing families are alleged to have gone back and forth between the land of the Sky people, Earth and the underworld. (Lewis 2015)

Indigenous beliefs of Pleiadian ancestry are certainly not limited to the Pacific. Some believe that all tribes in North America came from the Pleiades, in addition to certain indigenous tribes in South America who relate that their homeland is in the Pleiades.

The Hopi believe their ancestors came from the Pleiades, the place, or people they call Chuhukon, or, those who cling together, a reference it seems to that tightly grouped starry cluster, as it appears to the naked eye. Likewise, early Dakota legends speak of the Pleiades, or Tiyami, as the abode of the ancestors. (Lewis 2015)

This holds true for California and Arizona as well:

Some Yumans of Arizona and California say that their ancestors came from the Pleiades. (Kelley and Milone 2011)

Oral histories of indigenous people in Paraguay reflect this too:

An ancient Paraguayan tribe, the Abipones, worshipped them as their ancestors. (Dobrizhoffer 1763)

The mythology of the Cree attests to these same origins:

When you die your spirit returns south to the seven sisters . . . Other native oral histories, or legends, speak of an origin, if not in the Pleiades, then in the stars generally, or other constellations. The Cree, for example, arrived on earth from the stars, as spirits, and then became human beings. (Lewis 2015)

Wilfred Buck (2018), a teacher of Opaskwayak Cree mythology at the Manitoba First Nations Education Resource Centre, states that the aboriginal people came from the stars to Earth through a hole in the sky to learn about the human emotions they couldn't experience as spirits.

"Right below the grandmother spider is the Pleiades, the seven sisters," says Buck. "And that's called Pakone Kisik. The hole in the sky. And the hole in the sky is where we come from." (C. Taylor 2019)

"The Pleiades are a very interesting group of stars," Buck said. "When they're talking about a hole in the sky, they're referring to spatial anomalies, wormholes, they're talking about alternate realities here." (CBC News 2019)

What is amazing is that according to Pohnpeian legends, *a "blanket" with patterns on it* that was thrown over Pohnpaid is the *actual source of the petroglyphs!*

Cree mythology speaks of their people coming to Earth from the seven stars in spirit form first and then becoming flesh and blood. An extraordinarily similar scenario is *remembered* by native Hawaiian shaman Hale Makua and was shared by personal communication.

When we came as the first souls on the planet we were without bodies. Only souls. We came on a "ship" together. Because we were fragile and without a physical body yet, we were accompanied by the whales and dolphins who protected us.

Although these extraterrestrial ancestry claims seem preposterous, genome research has provided some eye-opening theories that DNA coding might actually confirm these indigenous oral histories.

The World Genographic Project has been testing haplogroups worldwide and until recently has had no cause for alarm, until it was discovered that between 4000–6000 years ago a small group of extremely unusual DNA was introduced into the population of Denmark. Geneticists have named it "Haplogroup I1" and have no idea where it came from. It only appears in the Nordic races and to small degrees in countries that have been invaded by Nordics, such as England and Ireland. No other group of people on the planet Earth have this DNA unless they have come in contact with Nordic peoples. It is the root cause for the Nordic appearance. All other Europeans and most humans have R, R1a, or R1b haplogroups. It is suggested that Nordic people have alien ancestry as they do have a large amount of distinctive DNA that is without explanation and is not found anywhere else. They resemble Pleiades aliens and appear to have been hybridized by the advanced Pleiades aliens in our ancient past. (truthfrequencyradio.com)

If Pleiadian contact at Pohnpaid or its environs is in actuality the case, it is no wonder that the Seven Sisters would be memorialized in such a profound and permanent manner as petroglyphs . . . especially if Pohnpaid was their "landing site or entry portal." According to "ET Genetic Code May be Found in Human DNA," an April 9, 2013, article in the *Huffington Post:*

> The scientists are suggesting that an advanced alien civilization "seeded" our galaxy eons ago with an ET signal that eventually found its way to Earth, implanting a genetic code into humans, reports Discovery.com. Physicist Vladimir I. Cherbak of al-Farabi Kazakh National University of Kazakhstan and astrobiologist Maxim A. Makukov of the Fesenkvo Astrophysical Institute refer to this far-out concept as "biological SETI."

VISITORS FROM AFAR?

Although the topic of alien visitation in our distant past is poison to mainstream academics, to ignore this "ET" petroglyph or other similar ones is to stick one's head in the conventional sand and choose to not explore all possibilities. As NASA has said:

> Consider again, therefore, the desirability of establishing symbolic/linguistic communication with ETI [Extra-Terrestrial Intelligence]. It is helpful to review some parallels from human existence that pose problems for us today. One of these is "rock art," which consists of patterns or shapes cut into rock many thousands of years ago. Such ancient stone carvings can be found in many countries . . .
>
> We can say little, if anything, about what these patterns [above] signify, why they were cut into rocks, or who created them. For all intents and purposes, they might have been made by aliens.

NASA isn't saying the markings were made by aliens, but that it might be useful to assume they are in order to reframe the way we go about looking for signals from other worlds, and how we attempt to make contact. (Vakoch 2014)

So countless and widespread are the examples of these "ET" figures and their accompanying visitation myths that volumes could be written about them, and have been. Therefore only a few in proximity to the Pacific area are included here.

Is it plausible that Pohnpei or the now submerged city of Kahnihmueiso could have been a landing site/portal for Pleiadians or other extraterrestrials—or a destination for an advanced human civilization from antediluvian eras?

One answer to this question may be furnished by another petroglyph at Pohnpaid.

Found etched into the gigantic outcrop of basalt is a caricature that resembles other rock art from around the world that looks alien in nature (fig. 6.183; plate 35). For example, the oversized head and circular eyes of Pohnpaid's petroglyph are similar to those found in other rock art from India and Pacific Rim locations.

It may be claimed that this "ET" petroglyph is merely a childish rendition of a human form; however, another more "human" glyph

Fig. 6.183. Humanoid (alien . . . ?) petroglyph, outcrop, Pohnpaid. Photo by Carole Nervig, 1992.

Fig. 6.184. Humanoid petroglyph, outcrop, Pohnpaid.
Photo by Carole Nervig, 1970.

exists in proximity, demonstrating an ability on the part of the etcher to distinguish and articulate individual features.

Or is the "ET" a distorted image of visions created during a shamanic trance? This is often true regarding *painted* rock art. It is doubtful that a trance would last long enough to allow for the chiseling through basalt . . . unless some kind of advanced laser technology was employed. In this case it might be advisable to allow the photograph to speak for itself.*

Enough said.

A CASE FOR DIFFUSION, MIGRATION . . . AND MU

The Pohnpaid site constitutes the largest assemblage of rock art known in Micronesia, with numerous motifs and configurations that are "out of place" or "out of time" with conventional historical time frames of Oceania.

---

*With all previous consideration given to the Pleiades, it must be said that the "extraterrestrial" petroglyph referenced in figure 6.183 (and plate 35) does not resemble descriptions of the Pleiadian race as given by human contactees and ufologists. Such reports normally describe them as being very human or Nordic-like.

It is not just one component of this site that doesn't conform to historic Pacific cultural identity; it's many. Even if the interpretations, as either "out of place" or as diffusional evidence in terms of cultural and geophysical placement, are not *all* definitive or correct, arguably some are. That such an abundance of criteria ascribed to places of power is found at Pohnpaid points to its significant role in a worldwide system of sacred sites. These criteria include the presence of stone circles, petroglyphs, cupules, running water, geodesic grid placements, and archaeoastronomical mechanisms, as well as legends of extradimensional portals, extraterrestrials, fertility themes, symbolic giants and little people, shape-shifting, sound-related rituals, and magic.

Additionally, strategic proximity to Nan Madol, which happens to be the largest sacred archaeological complex in the Pacific, must not be ignored given that Pohnpaid is part of the Greater Nan Madol complex (via geometric grid and archaeoastronomical alignments). The convergence of so many corroborating divergent criteria over millennia at Pohnpaid confirms at minimum the influence of, if not an actual location of, a civilization that appears to be of universal global origin.

The question remains, what was this antediluvian civilization, if not Mu? If Lemuria predates Mesopotamia, Australia, and Africa as the original source of all *subsequent* "cradles of civilization," often labeled as *picos* (navels) in their cultures, where are Mu's picos?

Pohnpei Island, with its Pohnpaid, Nan Madol, and underwater Kahnihmueiso complexes, is clearly a candidate.

Lest there be any doubt, James Churchward reiterates the obvious: Kahnihmueiso and Pohnpaid, both parts of Greater Nan Madol, encompassed *one of the **seven** sacred cities of Mu.*

The Legacy of Mu

Due to the continuing ignorance of the full extent of Pohnpaid's scope, and subsequent lack of comprehensive documentation, current archaeological findings are by necessity extremely limited. However meager, the interior megalithic site of Pohnpaid provides the most groundbreaking and profound evidence pertaining to its relationship with Nan Madol, ancient Pacific cultures and their global counterparts, and the Motherland civilization that predated Nan Madol.

POHNPAID UNVEILED

Besides Nan Madol, Pohnpaid is without a doubt the other *enormous* elephant in the Pacific room. Its early stages predate Nan Madol, serving either as a mountaintop temple component of Kahnihmueiso *or* to "mark the spot" of the drowned Kahnihmueiso culture, as did Nan Madol.

Anchoring and accessing the interdimensional "portal" of Pohnpei Island was the rationale for which both Nan Madol/Kahnihmueiso and Pohnpaid were created, before and after the Pacific cataclysm. However, *there will be no true revelation* about this "dual" site of shared purposes until a time when either the sunken city is found or science can understand the concept of interdimensional portals and can measure them. Until then the answer to why the ancients identified portals with megalithic structures will remain an enigma. Or in other words, until the overarching role of the submerged city Kahnihmueiso is understood, or at least seriously acknowledged in the context of Greater Nan Madol's identity and function.

In addition to Pohnpaid's stone circle(s) and monoliths, its hundreds of petroglyphs clearly demonstrate the legacies of an advanced and universal mother culture of Mu. The mere presence of megalithic circles implies an archaeoastronomical function; glyphs symbolizing celestial phenomena validate the presence of sky watchers. Archetypal symbols matching those worldwide are chiseled into its basalt boulders and outcrops as reminders of a past not yet fully understood. Sacred geometrical configurations connect Pohnpaid to Kahnihmueiso as well as line-of-sight alignments to Takaieu Peak, Nan Madol, then Kahnihmueiso/Nahmket—again confirming the interrelationships of these sites and the technical geodesic, geomantic, and astronomical know-how of their creators.

Glyph motifs and anthropomorphic megaliths speak to Pohnpaid's universal fertility/birthing/mother goddess identity, often overlooked on Pohnpei as a whole. Despite scanty findings *to date,* the fact that Pohnpaid has been accepted and investigated as an archetypal fertility site will enable different, more expansive perspectives about its function on Pohnpei Island and Micronesia—namely that of the goddess or divine feminine culture that preceded all others. The clear parallels between inland Pohnpaid and its sister goddess site of inland Menka on Kosrae Island (as well as both of their geographic relationships to Nan Madol and Leluh, respectively) are tangible. The obvious linguistic, megalithic, and fertility themes present on Pohnpaid reinforce the lore of the goddess at Pohnpaid, which is alive and well—and most importantly, finally *available for serious investigation* after all these years.

Once thoroughly scrutinized, Pohnpaid will provide a treasure trove of findings that will *transform* Micronesian, if not Pacific, anthropology.

ORAL HISTORIES INTERPRETED

Always universally controversial, and a subject never before broached *in a metaphysical context* at Pohnpaid and Nan Madol, are analyses, interpretations, and revelations based on Pohnpei's oral histories. But wasn't that exactly the cosmology they embraced? The metaphysical, the magical? How their minds worked?

Archetypal themes and characters of Micronesia join the cast of relics from Mu and its colonies, all reinforced by migrations back and forth. These remnants include shared origins of their existence, their magic, their deity, and their technologies. Investigation is needed into the identity of the folk hero of Isokelekel, mentioned earlier, and why the esoteric code of 333 is always used along with his name (see the appendix for more details). Also begging deeper examination is Isokelekel's relationships with winged serpents, amphibian lineages, and his being gifted 333 baskets (handbags) of seeds of life or esoteric wisdom. This is documented in my upcoming book *Nan Madol Revealed*. These associations point to earlier global traditions of the genesis of humanity as represented by images of handbags of the gods used to "seed" humanity with occult knowledge or with life itself, all vestiges of our shared mother culture of Mu. Turtle, eel (serpent/lizard/dragon), and even elephant themes are found in Pohnpei traditions. These representations may be either physically in stone or embedded in lore and ritual. They serve to reinforce singular cultural origins in primeval time frames.

Elsewhere in the world, similar sites, scenarios, and artifacts are continually being discovered, with older than expected time frames often confirmed by corresponding legends and geology. The "magic" of the ancients, including Pohnpei's magic, is now understood to be the result of various sophisticated astronomical, geophysical, geomantic, or engineering mechanisms. The serpent (eel, lizard, dragon) symbolizes sine waves, earth energies, and DNA/kundalini, while the octopus and spider symbolize earth grids. Megalithic configurations are identified as resonance generators/transducers and/or portals to other dimensions.

The bedrock of Mu's civilization was its deep understanding of living Mother Earth herself, physically and energetically enabling manipulation of her natural forces for positive ends—at levels our current society is barely aware of nor has attained.

MU OR LEMURIA?

Designations and definitions of Mu versus Lemuria* as applied to sunken landmasses of Oceania remain unclear and confusing. As mentioned previously but bears repeating here, when we speak of Mu/Lemuria, it's not

---

*For expediency, Mu/Lemuria will herein be considered as one and the same—Mu.

just as a particular landmass. We refer to Mu/Lemuria in a larger sense, encompassing *historical time frames and interdimensional time lines—or as phases* of a primordial enlightened civilization *of many different races.* That Mu/Lemuria subsidence took place in gradual stages adds to the difficulty of determining its definition, boundaries, and time frames. It has been most frequently described as one all-inclusive original continent, broken by seismic activity into three smaller landmasses, which were all submerged for the most part over eons.

In his book *The Lost Continent of Mu,* James Churchward's belief that Mu sank about fifteen thousand years ago springs from his viewing of ancient records from Tibet and the Troano Manuscript. Both describe a cosmic catastrophe during which the ocean fell upon the continent and destroyed all. Churchward's argument that the civilization of Mu dates

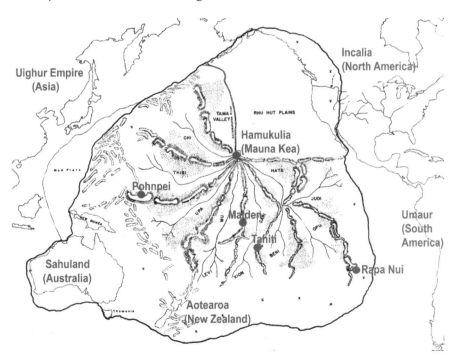

Fig. C.1. Continent of Mu "earliest" phase conceptualization, including Australia (Sahuland), Incalia (North America), Umaur (South America), and Uighur (Asia); various tribes: Tama, Chi, Thibi, Upa, Mu, Levi, Xion, Cari, Beni, Opu, Judi, Hata; and the cities found on Pohnpei, Hamukulia (capital once located on the Hamakua coast of Hawai'i Island), Malden Island, Tahiti, and Rapa Nui.
Map by Robert Stelle, 1952. Copyright by the Lemurian Fellowship.

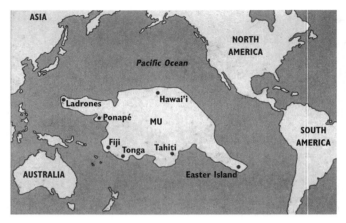

Fig. C.2. Sacred cities of the continent of Mu's
"middle" phase include Pohnpei.
Map by James Churchward, 1930.

back to more than fifty thousand years ago is based not only on Tibetan
records, but on discoveries by mineralogist and archaeologist William
Niven in Mexico of three civilizations buried beneath one another, with
strata of sand, gravel, and boulders between them.

For the majority of Pacific Islanders and even the ancient Jōmon
(14,500–300 BCE) of Japan, Mu (or its previously mentioned name-
sakes) pertains to sunken lands of Oceania, and for Hawaiian King
Kalakaua, it extended as far as the Indian Ocean (fig. C.3).

Sobata dwelling sites have been radio-carbon dated to the mid-
fifth millennium BC from Hokkaido in the north to the Ryukyu
Islands in the south. Their prodigious feats of navigation almost
perfectly parallel the distribution of Jomon earthenware finds made
along the East China Sea and the Sea of Japan, and may account for
Jomon pottery shards found on the other side of the Pacific Ocean,
in Ecuador . . . The late professor Nobuhiro Yoshida, President of
The Japan Petroglyph Society, states, "If they (the Sobata) were not
after all navigators from Mu itself—spreading its cultural influences
to both sides of the Pacific—then they may have been the direct
inheritors of a thallasocratic (naval supremacy) tradition from the
Motherland after its geologic demise." (Joseph 2006)

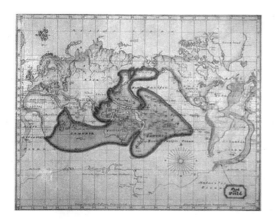

Fig. C.3. Chart of Mu/Lemuria commissioned by King Kalakaua, Kauai'i, 1886.

As depicted in the Lemurian Fellowship map (fig. C.1, p. 245), Hamukulia was the central "capital" or hub of Mu. It is noteworthy that Hamakua is in the northeastern district of the Big Island of Hawai'i, extending from the coast to the volcano of Mauna Kea. Home of the goddesses Poliahu and Lilinoe, the "white mountain" is the highest peak of the Pacific (and the world, if measured from the sea bottom). It has been revered for eons by indigenous tribes far and wide. More incredible is the listing of sixty-five people as Menehune, aka the Mu, by the 1820 census of Kaua'i.

> An 1820 census of Kaua'i by Kaumuali'i, the ruling ali'i aimoku of the island . . . listed 65 people as menehune (aka the Mu). (Joesting 1987)

Monumental confusion arises from *not distinguishing the Motherland, per se, from her colonies* (as delineated by James Churchward's exposure of ancient Tibetan texts). Mu's significant colonies include those *currently* identified as Uighur Empire, Kumari Kandam, Taiwania, Sundaland, Sahuland, Zealandia, the Americas, Atlantis, and Egypt—all of which are subject to various interpretations of prehistory.

What might currently be considered impossible migration routes would have been feasible before the inundation of the continent of Mu; landmasses were in closer proximity and currents differed from those of today.

Sanskrit and Tamil traditions refer to Lemuria as Kumari Kandam, the landmass connecting southern India to Australia/Sahuland, aka

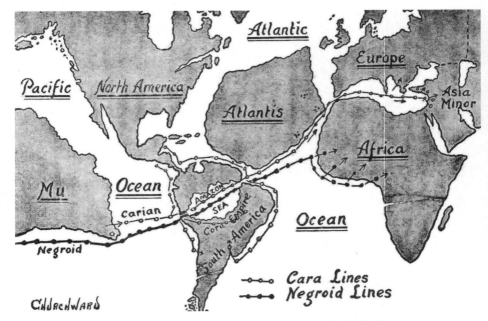

Fig. C.4. Lemuria, Mu, and colonies, circa 20,000 BCE,
based on Tibetan monastery map.
Map by James Churchward, 1930.

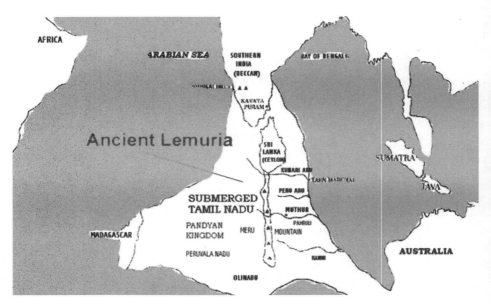

Fig. C.5. Kumari Kandam/Lemuria map.
Illustrator unknown.

the Kerguelen Plateau (fig. C.5). The Kerguelen Plateau (about a third of the size of Australia) was lost to the ocean between 30,000 and 3000 BCE. In 1999, the Joint Oceanographic Institutions for Deep Earth Sampling made an intriguing discovery in the South Indian Ocean using their research vessel *JOIDES Resolution*. The underwater Kerguelen Plateau was actually the remains of a lost continent that sank around twenty million years ago. It contains sedimentary rocks similar to those of India and Australia, indicating they were at one time connected.

> When sea levels fell during the Pleistocene ice age, including the last glacial maximum about 18,000 years ago, the Sahul Shelf was exposed as dry land. (Heyward, Pinceratto, and Smith 2006)

Once contained within the massive, original continent of Mu, Australia is the largest present-day remnant of Mu; some Pacific islands were once its mountain peaks. As sea levels rose, Sahuland (Sahu Shelf, Australia, Tasmania, New Guinea) and Zealandia (New Zealand, New Caledonia) detached from Mu in stages. Then during the past eighteen thousand to ten thousand years, Australia, Tasmania, and New Guinea separated from each other, as did the continent of Zealandia, which is now 93 percent underwater.

> The New Zealand continent [Zealandia] is unique: 93% of it is submerged, with huge areas of relatively shallow seas extending northwest as far as tropical New Caledonia and south-east to the scattered subantarctic islands. (Lewis, Nodder, and Carter 2013)

In addition to Sahuland, final phases of a sinking Mu are also demonstrated by the landmasses of Sundaland and Taiwania. Until about 110,000 to 12,000 years ago, Sundaland (the Sunda Shelf, Wallacea, Indonesia) was in extreme proximity to Sahuland (Australia, etc.; see figs. C.6 and C.7), as was Taiwania.

> Greater portions of Sundaland were most recently exposed during the last glacial period from approximately 110,000 to 12,000 years ago. (Hanebuth, Stattegger, and Grootes 2000)

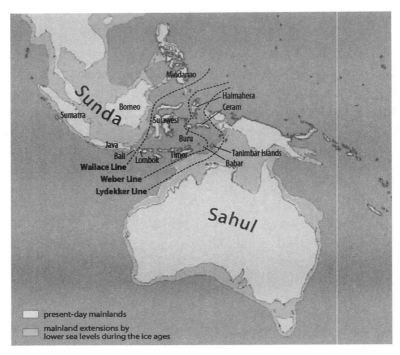

Fig. C.6. Sundaland and Sahuland in extreme proximity to one another as recently as 110,000 to 12,000 years ago.

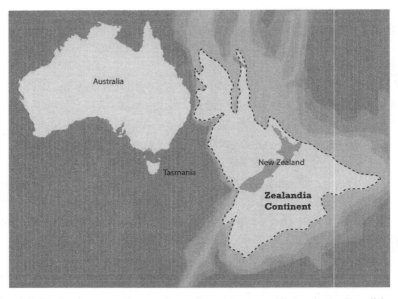

Fig. C.7. Zealandia map. Circa eighty million years ago, Zealandia broke off from Gondwanaland. Some say its formation could have occurred one billion years ago.
Map by Crystal Eye Studio.

Writer on human prehistory Stephen Oppenheimer, in *Eden in the East: The Drowned Continent of Southeast Asia,* posits that Sundaland and its upper regions were the origin locale of Austronesians. Recent findings by the University of Leeds suggest Sundaland was populated as early as fifty thousand years ago.

> Genetic research reported in 2008 indicates that the islands which are the remnants of Sundaland were likely populated as early as 50,000 years ago, contrary to a previous hypothesis that they were populated as late as 10,000 years ago from Taiwan. (University of Leeds 2008)

In basic alignment with Oppenheimer, researcher Daigu Sigua (n.d.) posits that Taiwania (Taiwan/Paiwan, aka *Mu*dalu, the shores of East Asia, Yangtze River Delta, Ryukyu Islands/Yonaguni, parts of Japan, the Korean Peninsula, Taiwan Strait, East China Sea, Japanese Sea) is the cradle of the Austronesian peoples, because both the Yangtze River Delta and the Ryukyu Islands (Yonaguni) have archaeological evidence suggesting human habitation from fifteen thousand years ago. By the end of the Ice Age, 11,400 years ago, Taiwan separated from the Asian continent.

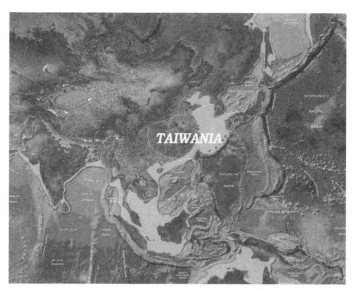

Fig. C.8. Map of Taiwania at the end of the Ice Age, circa 11,400 BP.
Image by Macadamer, 2018.

Fig. C.9. Uighur Empire, colony of Mu.
Map by James Churchward, 1930.

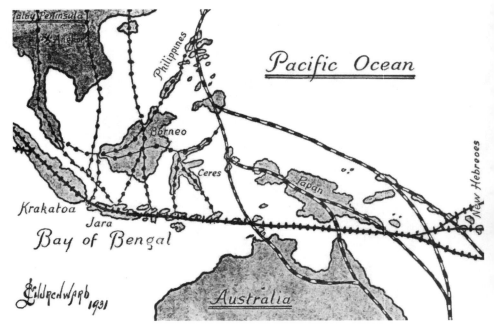

Fig. C.10. Sundaland migrations, "late" Mu phase.
Map by James Churchward, 1930.

Oppenheimer takes Southeast Asian migrations another step further, suggesting both linguistic and genetic links between Austronesians and the Saami (indigenous Nordic shamans) and Sumeria. This in turn points to an even further expansion of the Uighur Empire's culture.

In this respect, Uralic languages resemble Austronesian languages and the extinct orphan language Sumerian. Some linguists even suggest the possibility of a genetic link between Uralic languages and Sumerian (S. N. Kramer) . . . The Saami . . . may be genetically the closest survivors to the first immigrants from the East. A shamanistic culture, their legends record such migrations (Inger Zachrisson). Finnish mythology, as seen in their epic Kalevala, has clear Asian and Pacific echoes. (Oppenheimer 1998)

James Churchward (1931) has this to say on the subject:

Next to Mu herself, the Uighur Empire was the largest empire the world has ever known. From the Ural Mountains to the Pacific Ocean. They were the first colonists from Mu.

And per the blog on my-mu.com, written by Jack Churchward, grandson of James Churchward, James Churchward found the Naacal records in one of the Tibetan monasteries after a conversation with an old rishi. The records tell how the Naacals, seventy thousand years earlier and after a great flood, had brought to the Uighur capital cities copies of the Sacred Inspired Writings of the Motherland.

Taiwania is in close proximity to what was once the great Uighur Empire, a prominent colony of Mu. Taiwan (Paiwan, aka Mudalu) is central to an ancient migration route. Given all of this, the question is—considering primordial time frames yet to be validated—*from which direction did the migration flow?*

OUT OF AUSTRALIA OR OUT OF MU?

Some are familiar with the antiquity of indigenous Australians, said to date from 50,000 to 120,000 years ago (Royal Society of Victoria 2019), but few are aware of the Down Under links to Mu with its colony of Egypt (pyramids, hieroglyphs, and so on). Gympie pyramids and Gosford hieroglyphs in Australia have been dismissed by mainstream academia, especially the glyphs, as not a "perfect match" or being too "primitive" or that these glyph motifs were "not invented until 2,500 years after alleged to have been written." Precisely.

They originated in Mu, not Egypt . . . or at least the oldest of them. They could feasibly be *protohieroglyphs* as used in Mu that were later refined or altered in its Egyptian colony. As with any petroglyph site, there are layers upon layers; Gosford is no exception. It is possible that a temporal strata of hieroglyphs, from ancient Mu glyphs to later inscriptions done in historic times during the expedition to Australia by pharoah Khufu's son, all coexist at the same site . . . begging the question of how he knew Australia existed?

A possible answer might be—the same way other lineages of Mu knew to return and search for their lost Motherland in the Pacific.

Cultural remembrances of Mu were passed far and wide over generational eons as demonstrated by these very 250 Australian hieroglyphic petroglyphs. One hieroglyph precisely matches a symbol identified by James Churchward for "the Lands of the West in darkness." The three-pointed figure is Mu's symbol *as* the Lands of the West. "The sun without rays says that no light reaches Mu—she is in darkness—peaks only remain above the water. Mu is depicted here as being dead and in darkness with only points or peaks remaining above water. Kin no longer shines upon her . . . The Lands of the West at the time she was above water" (Churchward 1933).

Renowned alternative history researchers Stephen and Evan Strong bring to bear eye-opening evidence through structures, artifacts, and genetic evidence that resulted in their still highly controversial, yet plau-

Fig. C.11. *Left:* The lands of the West at the time she was above water;
Middle: Mu is submerged. No light shines upon her. She is in the region of darkness.
Right: The lands of the West are in darkness. No light shines upon her.
Illustrations by James Churchward, 1933.

Fig. C.12. Hieroglyph of Mu submerged, Gosford, Kariong, NSW, Australia.
Photo by Shaun Dench. Cropped from the upper left of the image and outlined for clarity.

sible, "Out of Australia" theory. This theory is based on the premise that humans inhabited Australia 50,000 to 120,000 years ago, predating the departure of *Homo sapiens* from Africa some 80,000 years ago.

> The one dimensional western scientific analogy together with archaeological findings are slowly moving the narrative closer to our stories of "The Dreaming," which tell us we have always been on this continent . . .
>
> Referring back to Wilson and Canns original calculations, their proposed timing of somewhere between 50–60,000 years stands on no less shaky ground than their genetic miscalculation. There are at least ten Australian sites claimed to be older than 60,000 years, granted every date is challenged by conservative critics, but even so, all are the products of respected academics . . .
>
> If just one date proves to be correct, irrespective of whatever

judgment is passed on the other nine, it can be confidently declared as a fact that Australia was not settled by African Homo sapiens 60,000 years ago. Whether the winning site turns out to be Lake George-fire-stick farming (120,000 years); Lake Eyre-skullcap (135,000 years); Jinmium-tools (176,000 years); Panaramittee-rock-engraving of saltwater crocodile (75,000 years); Rottnest Island-tools (70,000 years); Devonport-rock-engravings >115,000 years); Jinmium-art (75–116,000 years); Great Barrier Reef-fire-stick farming (185,000 years); Lake Mungo (WLH3—complete skeleton (61–65,000 years); or (WLH1) cremated bones (61,000 years); one out of the ten is sufficient to deny African entry. (Strong 2012)

Further, as anthropologist Alan Thorne told Reuters news service:

Neither of them (the skeleton or DNA) shows any evidence that they ever were in Africa . . . There's modern humans in Australia that have nothing to do with Africa at all." (ABC News 2006)

More evidence comes from researcher Bruce Fenton (2018):

There is no conceivable way in which the presence of humans in Australia 65,000 years ago can be explained by a migration moving slowly from Africa through Eurasia 60,000 years ago; even at the 70,000-year upper limit for dating this expansion, it simply does not make sense. Multiple genome studies have indicated that the ancestors of modern Eurasians diverged from their source population between 60,000 and 50,000 years ago . . . The reason for extreme doubt is that the oldest sample of African DNA yet recovered is 8,100 years old . . . With confirmation that humans were already living in Australasia 65,000 years ago, and that these people carried the oldest variants of the haplogroups considered ancestral for all modern Eurasians, we can redraw the migration map. Somewhere between 60,000 to 50,000 years ago, people carrying the identified ancestral lineages began to move through Asia, heading westwards toward Europe and Africa, reaching these lands 45,000 years ago. These migrants are almost certainly Australasians; no other interpretation better fits the evidence.

Fenton has identified a link between Australia and Turkey with what he claims are sacred Aboriginal *churinga* stones found at twelve-thousand-year-old Göbekli Tepe. Although Fenton does not specify Mu as the common element, Australia was part of Mu and Göbekli Tepe was one of her colonies.

Klaus Dona, artifact and archaeological researcher, directed Stephen and Evan Strong to another New South Wales site they describe as "no less than 19.77 meters of (tunnel) wall underneath a massive sandstone shelf that just shouldn't be there." They also state, "The technology needed to construct it cannot be found in any Original (Aboriginal Australian) tool-kit, or so the experts claim" (Strong and Strong 2019).

We've been arguing that ancient migratory routes may have been out of Australia . . . but could "out of Mu" be more accurate?

Technically, Australia was originally part of Mu continent, or at least one of the continents that comprised Mu, which would make it in closer proximity to both South America and Asia. Aboriginal beliefs passed down over eons and generations mimicked those of Mu,

Fig. C.13. Tunnel wall, NSW, Australia.
Photo by Stephen and Evan Strong, 2013.

especially regarding the sacredness of land and the Dreamtime. Perhaps early phases of a higher-dimensional, not-so-physical Mu more closely embodied or reflected the Dreamtime. Muvians did create natural landscapes, especially power places of natural beauty—their sacred temples. Information given on the website of Working with Indigenous Australians (2020) explains:

> According to Aboriginal beliefs, the physical environment of each local area was created and shaped by the actions of spiritual ancestors who travelled across the landscape. Living and nonliving things existed as a consequence of the actions of the Dreaming ancestors.

Astonishingly, recent genetic studies from Harvard Medical School link the indigenous peoples of Sahuland (Australia, New Guinea, Andaman Islands) with the Suruí and Karitiana peoples of the Amazon! Such findings demand a deeper examination and acceptance of the Strongs' "Out of Australia" theory as a more recent phase of "Out of Mu."

> Native Americans living in the Amazon bear an unexpected genetic connection to indigenous people in Australasia, suggesting a previously unknown wave of migration to the Americas thousands of years ago, a new study has found. (Dutchen 2015)

As for colonization in the opposite direction, markings of the Mu civilization appear in the cultures of Japan, Indonesia, Taiwan, Southeast Asia, India, and as far as central Asia, home to the Uighur Empire, the largest of Mu's colonies. It is more than coincidence that now extinct Denisovan DNA was discovered in a cave in the Siberian Altai Mountains, and near the border with Kazakhstan, China, and Mongolia. *Denisova hominins* are an extinct species or subspecies of archaic human that ranged across Asia before their extinction circa 125,000 years ago.

> [In] 2019, Greek archaeologist Katerina Douka and colleagues radiocarbon dated specimens from Denisova Cave, and estimated that Denisova 2 (the oldest specimen) lived 195,000–122,700 years ago. Older Denisovan DNA collected from sediments in the East

Chamber dates to 217,000 years ago. Based on artifacts also discovered in the cave, hominin occupation (most likely by Denisovans) began 287±41 or 203±14 ka. (Douka 2019)

More recently, Denisovan DNA appeared in 160,000-year-old remains from the Tibetan Plateau or "Roof of the World"—and home of the monastery housing the Inspired Sacred Writings of Mu.

But new fossil evidence reveals that these ancient human relatives also inhabited the Tibetan Plateau . . .
    Though Denisovan fossils have been found in only two locations, some Denisovan DNA is retained in contemporary populations of Asian, Australian and Melanesian people, said Jean-Jacques Hublin, a study co-author and director of the Department of Human Evolution at the Max Planck Institute for Evolutionary Anthropology in Leipzig, Germany. (Weisberger 2019)

Richard Roberts, director of the Centre for Archaeological Science at the University of Wollongong, even suggests that Denisovans first discovered Australia prior to *Homo sapiens.*
    Although Asian people retain some Denisovan DNA, Australian Aboriginals and Melanesians have between a 3 percent to 5 percent match to this gene; Papuans have about 6 percent. This percentage is remarkable given that there is no earthly parallel, according to Stephen and Evan Strong.

The percentage of Denisovan DNA is highest in the Melanesian population (4 to 6 percent), lower in other Southeast Asian and Pacific Islander populations, and very low or undetectable elsewhere in the world. (Genetics Home Reference [now Medline] 2020)

And if that were not strange enough, Denisovan DNA demonstrates an admixture with an unknown archaic human population, an unidentified ancestral hominid species *unlikely to be either Neanderthal or Denisovan.* But more recent genetic modeling of the Melanesians has revealed a third possibility, unlikely to be either Neanderthal or Denisovan, a different human ancestor that may be an extinct, distinct cousin of the Neanderthals. "We're missing a population, or we're misunderstanding something about the relationships," researcher Ryan Bohlender told Science News. "Human history is a lot more complicated than we thought it was" (quoted in Saey 2016).

Another author posits, "The more divergent Denisovan mtDNA has been interpreted as evidence of admixture between Denisovans and an unknown archaic human population" (Malyarchuk 2011).

Could there be a third ancestor as well? It seems increasingly clear that a third ancestor might explain the mysterious lineage of groups like the Melanesians and perhaps others. The study revealed "DNA that was very similar to that of the Denisovans, but distinct enough for the researchers to suggest that it could have come from a third, unidentified hominid" (BEC Crew 2016).

The plot thickens in the Philippines.

Callao Cave on Luzon, the largest island of the Philippines, was at one time home to an extinct species of humans known as *Homo luzonensis*. Archaeologist Armand Mijares of the University of the Philippines discovered the sixty-seven-thousand- to fifty-thousand-year-old fossils that attest to this. Could these be survivors from Mu or their descendants? Luzon's Mount A-*mu*-yao, near the towns of Ga*mu* and A-*mu*-lung, is the place revered "as the place ancestors landed in a canoe after escaping the Great Deluge," according to Frank Joseph's *The Lost Civilization of Lemuria*. Twenty-five percent of words in the native language of the Philippines are from Sanskrit and Tamil, according to Wikipedia. And, as Klakring and Hallen (1998–1999) point out, "One of the first non-Austronesian languages to have a major impact on the Tagalog language was Sanskrit."

And so it goes. Each day brings changes to what once was historical "fact."

New breakthrough discoveries, whether anthropological, genetic, linguistic, chronological, mythological, biological, nautical, or geological, have always forced changes in historical paradigms, usually pushing them farther into the past.

Yet third-dimensional evidence is only one paradigm by which to explore Lemuria. To understand this past civilization, minds must be open to the nature of its other dimensional reality, as foreign and divergent as it may be from our present one.

STATES OF CONSCIOUSNESS

The states of consciousness of its inhabitants provide another basis for describing Mu or distinguishing Lemuria from Mu. Initially, when races were "seeded," vibrational levels of the beings inhabiting Lemuria were extremely high, as was necessary for inhabiting fourth- and fifth-dimensional consciousness. In time, their consciousness lowered or "fell" as the planetary vibration was transformed gradually into third-dimensional reality. Based on this rationale, "Lemuria" might describe the earliest phases of the Motherland, and "Mu" the later, with physically denser phases more easily remembered.

Hawaiian traditions are very clear about their "emanation from nonphysical" origins to Mu. They came descending in the space *over* water, *not through it*, but as a flow from the "stratum of heaven" at "the beginning of the human era." Obviously, historical migrations of later days were on *wa'a* (canoes), but not the first waves of progenitors known as the Mu. In *Children of the Rainbow*, Leinani Melville explains how sophisticated native Hawaiian spirituality was completely misinterpreted by the missionaries. Taught traditional Hawaiian religion, mythology, and sacred symbols by Native Hawaiians and based on information from the Hawaiian creation chant Kumulipo, he leaves no question as to the reality of Mu being their terrestrial Motherland, known by several names, including Ta Rua and Havai'i-ti. This would of course account for their higher levels of consciousness in the Motherland's formative stages, from which their religion of Tahuanism stemmed. It is no surprise, then, that the Egyptians (latter-day Mu colony) used the same name, Ra, for their solar deity as the Mu used for theirs, Te Atau Ra.

Sophisticated technological feats in myths and oral histories may be attributed to the highly evolved states of consciousness of Muvians, typically categorized as magical events. Their cosmological perspective and achievements provide insight into comprehending our current planetary transition of lower to increased levels of vibration/resonance, specifically to experiencing the transition to fifth-dimensional reality in our physical bodies.

Forms of their "magic" allowed the Mu access to more than one level of consciousness and to utilize phenomena such as shape-shifting, telepathy, and levitation. It also allowed them to "mold" stone and create landscapes. Telepathic communication eliminated a need for written language; visual communication was typically by symbols or petroglyphs whose resonance and meanings were transmitted or "felt" tactilely, not just visually. Thus some truly *ancient* and *potent* glyphs are impossible to interpret only by their visual graphic motifs; they must instead be felt.

Shape-shifting bodies or their parts was another type of "magic" used extensively by Muvians or their cultural descendants. More than coincidental, legendary story lines of Pohnpei and Oceania conclude with someone—a shaman, demigod, or human being—turned into a stone, a tree, or a bird, for instance. Often a part of pagan beliefs, the occurrence of shape-shifting, especially into stone, is so plentiful and consistent in oral histories it merits examination in order to understand the nature of Mu.

Changing the molecular structure of stone with their "minds" (mystic technologies) made it malleable, and as such, intricate geometrical shapes could be formed by this process. Or it became "light" enough to levitate—all "magic" in terms of our current, almost nonexistent, spiritual technologies. Yet countless megalithic sites and oral histories attest to such feats, including the flying stones of Nan Madol!

> The architects of these (Jomon) monoliths are described as Keepers of Stone thousands of miles away in Tiwanaku; the Waitaha of New Zealand also received a group of such master craftsmen, whom they describe as "with narrow eyes from the north after the flood," magicians capable of "shaping rock without breaking its spirit." (Silva 2019)

Clearly concepts of Mu/Lemuria are inconsistent, confusing, and difficult to grasp. Sinking landmasses, numerous colonies, eons of time, and limited or submerged evidence—all are culprits. Added to this mix are the esoteric factors of multiple states of consciousness or the unfamiliar or "magical" dimensional realities they occupied. No wonder many academics or those with limited mindsets refuse to broach the topic.

Perhaps the most expedient way to define Mu or Lemuria would be as an all-inclusive one: an *enlightened* civilization that existed over a vast expanse of time and multiple dimensional realities that, before its submergence, had its geographic origins in the Pacific Ocean but became culturally diffused outward though its survivors and colonies.

To understand Mu as the Motherland, she must also be differentiated from one of her colonies, Atlantis.

MU VERSUS ATLANTIS

Ignorance assigns many megalithic sites to Atlantis. Not the case. More often than not, many of these ancient sites were *within* Mu's colonies but located *outside* Oceania. That said, there was an extended period of time when Mu and Atlantis coexisted, thus adding to the confusion and incorrect attribution of cultural images and monuments to Atlantis rather than to its Motherland.

> Atlantis disappeared very quickly into the ocean and our Third World, Kásskara [Lemuria], disappeared very slowly. (Hopi elder Oswald "White Bear" in Hamilton 2020)

Unlike its once-colony Atlantis, reported by Plato as gone "in a single day and a night," Mu went slowly in stages, long before Atlantis, but again, with some overlap. Migrating survivors of *all races* went to known colonies, while others established new cultural centers. Remembrances of the homeland, although scattered, eventually motivated some Pacific Rim cultures to reverse-migrate back into the Pacific to search for their lost lands. Whether consciously or not, at some level they were drawn back to their Motherland.

Gary A. David (n.d.) explains that in addition to Hopi legends of sailing eastward on reed rafts across the Pacific Ocean from the previous Third World, which was destroyed by a deluge, to the current Fourth World, many cultural and linguistic similarities exist between the peoples of the South Pacific and those of the American Southwest. The astronomical and navigational skills possessed by these globally dispersed serpent seafarers (sometimes called the Nagas) must have been the common currency of the day.

Inhabitants of submerged landmasses and remaining mountain peaks of the Pacific Motherland are identified as more spiritual, intuitive, emotional, and creative. They are deemed to be less dense physically and less aggressive. They are also considered to be life-seeding, matrilineal, right-brained, ancestor-revering, and nature-loving.

To the contrary, the inhabitants of the "fatherland" of Atlantis, Mu's younger, smaller counterpart in the Atlantic, are described as patrilineal, left-brained, less spiritually evolved, more physically dense, and technology-loving. Atlantis was partially populated by colonizers and then later by survivors of Mu along with other peoples from unidentified locations.

The point is that contemporary civilization has devolved in many ways since Mu/Lemuria. Atlanteans hastened this process with their technological addictions. The loss of balance between the feminine and masculine principles and between genders has resulted in a more disharmonious planet—a pivotal reason to examine the wisdom of the Motherland.

MEGALITHIC LIBRARIES OF MU

That civilization may be much older and much more mysterious than we have been taught is becoming apparent with each passing day and decade.

GRAHAM HANCOCK, 2019

Fortunately, anthropological findings provide both physical and cross-cultural validation of the Motherland—cultural diffusion par excellence.

Much has been written over recent years by both alternative and even, occasionally, not so alternative sources about the matching of various architectural structures and symbols from supposedly unrelated civilizations. *The point they repeatedly miss is that Mu, their mutual Motherland, is the source of this connection.* Atlantis is too limited and too young be the *original* source, although as a colony of Mu it maintained and then later passed on aspects of this shared culture and cosmology along with its own traditions.

Mu's existence answers many questions in alternative history—the elephant in the room.

Because Mu/Lemuria existed prior to the Great Flood or cataclysm, it is no wonder that material evidence of Mu is hard to come by; most prehistoric coastal regions are now submerged. Underwater archaeologists Jonathan Benjamin and Geoff Bailey (2017) write that one third of the continental landmass was submerged as recently as 65,000 years ago, the earliest date published for human entry into Australia and New Guinea.

Megalithic libraries are the only irrefutable evidence remaining from Mu and her colonies; stories in stone may be hidden but cannot be distorted or forgotten or destroyed as can oral histories and legends. These "libraries" are scattered worldwide and speak of spiritual or "natural" technologies often beyond our recognition and comprehension. The very relationship of Mu with her colonies explains the transmission of and resemblance to certain cosmologies, structures, and symbols across the cultures of the world.

From a plethora of examples, a few striking matches between rituals and symbols follow. These proverbial images, *worth more than words,* show unsuspected and unorthodox links between otherwise diverse cultures. Archetypal or cosmological themes and symbols of the turtle, serpent/eel, and elephant all originated with Mu.

Hindu cosmology combines all three—the serpent, the elephant, and the turtle—to represent the foundation upon which the mountain/earth is balanced so that the sky does not fall down (fig. C.14, p. 266). Variations of this archetypal concept appear as the avatar turtle Akupara/Vishnu supporting a pivoting Mount Meru, and a serpent as the cord for the "churning of the Milky Ocean" to achieve balance. "In the Hindu legend of the *Churning of the Milky Ocean,* the gods and the demons churned the Milky Ocean in order to acquire the Nectar of Immortality. In this grand spectacle, Vishnu, the preserver of the cosmic order, had taken the form of a massive tortoise (*Kurma Avatar*) in the middle of the Milky Ocean. His humped shell acted as a pivot for Mount Mandara or Mount Meru, which served as the churning stick, while the serpent Vasuki was the cord for the churn" (Dev Misra 2016).

"World turtles" with "pillars" on their shells are also found in China (fig. C.16), Mongolia, and even Mexico (fig. C.15), while indigenous American myths tell how the Great Spirit created their homeland by placing Earth on the back of a giant turtle.

Fig. C.14. Hindu cosmogram.
Illustration by Thunot Duvotenay, 1843.

Fig. C.15. Turtle with pillar-mountain, Mexico
Photo by Bibh Dev Misra,
Museo Anthropologico, Mexico City.

Fig. C.16. Bixi turtle pillar, China.
Photo by Yingna Cai.

Focus will first turn to the omnipresent turtle, both material and iconic, as inherited from Motherland cosmologies.

THE TURTLE AND
THE FOUR DIRECTIONS

One of the oldest and longest-living animals on Earth, the sacred turtle symbolizes cross-culturally the creation of the landmasses of the world, Mother Earth, the four directions, and in some cases the literal markers of land boundaries.

> At the beginning of this cycle of time, long ago, the Great Spirit came down and He made an appearance and He gathered the peoples of this earth together—they say on an island which is now beneath the water—and He said to the human beings, "I'm going to send you to four directions and over time I'm going to change you to four colours, but I'm going to give you some teachings and you will call these the Original Teachings and when you come back together with each other you will share these so that you can live and have peace on earth, and a great civilization will come about. (Brown 1986)

"At the beginning of this cycle of time" is a clear reference to the Motherland culture of Mu, from which the races of humanity were sent in four directions. *"On an island which is now beneath the water . . . Great Spirit said . . . send you to four directions and over time . . . change you to four colours."*

Thus originated the significance and cultural diffusion of the four directions and four colors (races) to indigenous peoples. (Renowned psychic Edgar Cayce described how each race that was originally "seeded" had a different aspect of spiritual growth to work with related to the five physical senses, suggesting an esoteric rationale for the creation of four races.)

Not restricted to any one continent, turtle veneration and ceremonies reenact ancestral departures from Mu. The origins of this, however, are so old that the details are lost yet are of such consequence they can never be totally forgotten.

Among the indigenous peoples, what remained were consistent representations of the four directions of migrations via turtle imagery or the archetypal concept of the mystical turtle supporting earth and sea on its back. Sculpted stone turtles often display graphic indications of these alignments and are frequently placed as land border markers. They are always oriented to the *four directions* and *land,* for the turtle reiterates the shape of Mother Earth, aka Turtle Island. Native Hawaiians also connect the turtle with migrations. Indeed, their legends tell how the first people to arrive in Hawai'i were guided by the *honu* (turtle).

And yes, as we have established, the "four directions" are indeed the four literal and practical directions (north, east, south, west) utilized in astronomy, navigation, and other sciences. They also reference the sacred four elements (earth, air, fire, water, or liquid, plasma, gas, solid) or, according to James Churchward, "the Deity and his Four Great Primary and Creative Forces" (or archangels)—all of which demonstrate their symbolic potency in relationship to their origins in the Motherland culture. The turtle connection to direction is validated by their internal mechanisms that allow them to navigate utilizing the Earth's magnetic field.

Fig. C.17. Ofai Honu (turtle stone) and its petroglyphs, Bora Bora, French Polynesia.
Photo by Arthur Baessler, 1896; inset by K. P. Emory, 1934.

It could even be said that the four directions are embedded in physical turtles, as witnessed by the Ecuadoran snapping turtle's belly.

Turtles can use the magnetic field as a sort of map. It gives them positional information . . . employ geomagnetic imprinting to navigate . . . turtles can sense both the magnetic field's intensity and inclination angle. (Putnam 2011)

As to be expected, these turtle sculpture legacies are found worldwide, often placed in strategic locations as altars in front of temples or pyramids, as four directional markers, as markers of land borders (as we have established), and for ceremonies. Nan Madol is no exception, as the list below shows.

Komkorun, Mongolia (Uighur): With remnants of what once were pillars on their backs, four turtles surround the ancient city, marking four borders and four directions.

Linggu Temple, Wangsan, China: Missing the "pillar" once attached to its back, a turtle sculpture dated to 515 CE lies in front of the Linggu Temple.

Siem Reap, Angkor, Cambodia: In 2020, archaeologists led by Chea Socheat unearthed two Hindu sculpted turtle stones and a seven-headed Naga stone at the Kandal Srah Srang Temple site (fig. C.18). One turtle had a rectangular lid that opened to reveal an unidentified plasma/gel substance in the hole (shown in a 2020 video by Praneen Mohan, explorer of ancient history and megalithic sites); the other had a triangular lid over another container holding polished quartz crystals and thin bronze wires.

Buried around the Kandal Srah Srang temple premises were two metal tridents, hundreds more crystals, and a broken sculpted Naga stone (seven-headed serpent deity, such as the one seen in fig. C.19) with a circular, multiringed petroglyph incised upon its chest suggesting a resonance or frequency pattern. Mohan (2020) describes it:

Very high quality metal objects with no trace of rust or decay . . . crystal quartz and bronze wires side by side . . . Are these religious

Fig. C.18. Turtle stone, Kandal Srah Temple, Siem Reap, Angkor, Cambodia.
Photo by APSARA, the Authority for the Protection of the Site and Management of the Region of Angkor, 2020.

tridents, or are they antennas used for radio communication? . . . As soon as these were found, locals started to come in and pray in large numbers, because they felt a strange energy radiating from them . . . they performed all sorts of rituals on these artifacts and crystals.

The question remains whether these artifacts were "spiritual" in nature or components utilized in technology. Or both?

James Churchward describes the trident as the royal scepter of the Empire of the Sun, aka Mu, noting their prominence in Angkor as well

Fig. C.19. Seven-headed Naga Hindu deity, Phnom Penh, Cambodia.
Illustration by James Churchward, 1933. The circular frequency mandala as recognized by Praneen Mohan on the Naga at Kandal Srah Temple.

as use by the Uighur cultures twenty thousand years ago. Poseidon was the first king of Atlantis, a Mu colony, and his trident is a legacy of the Motherland.

Trident symbolism combines with the feather, symbol of truth, to create the Crown of Mu, explains Churchward. "Three feathers were the ornament of the headpiece of Ru Mu, the King High Priest of Mu" (Churchward 1933). This very same combination of a trident and three feathers is found in Inca, Mauritius, Maori, and Paiwan/Taiwan cultures (see the figures on the next page). Manco Capac's trident staff (fig. C.23) adds a component similar to Thor's hammer, often considered a derivation of Mu's T symbol. Similarly, the Shiva sculpture at Mauritius's sacred Lake Ganga Talao holds a matching trident (fig. C.24). In another familiar example:

> The crown of Poseidon is shown as having three points, the numeral of the Motherland. His scepter was a trident, again showing Mu to be suzerain. The trident was the form of the Uighur scepter 20,000 years ago and later we find it as the scepter of the Khimers of Cambodia . . . A dose [sic] examination of the carvings on all of the structures at Angkor show them crying out: "Motherland! Motherland! Mu, the Motherland!" The royal lotus, the symbolic flower of Mu, is profusely used in the decorative carvings. The trident, the royal scepter of the Empire of the Sun, is prominent. The headdresses of many of the figures carry the numeral symbol of Mu. All buildings, except the last at Angkor Vat, face the east, the direction of the loved and revered Motherland. (Churchward 1933)

To underscore the symbolic turtle presence in front of temples as vestiges of Mu, here are a few examples of note:

Candi Sukuh, Java, Indonesia/Sundaland: Twin turtle altars lie in front of the pyramid stairway. In Hindu mythology, the tortoise symbolizes the support of the world and is an avatar of the god Vishnu.

Wangsan, Korea: Gwigamseok, a 127-ton turtle-shaped rock, is believed to be a power spot of pure energy, the ultimate source of ki—the nonphysical energy of all life.

Fig. C.20. *Left:* High priest Ra Mu,
from Mu tablets found in Mexico by Niven.
Right: Ancient Mu crown.
Illustrations by James Churchward, 1933.

Fig. C.22. Paiwan/
Taiwan aboriginal
three-feather
headdress.
Photo by Yali Shi.

Fig. C.21. Topa Inca Yupanqui,
Inca ruler, with trident staff
and three-feather crown.
Illustration by E. Osorio.

Fig. C.23. Manco Capac, first Inca emperor,
Cusco, Peru.

Fig. C.24. Shiva at Ganga Talao, sacred lake
on island of Mauritius, near Madagascar.
Photo by Gowtumbac.

Yonaguni, Ryukyu Islands, Japan: Reminiscent of the Egyptian turtle altar at Abu Ghurab is one submerged at the Yonaguni complex. It lies just before the apex of a V-shaped trench that faces due north.

Niuserre, Abu Ghurab, Egypt: This sun temple altar once held an obelisk oriented to *four* directions. *Niuserre* means "delight of Ra" in that Ra was satisfied by the obelisk's orientation to the four directions, circa 2400 BCE. Mehler (2002 and 2014) states that Ebd'El Hakim Awyan, teacher of ancient Kemet, said that the site was designed to expand spiritual awareness through the use of harmonic resonance transmitted through the alabaster platform that enabled one to connect with the sacred energies of the universe, known as *neters*. Kemet teaches that the neters "landed" in physical form at this "portal."

Great Plaza, Copan, Honduras: One head of the Mayan cosmic turtle altar that supports the Earth is facing north, and the other is facing south.

Uxmal, Yucatan, Mexico: Carefully carved turtle statues adorn the cornice on the four sides of the Temple of Turtles frieze.

Jaina, Campeche, Mexico: A limestone turtle oriented north-to-south beneath a ball court commemorated the first built *horizon* in an artificial island, constituting a gateway to the underworld.

Generally, "Maya worldview reveres sea turtles, whose profile not only reiterates the shape of the universe, but also whose nature shows a unique capacity to thrive in all three realms, as a stellar icon near the celestial heart and by reproducing solely on land while living in a watery otherworld" (Williams-Beck 2015).

On Fakahina Atoll, French Polynesia, turtle rituals were performed to establish and sanctify marae; there and on many islands, as we've established, the term relates to stone temples. As well as the coral-slab altar, the people built a cist or ceremonial "seat" for offerings, which was used by the officiating tribal leader. Similar ceremonies were also held on Tongan maraes.

According to tradition, ceremonially butchered offerings of turtle meat were made on an altar-like platform in the Marae. Parts of

Fig. C.25. Mayan cosmic turtle altar, Copan, Honduras.
Photo by Peter Wendelken, 1984.

Fig. C.26. One of four turtle border markers, Karakkorum, Mongolia.
Photo by Dom1.

Fig. C.27. Turtle altar, Yonaguni, Japan.
Photo by Chris Wilson.

Fig. C.28. Niuserre sun temple, 2400 BCE, in front of pyramid, Abu Ghurab, Egypt.
Photo by Jim Henderson, Ancient Egyptian Foundation.

the turtle were cooked in separate ovens, then shared according to a strict hierarchy . . . The turtle's head and heart were reserved for the highest-ranking individuals . . . Guillaume Molle's . . . dig uncovered . . . bones of the ritual turtle offering . . . This was really exciting—it's like finding the foundation stone of a cathedral. Before building a Marae, the site was sanctified by sprinkling salt water over coral branches taken from the sea . . . The people then built the structure and ceremonial platforms around this first offering so we're seeing the very first gesture of the people marking the construction of this sacred site . . . To the Polynesians, the turtle was seen as the embodiment of the ancestors and clans. (Faure-Brac, n.d.)

Elsewhere in Polynesia, turtle petroglyphs are consistently located in sacred domains, near the sea, at ceremonial ahu or marae, and occasionally as boundary markers. Of religious significance, turtles were considered *amakua* (ancestral spirits) and/or were associated with the voyaging to the afterworld, assisting in safe passage of the spirit after death. Of Polynesia it is said:

Caves sites, cliff edges, tidal zones, lava flow, volcanic craters, fresh water springs and ceremonial structures: these all seem appropriate locations for turtle motifs, considering that this animal was regarded to travel between the worlds of the living (on the surface) and the ancestors (down below). (Meijer 2012)

Elsewhere in the world, similar words are shared by a Mohawk elder:

Our old stories tell how we traveled from the Sky World to find ourselves a place on Turtle Island. (Beaton 2020)

As with most indigenous cultures, often as an inheritance from Mu, the turtle holds equivalent stature and consequence in cultural traditions of the eastern Caroline Islands of Micronesia.

Pohnpei Island is in fact an island made up of "turtle" districts, or *wehi,* a literal, not just archetypal, representation of land (Mother Earth).

In Pohnpeian language, *wehi* means "turtle." And because of its

Fig. C.29. Nanweias turtle rock, Nan Madol, Pohnpei.
Photo by Adam Thompson, 2013.

Fig. C.30. Twin turtle dais flanking pyramid of Candi Sukuh, Java, Indonesia.
Photo by Anandajoti Bhikkhu.

Fig. C.31. Bacab turtle mask of the Maya.
Photo by Hadi Nikbakht.

conceptual significance and inherent symbolization of "earth," perhaps the term *wehi* was initiated to designate the three major land divisions of Pohnpei: Wehi Madolenihmw, Wehi Kitti, and Wehi Sokehs.

As the majority of lore about the Pohnpaid megalithic site is lost, it cannot be firmly established that its turtle petroglyph motifs (see fig. 2.11, p. 41) relate to specific religious ceremonies or fishing. That said, when the site is *thoroughly* documented, other material findings could conceivably validate Pohnpaid's relationship with the turtle and in turn, with Mu and ancient Kahnihmueiso.

The eel (aquatic serpent) and the turtle were the basis of Pohnpeian religion as its main totem characters. The possibility exists that memorialization of the four directional Mu migrations at Nan Madol may be witnessed by the consistent use of the number 4 in conjunction with the turtle in rituals.

Just as at other world-class sacred sites, there is indeed a turtle-shaped rock in Nan Madol. Used in Pohnpei's most important religious ceremony, the annual Pwung en Sapw, were the turtle, the number 4, and the eel.

The magical pool Na*mu*eias on the nearby islet of Idehd kept turtles used for these rituals. Were the turtles perhaps being "prepared" in these magical waters?

After an elaborate canoe procession from Nan Madol to Takaieu (the pyramidal peak) and back, four turtles were placed four times (or four turtles at a time) on the "turtle stone" Nanweias by priests. The sacrificial turtle was then taken to Idehd to elicit the "blessings" of the holy saltwater eel *Mu*an (Nan Samwol). A medium between the people and the ruler's god, the turtle was offered as tribute and atonement.

Muan's acceptance or consumption of the turtle indicated that "the honored spirit of the land" was pleased with human conduct on Pohnpei.

> According to Masao Hadley, every June and July, a great ceremony called Pwung en Sapw or Aponalap took place "which consecrated and gave power to the kinds of rituals which concern respect for the high chiefs." Missionary Luther Gulick reported this a seventeen-day affair involving chiefs, priests, food, sakau (kava), drinking, dancing, blowing couch shells and communing with spirits, culminating at the islet of Idehd. This process also included a ritual canoe "flotilla" to Takaieu, the pyramidal guardian peak of Madolenihmw Bay and component site within Greater Nan Madol archaeo-astronomical and sacred geometrical alignment complex. (Nervig 2001b)

Religious ceremonies on neighboring Kosrae Island's sacred city of Leluh also involved turtles and the number 4. More humane than Nan Madol's, in which the eel devoured the turtle, the Kosrae turtle ceremonies were "catch and release."

The months-long Epan feast was held every four to six years. On its last day a special turtle ceremony called Sar-ik was performed, wherein canoes of high-ranking chiefs each brought a turtle to Leluh, as representation of the thunder god Nösünsap (husband of goddess Sinlaka). According to relentless historical researcher and Kosrae resident Maria Grazia Fanelli Stephens (based on research by Ernst Sarfert and Ross Cordy), the similarity between Leluh and Nan Madol rituals was that each canoe held four decorated men who held a turtle by its four legs. They lifted the turtle and then hit it four times on the platform of the canoe while a fifth person counted along "one, two, three, four." After all the turtles lay in presentation to their respective chiefs, they were released unharmed into the ocean and a daylong regatta commenced in Leluh Harbor.

On Kosrae Island, the eel was not part of the Epan feast, but it was honored in ceremonies at Menka, the temple complex of the goddess Sinlaka. On Pohnpei, both eel and turtle were honored in the Nan Madol annual ritual, but worship of the eel goddess Ilake came first. It was likely tied to the "rock and tree" people whose nature focus resembled that of Mu (the creators of Pohnpaid?). Perhaps these earlier ceremonies might have been without the sacrifice of a turtle. After all,

Olsipha and Olsopha were to have brought a "new" religious ceremony to Nan Madol—clearly one less goddess oriented—where the turtle was ritually sacrificed and then eaten.

Elsewhere in Micronesia the turtle is revered as sacred, in addition to its importance as food and adornments. A vast "turtle cave" on Paata in the Faichuuk District of Chuuk State houses a large turtle stone (fig. C.32). The cave includes a paved stone pathway, suggesting significance of the site; one might only imagine what rituals took place within, as its function is unclear.

Fig. C.32. Turtle Cave and stone, Paata, Faichuuk District of Chuuk State, Micronesia.
Photos by Lee Arkhie Perez, 2020.

Along with the turtle, the elephant and serpent/eel/lizard/dragon/mo'o are cultural fragments of Mu dispersed just as far and wide; both are linked cosmologically and, upon occasion, physically. That a serpent holds together the cosmos as symbolized by the elephant's body shows a clear link between these two Lemurian archetypes across Pacific cultures.

EELS AND ELEPHANTS IN THE ROOM

Predating Nan Madol was the worship of a freshwater eel (aquatic serpent) goddess Ilake, comparable to a mother earth goddess. Later, a saltwater eel gained domination at Nan Madol. Here it became a living representation of the Great Spirit during the annual ceremony of redemption held on the islet of Idehd. This ritual combined both sacred turtle and holy eel, as did other Mu traditions noted above. Of note is that the name of this eel was Muan (Nan Samwol).

> At the center of this extended ritual was the great marine eel Nan Samwol. It was kept in a pen or pool beneath the once soil surface of Idehd. This eel represented the Great Spirit. Only one special priest, Nahnmadau en Idehd, was allowed in the enclosed portion of Idehd where he cast a spell or prayed to Nan Samwol. The eel responded by rising up and out of his pen looking angry.
>
> At this point the priest would perform the "Prayer of Nahnishohsapw," a right of atonement. First he would ask the eel, who symbolized the Great Spirit, for forgiveness himself and his sins throughout the year, then for his fellow priests, then the Sahu Deleur or Nahnmwarki and other chiefs, and finally for everyone.
>
> Usually all went well; Nan Samwol returned to his hole with a peaceful, happier appearance while Nahnmadau en Idehd offered the turtle stomach. After eating, the eel would settle into his hole and the annual ceremony was successful and complete. (Nervig 2001a)

There are other iconic links than serpents and turtles to be considered—with elephants! According to Ritu Shukla in the April 4, 2019, article titled "Symbolic Description of Lord Ganesha" in the *Times of India* online:

Lord Ganesha's belly represents the whole cosmos, the seven realms above and below and the seven oceans are inside Ganesha's cosmic body. These are held together by the cosmic energy (kundalini) symbolized by the huge snake around him. The snake that runs round his waist represents energy in all forms.

That Nagas, Naacal Mayas, or "Serpent People" migrated from their submerged Motherland Mu (aka Rutas/Rua) is not only found in the Tibetan tablets (originally from Burma) that James Churchward came across in northern India. The Naga "serpent" seafarers appear

Fig. C.33. Sakya Monastery, Tibet, where eighty-four thousand wooden books were discovered in 2003. The books in this library or others similar to it may have been read by early researchers such as James Churchward, in a quest to discover the secrets of Mu.
Photo by Richard Mortel, 2018.

repeatedly in Vedic scriptures and Hindu legends of India, according to Mark Amaru Pinkham's *The Return of the Serpents of Wisdom*. Naga Mayas also headed to Tibet and China, there establishing the Uighur Empire.

As for the elephant archetype Ganesha, aka Su*m*ukha, it is worshipped by Hindus of India and also revered by Thai Buddhists—which is to be culturally expected. Both groups evolved from the Bön shamanism of Nepal, more closely related to Mu.

Less expected are the pre-Columbian elephant motifs in the Americas, especially when used in conjunction with a pyramid. This combination speaks of a huge cross-confirmation of Muvian oceangoing diffusion.

As discussed previously, mammoth or mastodon or Ganesha imagery appears in North, Central, and South America. Its prominence at the apex of pyramid-shaped stones found in Ecuador renders the elephant elevated with a special status, even that of a deity. Of major interest is that the stone artifact found in Burrows Cave, Illinois (fig. C.35), is not only duplicated in South America (fig. C.34) but also coupled with paleo-Sanskrit text and, according to Russian proto-language specialist Hauty Phitikove, may relate to the ancient Sindh (Harappa) country of Hindustan.

And it is not only the elephant and pyramid combinations that coincide. Tablet layouts also include a sun, horizontal lines, and script, all a match on these lithic artifacts from both Americas. Their translation might speak of a cataclysm that created a cave in which a broken "mechanism" is hidden? Sounds like Mu again. Take this translation:

> The bed of death is where the beating made a cave. There dwells the lamed mechanism. There lies the dish that tipped the top and shagged all. (McCulloch 2016)

In pre-Columbian Central America, Ganesha is frequently depicted in Mexican manuscripts as well as in temple ruins, with a similarity to Chinese versions. The serpent is likewise no stranger to all indigenous cultures of the Americas. As we know, one of their great gods is in fact a winged serpent known as Quetzalcoatl or Kukulkan.

Fig. C.34. Elephant stone, Tayos Cave, Ecuador,
from the Father Crespi Collection.
Photographer unknown.

Fig. C.35. Elephant stone, Burrows Cave, Illinois.
Photographer unknown.

In his 1989 book *Nu Sun: Asian-American Voyages,* anthropologist Gunnar Thompson was one of the first "time dectectors" to document the links between Asia and Central America and to demonstrate specific similarities between certain Chinese cultural images of elephants and those of the Maya. What is remarkable is the graphic similarity between the elephant images of Central America and China.

Fig. C.36. *Left:* Mayan elephant Stele B, Copan, Honduras;
Center: Tlaloc, Maya rain god, Yucatan, Mexico; *Right:* Nu Sun Chou bronze, China.
Drawings by Gunnar Thompson, 1989.

As mentioned previously, the Hindu god of luck, Ganesh, was perhaps worshipped in Central-South America. Images of a god with an elephant's trunk have been excavated in plenty of Mexican manuscripts and in temple ruins in Central America (Mundkur 1980).

Another occurrence of particular interest is the use of the circled cross and enveloped cross motifs in conjunction with the elephant trunk at the Mayan site of Uxmal in the Mexican Yucatan. Both of these cross patterns are found at Pohnpaid. The elephant trunk also displays a swastika, that according to James Churchward, originated in Mu, not in India.

"Out of place" elephant imagery reared its unlikely head in another *theoretically* unrelated location . . . Pohnpaid!

As astonishing as the presence of a megalithic elephant head and trunk (and body underground?) at the Pohnpaid inner stone circle may be, even more so is how the author was predestined to recognize this elephant megalith during her first exposure to the site, as related in chapter 1 (recall fig. 1.15, p. 23). As mentioned in that chapter, it is noteworthy that the Pohnpeian elders recognized the rock's significance by taking a photograph of it, but as important is that the photograph was pressed upon me by my friend.

The rationale for why this megalith was evidently so important for the author to find was never given. Its *preordained discovery and recognition* remain the only clue, as there are no traditional accounts of presumed ceremonies or other functions at the Pohnpaid site. The only plausible explanation as to why a gigantic stone elephant would be at Pohnpaid is as a legacy of Mu, possibly in the form of the Hindu elephant deity. Ganesha statues are often a focal point in temple complexes of Mu colonies. Pohnpaid evidently is no exception.

Whether the elephant stone at Pohnpaid was contemporary with Kahnihmueiso or created later by ancestors as a memorial to Ganesha or Kahnihmueiso is debatable. What is clear is that its location on Pohnpei in the middle of the Pacific Ocean attests to cultural imagery diffusing from *both* directions outward: the Americas and Southeast Asia.

MU "LOGO"

Conceivably, the most exciting documentation of the existence of Mu and its colonies was a site discovered off the coast of Venezuela by underwater archaeologist Miguel Angel Prieto (1983) of Simón Bolivar University. Dated at ten thousand to thirty thousand years old, the site consists of rock art and dozens of man-made structures. Astoundingly, the Venezuelan petroglyph depicted on the next page (fig. C.37) is identical in design to the symbol that, according to James Churchward, represents Mu (fig. C.39). The Venezuelan submerged "Mu symbol" is clearly the oldest to date, but certainly not the only one amidst Mu colonies. (See the appendix for more examples.)

The Chumash tribes of Southern California's coast are clear about their origins being a sunken homeland to the far west in the Pacific Ocean. Their migration to the Santa Rosae (then a contiguous landmass of northern Channel Islands) left human skeletal remains off Santa Rosa Island that have been deemed to be approximately thirteen thousand years old.

> University of Oregon archaeologist John Erlandson says . . . in the Channel Islands . . . the oldest artifacts are in the ocean off of Santa Rosa Island, and could be 13,000 years old. (Orozco 2017)

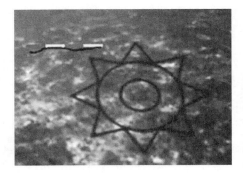

Fig. C.37. Undersea petroglyph, 30,000–10,000 BCE, Venezuela. Documented by Miguel Angel Prieto and Luis Felipe Valera in the 1960s and 1970s.

Fig. C.38. Rock art, Chumash Painted Cave State Park, California. Photo from the collaboration between CyArk, California State Parks, and Santa Ynez Valley High School, 2021.

Fig. C.39. Royal escutcheon of Mu. Illustration by James Churchward, 1933.

Fig. C.40. Symbol of the Mound Builders of the United States. Illustration by James Churchward, 1933.

Additionally, David Reich, a population geneticist at Harvard Medical School, found a "perplexing connection between a forty-two-hundred-year-old human in the Central Andes and ancient inhabitants of the Channel Islands off the coast of California" (Callaway 2018).

Weighing in on the matter from a local perspective and as cited in a 1999 *LA Times* article by Gary Polakovic, "Channel Island Woman's Bones May Rewrite History," Paul Varela, executive director for the Chumash Interpretive Center, says:

> If you ask a Chumash person, they will tell you they have been here forever. We've always been here.

That the Chumash physically resemble the ancient Japanese Ainu as a *result of a coastal migration* via the Bering Strait should not be a foregone conclusion. The Chumash are clear about their submerged homeland directly to the west, while in Ainu, Hawaiian, and Maori cultural traditions, coming from Mu is a given.

> As a matter of fact, Ainu [language] shows a great typological closeness to Quechua and Inga, which belong to the American Indian languages. (Tambovtsev 2008)

More evidence of Mu migration to the Americas is the link between the genome of a 10,400-year-old individual from southeastern Brazil to Australasian groups (including Papua New Guineans and Aboriginal Australians) documented in 2015 by David Reich, Harvard Medical School, and Eske Willerslev, a paleo-geneticist at the University of Copenhagen and the University of Cambridge (as discussed in Callaway 2018).

Gary Polakovic, in the same *LA Times* article cited above, says:

> Many scientists say that the old skeletons found in the past few years around the Western United States do not resemble modern Native Americans . . . Some of them bear striking resemblance to a very ancient race called the Ainu, a maritime people who were forerunners of Polynesians and long ago occupied Japan and China, said Douglas W. Owsley, head of anthropology department at the Smithsonian Institution's National Museum of Natural History.

Might all of these genetically linked populations share the same Motherland? Australasians, indigenous Brazilians, Ainu, and Chumash could have left their common inundated lands from the *central* Pacific and disseminated outward in opposite directions, whether as colonizers or postdiluvian survivors.

More telling is the stunning Chumash rock art that replicates numerous variations on the Mu "logo" motif.

Mu "logos" now exist throughout what was once Mu, namely its colonies, as the continent for the most part no longer exists. The information that James Churchward came up with was based on Tibetan records and not considered "legitimate" by academia. But regardless of any source, this consistent motif of the Mu logo is, in fact, distributed worldwide and points to an ancient mother culture.

Fig. C.41. Rock art, 3000 BCE, East Timor, Southeast Asia.
Illustration by Asmus Koefoed.

Fig. C.42. Royal fan, Marquesa Island, French Polynesia.
Illustration by James Churchward, 1933.

Fig. C.43. Mu logo geoglyph, Guatacondo Ravine, Chile.
Photo by Jose Pérez de Arce.

Fig. C.44. Jade, Lingjiatan Site, 5,300–5,800 years old. Anhui Museum, Hefei China. Photo by Cangminzho.

Fig. C.45. Mu logo pendant and Mapuche "purse" earrings, Chile. Photo by Jose Pérez de Arce.

These images are but a few of many Mu "logo" examples that span both the Pacific and Atlantic oceans, from Indonesia to New Guinea to the Pacific islands to the Americas to the Canary Islands to Europe. And, according to Churchward, this design specifically depicts the lost lands of the Empire of the Sun, the Motherland of Mu.

It could be argued as well that the enveloped cross petroglyph found at Pohnpaid was a variation on the Mu logos discussed above. (A multitude of graphic variations on this Mu motif are found in the appendix.)

Pohnpeian linguistic links to Mu might be as valid as lithic ones, yet it is the sum total of innumerable connections, some concrete and others not so, that point to the obvious conclusions.

MU, THE PACIFIC ROSETTA STONE

Every truth passes through three stages before it is recognized. In the first stage it is ridiculed, in the second stage it is opposed, in the third it is regarded as self-evident.

ARTHUR SCHOPENHAUER

Nan Madol is a *legacy* of the civilization of Mu, a graveyard to commemorate Mu's "shining" city Kahnihmueiso; it is a monument to identify the sunken city's location, thus both are one and the same in terms of places of power status. Guided by ancestral memory and "magic," progeny of this lost civilization returned to locate this energy "portal" and reestablish it. Nan Madol/Kahnihmueiso is one of many examples of a "site upon a site."

> Silten [the Pohnpeian writer] is quite explicit. After searching out a site for (in which to locate) their mana, the pair "returned to the Southeast, near this shining town (Kahnihmueiso). This place was good for the seat of their mana (spiritual power) to be there for it faced Upwind Katau." (Petersen 1990)

A portion of the information herein about Nan Madol/Kahnihmueiso, Pohnpaid, and the Motherland culture of Mu is by its very nature difficult to substantiate by conventional means. That said, a significant amount of evidence provided *is physically verifiable and demands examination before being casually dismissed.* Even if certain analyses, interpretations, and conclusions appear far-fetched or even self-contradictory, the point of this book is to ignite awareness of the enormous potential held in these sites and to motivate creative and meticulous investigation. Nan Madol/Kahnihmueiso and Pohnpaid add more pieces, not just to the Nan Madol puzzle, but to the legacies of Mu embedded in Oceania and beyond.

> Since at least 65,000 years ago, the recently published earliest date for human entry into Australia and New Guinea, one third of the continental land mass has been drowned by postglacial sea-level rise. (Benjamin and Bailey 2017)

What must never be forgotten while examining the reality of the Motherland Mu is that the vast majority of evidence testifying to her existence lies on the ocean floor. *Mountaintops are not for permanent human settlements, nor cultivation, nor technological facilities.* With the exception of an occasional shrine or temple, the populace always clings to shores or plains. Urban centers and agricultural endeavors create material remains and artifacts, not the highest peaks of landmasses—thus the dilemma of proving the existence of Mu.

Greg Taylor (2019) puts it like so:

One of the important aspects of reading works that put forward new ideas and challenge the orthodoxy is to recognise that not all "leads" will pan out to be true.

Graham Hancock (2019), writer and former journalist whose so-called "pseudo-archaeology" books have sold millions of copies says:

For a writer such as myself, with a controversial, non-mainstream view of the past, to face pushback on this scale is a sure sign that the archaeological establishment feels the ground moving under its feet.

After exploring a variety of possible scenarios and interpretations, conventional and unconventional, ambiguity still reigns. Only time and meticulous exploration with new technologies will resolve questions about the birth and original identity of Nan Madol and Pohnpaid. Untold revelations await the discovery and documentation of Kahnihmueiso.

IN THE END . . .

The wisdom that allowed the culture of Mu to stay connected to earth energies provides answers not only to Nan Madol, Kahnihmueiso, and Pohnpaid's mysteries, but also to the workings of her global sacred sites and energy grids. How this network of "navels" or portals functions as Earth's acupuncture meridians and interdimensional access points explains the many *whys* of these enigmatic Pohnpei sites as well as others worldwide. Validating and *reigniting* these systems offers a new paradigm for solving the enormous environmental and societal problems of these transitional times . . . or at the very least, acknowledging the importance of working for, not against, Mother Earth.

By acknowledging that a civilization put nature first, paid equal homage to females, valued balance between the divine masculine and the divine feminine paradigms, and might also have excelled in advanced technologies of spiritual/earth energy principles beyond our current grasp can provide insights and pathways for how to create a similar *paradise*, here and now.

Humanity was left with megalithic clues—the Pacific elephant in the room—so we might reach and surpass the wisdom and enlightenment of what was once known as Mu.

> *In the time of the Seventh Fire, a New People would emerge. They would retrace their steps to find the wisdom that was left by the side of the trail long ago. Their steps would take them to the elders, who they would ask to guide them on their journey. If the New People remain strong in their quest, the sacred drum will again sound its voice. There will be an awakening of the people, and the sacred fire will again be lit. At this time, the light-skinned race will be given a choice between two roads. One road is the road of greed and technology without wisdom or respect for life. This road represents a rush to destruction. The other road is spirituality, a slower path that includes respect for all living things. If we choose the spiritual path we can light yet another fire, an Eighth Fire, and begin an extended period of Peace and healthy growth.*
>
> GRANDFATHER WILLIAM COMMANDA,
> CIRCLE OF ALL NATIONS PROPHECY OF
> THE SEVEN FIRES OF THE ANISHNABE,
> FROM ANCIENT WAMPUM BELT

APPENDIX

Symbols of Mu

Numerous comparisons between petroglyphs from Pohnpaid with others discovered worldwide are found in chapter 6, "Pacific Crossroads," and in the conclusion, "The Legacy of Mu." Although a few of the following comparisons of motifs are between those *not found* at Pohnpaid, they nevertheless reinforce the case that they all originated from a shared Motherland.

How Mu identified herself was varied but according to Churchward took the form of three types of symbols: her royal escutcheon, three triangles, and her "logo," which consisted of a central circled cross with a varying number of "points" radiating from its center. Mu's cosmology was also represented by a different symbol configuration. Versions of all of Mu's symbols span the globe. Without the prolific findings of James Churchward's *The Sacred Symbols of Mu,* based on ancient Tibetan texts, identification of any one symbol's origination in Mu as well as comparisons to their legacies would be challenging to accept, as would the following information. Whether conventional history takes James Churchward seriously or not, evidence of his Mu symbols is found on continents and cultures far and wide. One might dismiss his theories of Mu, or the oral histories from Oceania, but the matching motifs and multitude of occurrences make the case for cultural diffusion from an ancient central source, a universal Motherland.

ROYAL ESCUTCHEON OF MU

For clarification on the difference between an escutcheon and a more conventional logo or symbol, a definition is called for at this point.

An escutcheon is a shield or emblem bearing a coat of arms. That it is found upon a coat of arms connotes a culture, country, or geographical domain, as was the Motherland of Mu.

Fig. A.1. Royal escutcheon of Mu.
Illustration by James Churchward, 1933.

Fig. A.2. Bentendo Temple, Tokyo, Japan.
Photo by Stuart Matthews, 2017.

Fig. A.3. Base of Chandi Sukuh Temple pyramid, Java, Indonesia.
Photo by Anandajoti Bhikkhu.

Fig. A.4. Pict stele, Scotland, known as Rodney's Stone.
Photo by Ann Harrison.

Fig. A.5. Tukanos, Del Vaupé, Colombia.
Photo by Gerardo Reichel-Dolmatoff, 1977.

Fig. A.6. Egg serpent redeemer, Mithras.
Illustration by Thomas Maurice, circa 1790s.

Fig. A.7. Indigenous stele, Taiwu, Paiwan (Taiwan).
Photographer unknown.

Fig. A.8. Petroglyph,
Madolenihmw, Pohnpei.
Illustration by Paul Hambruch, 1911.

Fig. A.9. Egyptian goddess
Hathor, wood, 715 BCE.
Photo by Jgaunion.

TRIPLE TRIANGLE, CODE 333

Although not in the form of a symbol, the triple triangle is embedded in the oral histories of Nan Madol. It is never omitted. The 333 code will be examined in more detail in the author's next publication currently titled *Nan Madol Revealed*.

The topics of 333 and Isokelekel are ripe with universal esoteric symbolism and unanswered questions. This has been demonstrated even in modern times. The synchronistic issuance of the first thirty-three-cent Nan Madol stamp in conjunction with the United States Postal Service in 1985 is one example. The author's direct personal experiences connecting sacred stones on a heiau on Molokai, Hawai'i, with the inherent spiritual power of Nan Madol's 333 stones is another. Neither would be considered to be "material evidence" of 333 "magic" by conventional academia.

In even the briefest narratives on Nan Madol, there are no incidences of Isokelekel's story told without alluding to the number 333—whether in reference to the stones or the warriors that accompanied him during his overthrow of Nan Madol. Considering the multitude of

Fig. A.10. What remains of the 333 magical stones of Idehd Islet, Nan Madol.
Photo by Carole Nervig, 1970.

contradictions in other details of Isokelekel's arrival(s) on Pohnpei (and Pohnpeian oral histories in general), the number 333 is always mentioned. Even when as obscure or odd as the mention by Luelen Bernart (1977) regarding provisions on Anhd Atoll: "Now this man [Soulik en Anhd] had prepared some gifts for them, some baskets of breadfruit seeds, 333 of them."

Despite its consistent use, detailed physical descriptions of either Isokelekel's 333 companions or the 333 physical stones are virtually absent in oral histories. Perhaps this absence is an indication of 333 being a code, or a universal symbolic reference?

Fig. A.11. Triforce bronze emblem,
Shinobazu Temple, Japan.
Photo by Frank Joseph.

Fig. A.12. Guanche tablet, Canary Islands.
Photo by Phil A. Crean.

Fig. A.13. Three triangles represent Mu;
the dots represent ten lost tribes.
Illustration by James Churchward, 1933.

MU "LOGOS"

In addition to the royal escutcheon and the triple triangle, Mu identified herself with what could be referred to as a "logo" found in indigenous symbols across the globe.

Fig. A.14. Geoglyph, Atacama, Peru.
Photo by Gerhard Hüdepohl.

Fig. A.15. Rock art,
Lena Hara Cave, 100,000 BCE,
East Timor, Southeast Asia.
Illustration by Asmus Koefoed.

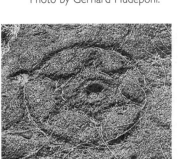

Fig. A.16. Petroglyph,
Waikoloa, Hawai'i.
Photo by Maria1986nyc.

Fig. A.17. Forehead ornament,
West Solomon Island.
Courtesy of the Barbier-Mueller
Museum. Photographer unknown.

Fig. A.18. Minoan mold,
Crete.
Photo by Olaf Tausch.

COSMOGONIC DIAGRAMS

Ives Washburn, publisher of Churchward's *The Sacred Symbols of Mu,* explains the cosmogonic symbol as follows: "The central circle is a picture of the sun and deity whose Abode is Heaven. The twelve divisions, formed by the crossing of the two triangles, are gates to Heaven where dwells the Heavenly Father. These gates symbolize virtues, the twelve

Fig. A.19. *Left, top:* Mu's cosmogonic diagram symbolizing the eight roads to heaven. *Right, top:* Babylonian; *Left, bottom:* Chaldean; *Right, bottom:* Hindu. Diagrams by James Churchward, 1933.

great earthly virtues, which man must possess before he can enter the gates." Churchward himself further explains: "The ribbon with eight divisions symbolizes the eight roads to Heaven" (Churchward 1933). Churchward demonstrates with the examples on the preceding page that cosmogonic symbols are found globally.

A central circle surrounded by divisions, and with a "ribbon" or "scallops" at its bottom, is also seen around the world.

Fig. A.20. Mayan solar glyph,
Uxmal, Mexico.
Illustration by
William H. Holmes, 1883.

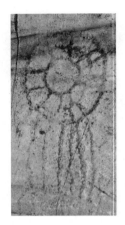

Fig. A.21. Bidzar glyph,
2500–1500 BCE,
Cameroon, Africa.
Photo by 2ddanga.

Fig. A.22. Prehistoric sun
glyph, Scandinavia.
Photo from the
Underslös Museum, Sweden.

Fig. A.23. Caiapós culture,
500 BCE, Amarolândia, Brazil.
Photographer unknown.
Shown by Mirekulous, Tumblr.

Fig. A.24. Petroglyph, Castillo, Nueva Suiza, Panama.
Photo by David Dell.

Fig. A.25. Petroglyph, Mara Rosa, Goiás, Chile.
Photo by Marciel Mendes de Avelar Pereira, Archaios Mundus.

Another globally dispersed symbol that refers to Mu, or the "Mu logo," is the T symbol.

THE T SYMBOL

In his *The Sacred Symbols of Mu,* James Churchward translates many symbols he viewed in the Tibetan manuscripts. One of the most ancient unchanged words throughout time was *Tau* or the T glyph, the emblem

Fig. A.26. Petroglyph, Pohnpaid.
Illustration by Paul Rainbird and
Meredith Wilson, 1999.

for Mu that symbolized its submersion and resurrection as well as the sacred Tree of Life from the Garden of Eden, aka Mu. The Southern Cross constellation—always significant in middle to southern Pacific cultures—is represented by the T symbol as well.

A handful of T symbols scattered here and there does not automatically constitute a shared origin; consistent recurrences spanning distances and cultures *do* . . . with or without the acceptance of Churchward's findings. Their presence speaks for itself. Prominent appearances at sophisticated ancient sacred sites and upon ancient artifacts disclose a common genesis and identity of their builders—the figurative children of Mu (of all races) fanning away by water and air, as symbolized by the two arms of the T.

The same "fanning away" T theme is found in numerous cultural traditions. Linguistics scholar Marinus Anthony Van Der Sluijs notes the consistent imagery of the "losing of tree branches" or "separation from the Tree of Life (T)" to symbolize the original dissemination of the races after a cataclysmic inundation. In this he cites Kiribati and Aztec traditions, among others. Of note is that both refer to linguistically linked *Samoa* and *Tamoa*nchan (samoa, tamoa) as the original location of the tree, thus demonstrating diffusion from a Pacific origin.

> For the people of Kiribati . . . the dissemination of the first people across the world took the form of exile from the "tree of life" . . . Micronesians of Kiribati held that the people had formerly dwelled upon "the tree of Samoa", a marvelous tree . . . of many branches", were scattered over the earth when the tree was brought down . . . For the Aztec, too, the breaking of the tree in Tamoanchan was the signal for expulsion from paradise, the rupture between heaven and earth, and the beginning of differentiation. (Van Der Sluijs 2011)

For at least three thousand years, the Deluge has been commemorated by the Ama tribe of Japan, who believe they are direct descendants of the ancient civilization from the eastern Pacific Ocean, according to writer Frank Joseph. Genetically linked to the Jōmon, these free-diving Ama females honor Mu by carrying a tree branch through the water as their annual ritual.

> At dawn, the celebrants gather on the beach to face the dawn and pray for the souls of their ancestors, the Sobata. Following purification with seawater, a designated leader walks into the ocean, up to his neck, bearing a small tree branch in his hand. After a pause, he turns to face the shore. Emerging from the water, he is greeted with the wild beating of drums and joyful chanting, as though he had survived some catastrophe. (Joseph 2006)

Along these lines it is linguistically telling that, in Chinese, *timber* means *mu*.

> The word for "timber" in Chinese is mu. In Japanese and Korean, mu signifies that which does not exist, referring perhaps to the vanished Nirai-Kanai signified by the tree branch carried through the water by the Ama celebrant. (Joseph 2006)

Ancient Hawaiian tradition supports Churchward's findings regarding the T symbol. The Tau Rua, visually a fat T symbol resembling a mushroom, was an ancient way to depict the tau symbol T from which the *four directions* of light spread to the world, according to Leinani Melville. (Ta Rua is the Hawaiian name for Mu, thus Tau Rua, cross of Mu.)

> Ta Rua was the native country of the Mu who were the earliest race of human beings and who organized this world's original civilization. (Melville 1969)

The mushroom-shaped T is also found in conjunction with the "seven serpents" of wisdom (notably, there have never been snakes Hawai'i) in the motif of an *orbor* or "shell of life," symbolizing the infusion of life by breath, with a triangle symbolizing "residence of divinity" and two lateral serpents representing God and Goddess.

The centerpiece is drawn in a very ancient form of writing tau for cross. The rays spreading from the lamp symbolize the flowing of light from God and Goddess to the four directions of this world. The two lines outside the diamond indicate this is the Cross of God and Goddess. (Melville 1969)

T

Fig. A.27. Tau Mu symbol (Tammuz cross).
Illustration by James Churchward, 1933.

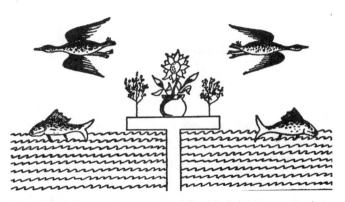

Fig. A.28. Submerged survivors of Tau Mu left by water and air.
(Note how this forms a T in the image.)
Illustration by James Churchward, 1933.

Fig. A.29. Yaxche sacred tree, Mayan.
From *Sacred Mysteries Among the Mayas and the Quiches, 11,500 Years Ago* by Augustin le Plongeon, 1886.

Fig. A.30. Tau Rua,
ancient Hawaiian divine cosmology.
Illustration by Leinani Melville, 1969.

Fig. A.31. Ancient Hawaiian divine
cosmology depicts seven serpents
radiating from triangle godhead and
a mushroom over the Earth globe.
Illustration by Leinani Melville, 1969.

Among the Maya, the Ik glyph (T) is one of the most sacred symbols, signifying wind, breath (breath = life), and spirit, and makes an appearance on the sacred elephant! It also represents a sacred day in the Mayan calendar that is linked to the birth of the feathered serpent Quetzalcoatl.

A transcendental synthesis of human religious experience is inherent in the word te, Sacred Tree, which emerged from the words teol and teotl the names of God the Creator in Mayan and Nahuatl. These most revered and sacred words of the ancient people, symbolized by the Sacred Tree, were represented in the Mayan hieroglyphs as the symbol 'T.' Additionally, this symbol represented the air, the wind, the divine breath of God. (Men 1990)

It is more than interesting that the T-shaped monoliths at Göbekli Tepe (another "navel of the Earth" portal site comparable to Greater Nan Madol) were built "submerged" into the landscape, then later buried under soil, demonstrating the symbol T representing "below." Was this the honoring of their lost Motherland of Mu, now underwater . . . the underworld?

It (T symbol) is simply the gesture sign for, "below" . . . Thus the "T" indicates the combination of vertical and horizontal places . . . We also learn that the entire Circle of the structure was intended to be conceived as, below the surface, in other words as part of the underworld . . . That the floor of the structure was made to hold rainwater runoff that represented the waters of the underworld . . . It was believed that the spirits of the deceased fell into the watery underworld and were carried by the current or streams of water (represented by the Imagery of Serpents) until they arose to a spring (the water source) viewed as a portal to the sky. Such areas were called the Navel of the Earth or the Center of the Earth and held in great reverence as waiting-places of the spirits. (Richey 2019)

To date, nine T pillar sites have been documented in Turkey—not to mention others spanning Europe—from the mystic Tau of the Egyptians and Chaldeans, representing the gods Mithras, Attis, and their forerunner Tammuz, consort of Ishtar, to the Nordic hammer of Thor. Even more remarkable, a T was drawn on the forehead of Norse pagans to initiate them, explains Harald S. Boehlke, suggesting a Mu origin for present-day baptism rituals.

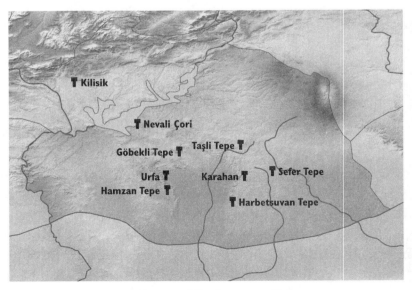

Fig. A.32. Map of T pillar sites in Turkey.
Illustration by Joe Roe

Fig. A.33. T pillars, Göbekli Tepe, Turkey.
Photo by Emiralikokal.

Fig. A.34. Taula paleolithic
ruins, Trepucó, Spain.
Photo by Hector Martinez Troyano.

The cross symbolized the first letter in the name of the old dead and resurrected Sun god Tammuz and the son of the Moon goddess, The Queen of Heaven. The "Tau" (T), precursor of today's cross, was drawn on the forehead of the (pagan) initiate. (Boehlke 2000)

The indigenous Americans utilized the T symbol consistently as the shape of sacred site "doorways"—gates or interdimensional portals. Would this explain the painting of Ts on participants of Australian Aboriginal ceremonies? Researchers of Göbekli Tepe also drew this connection:

In summary, we have drawn a semantic link between the dominant symbolism of Göbekli Tepe, T-pillars and H-symbols, and the words for god and gate in the Luwian script. (Seyfzadeh and Schoch 2019)

An adaptation of the basic T is found embedded in the archetypal Tree of Life image from Mayax (the Mayan lands, sometimes called Mayapan) to Egypt, even making an appearance in Solomon's seal.

Fig. A.35. T-shaped window, Mayan, Palenque, Mexico.
Photo by David Esser.

Fig. A.36. False doorway in the shape of a T, Amaru Muru, Peru.
Photo by Adwo.

Fig. A.37. Kiva doorway, Anasazi, Casa Rinconada,
Chaco Canyon, New Mexico.
Photo by the U.S. National Park Service.

So where might the T symbol be found on Pohnpei Island?

To date, no T megaliths have been identified. If indeed present, they would most likely be upon stones under the ground at Pohnpaid, or drowned with Kahnihmueiso. Pohnpaid has yet to be thoroughly documented; Kahnihmueiso will never be, unless new underwater technologies become available. That said, a T-shaped petroglyph was documented at Pohnpaid by Rainbird and Wilson.

Reports of a single ideogram T inscription or tau on submerged basalt near Nakapw Island in the Nan Madol vicinity by David Childress have yet to be documented; claims by Frank Joseph that they match those found at Yonaguni are as well unsubstantiated.

Tau does exist as a significant Pohnpeian word, even if it doesn't refer to a lithic monument. The *T* and *D* in *tau/dau* are interchangeable and pronounced as a combination of the two letters. *Tau/Dau* literally means a "channel," "canal," or a "passage in a reef." In a more esoteric context *tau/dau* could refer to a divine energetic bridging mechanism or passageway (quantum wormhole?). *Dau* is also a syllable in the name of Pohnpei's highest god, Taukatau/Daukatau.

Dau Katau is an honorific title, rather than name, of god Nahnsapwe (Bernart) or rain god (Petersen). Some legends credit Dau Katau with creating Pohnpei by breaking the landing rock of the first canoe into eight pieces (Hambruch). The god supervises all other deities. With Katau being the name for the spirit world, it could be literally interpreted to mean "channel of the spirit/sky world," i.e., energy portal or holy spirit, rather than an anthropomorphic deity.

These are just a few of countless motifs seen the world over. Other archetypal symbols that speak for themselves by their similarities include but are not limited to the Ouroboros, the *chacana,* the "stone purse," a goddess spread-legged with vagina exposed, the T and H symbols, egg and serpent motifs, as well as pillars and gates representing portals to other dimensions.

By demonstrating the relationships between the above symbols as well as those found throughout this book, it has always been my sincere intention to provoke deeper investigation not only into the Pohnpaid site, but into unearthing the complete and accurate picture of our distant past in the Pacific.

What better place than one written in stone?

According to United States Geological Survey, 90 percent of an iceberg lies below the waterline; Pohnpaid's potential is the same. Literal and figurative secrets are still hidden, not only underneath the jungle's camouflage and under the ground of the site, but incised upon the buried underbellies of its megaliths.

Even if the fire to dig deeper is lit by my theories judged controversial, so be it. I dare the jungle to be cleared to prove me wrong.

References

ABC News. 2006. "Australia Challenges Out-of-Africa Theory." *ABC News* online (Jan. 7).

Ahmad, M. S., and Awwad M. Zihlif. 1990. "Some Magnetic and Electrical Properties of Basalt Rocks." *Materials Letters* 10, no. 4–5 (November): 207–14.

Aluli, Noa Emmett, and Davianna Pomaika'i McGregor. n.d. "'Aina: Ke Ola O Na Kanaka 'Oiwi Land: The Health of Native Hawaiians." United States National Library of Medicine, available online.

Andrews, Munya. 2004. *The Seven Sisters of the Pleiades: Stories from Around the World*. Australia: Spinifex Press.

Argue, Debbie, Colin P. Groves, Michael S. Y. Lee, and William L. Jungers. 2017. "The Affinities of Homo floresiensis Based on Phylogenetic Analyses of Cranial, Dental, and Postcranial Characters." *Journal of Human Evolution*. (April 21 online; June print): 107–33.

Art Encyclopedia. n.d. s.v. "Venus Figurines." Encyclopedia of Art Education website accessed January 6, 2022.

Athens, J. Stephen, and Jerome V. Ward. 2001. "Paleoenvironmental Evidence for Early Human Settlement in Palau: The Ngerchau Core." In *Pacific 2000: Proceedings of the Fifth International Conference on Easter Island and the Pacific,* edited by Christopher Stevenson, F. J. Morin, and Georgia Lee, 167–78. Los Ojos: Easter Island Foundation. International Archaeological Research Institute.

Attenborough, David. 2016. *The Waterside Ape* broadcast. BBC Radio 4.

Aveni, Anthony F., and Horst Härtung. n.d. "The Cross Petroglyph: An Ancient Mesoamerican Astronomical and Calendrical Symbol." Available online.

Baker, Douglas. 1952. *The Seven Rays: Key to the Mysteries*. Newburyport, Mass.: Red Wheel/Weiser.

Barrow, Valérie. 2015. "Kariong Research: Phoenicians and Egyptians in Australia." Website of Valérie Barrow (August 20).

BBC News. 2002. "Lost City 'Could Rewrite History," BBC News website (January 19).

———. 2016. "Neanderthal Stone Ring Structures Found in French Cave." BBC News website (May 25).

Beardsley, Felicia, and Umai Basilius. 2002. "Sengall Ridge, Belau: Burials, Spirit Walks and Painted Pottery." In *The Melaka Papers: Proceedings of the 16th Congress of the Indo-Pacific Prehistory Association,* Melaka, Malaysia (July 1–7, 1998), edited by P. Bellwood, D. Bowdery, F. Beardsley, D. Bullock, S. Keates, and S. Phear, 147–51. *Bulletin of the Indo-Pacific Prehistory Association,* vol. 22.

Beaton, Danny. 2020. "Mohawk Elder, Defenders of Our Sacred Mother: Native Wisdom Keepers Speak Out." Cultural Survival website.

BEC Crew. 2016. "Pacific Islanders Appear to Be Carrying the DNA of an Unknown Human Species." ScienceAlert website (October 25).

Beckwith, Martha. 1914. "Field Notes." Hawaiian Sources Collection, Bishop Museum Library, Honolulu, 384–97, as cited by the National Park Service website, "Hawai'i Volcanoes."

Bednarik, R. G. 2008. "Cupules." *Rock Art Research* 25, no. 1: 61–100.

Bell, H. C. P. 1901. "Sakwala Chakraya: Archaeological Survey of Ceylon: North-Central and Central Provinces. Annual Report." Ceylon [Sri Lanka]: H. C. Cottle.

Bellwood, P. 1978. *Man's Conquest of the Pacific.* Auckland, Australia: William Collins.

Benjamin, Jonathan, and Geoff Bailey. 2017. "Coastal Adaptations and Submerged Landscapes: Where World Prehistory Meets Underwater Archaeology." In *From Hunter-Gatherers to Farmers: Human Adaptations at the End of the Pleistocene and the First Part of the Holocene. Papers in Honour of Clive Bonsall,* edited by Monica Mărgărit and Adina Boroneanţ, 169–83. Târgovişte, Romania: Editura Cetatea de Scaun.

Bernart, Luelen. 1977. *The Book of Luelen.* Honolulu: University Press of Hawai'i.

Blackburn, Thomas. 1967. "Some Examples of Ponapean Folklore." *Journal of American Folklore* 80, no. 317: 247–54.

Blong, Russell. 1982. *The Time of Darkness: Local Legends and Volcanic Realtiy in Papua New Guinea.* Seattle: University of Washington Press.

Boehlke, Harald S. 2000. *The Viking Serpent*. Bloomington, Ind.: Trafford Publishing.

Brown, Lee. 1986. "North American Indian Prophecies." Prophecy as told at the Continental Indigenous Council, Alaska. Available at Bahá'í Library Online.

Buck, P. H. (aka Te Rangi Hiroa). 1932. *Bishop Museum Bulletin* 92 (April). Honolulu, Hawaii.

Buck, Wilfred. 2018. *Tipiskawi Kisik: Night Sky Star Stories*. Manitoba: Manitoba First Nations Resource Centre.

Callaway, Ewen. 2018. "Ancient Genomics Is Recasting the Story of the Americas' First Residents." *Nature* (November 8).

CBC News. 2019. "'Legends of the Northern Sky': Movie Explores Cree Culture's Connections to the Stars." CBC News website (April 10).

China Daily. 2005. "World's Oldest Observatory Discovered in Shanxi." *China Daily* website (November 1).

Christian, F. W. 1967. *The Caroline Islands: Travel in the Sea of the Little Lands*. London: Frank Cass & Co. Ltd.

Churchward, Jack. my-mu.com blog.

Churchward, James. 1931. *The Children of Mu*. New York: Ives Washburn.

———. 1933. *The Sacred Symbols of Mu*. New York: Ives Washburn.

Clay, A. T. 1910. "An Ancient Plow." *Museum Journal* 1, no. 1 (June): 4–6. Accessed January 10, 2022 on the Penn Museum website.

Cochrane, Ev. 2001. *The Many Faces of Venus*. Aeon Press.

Constellation of Words. "List of Stars." s.v. Pleione. Constellation of Words website. Accessed January 7, 2022.

Cook, Robert G. 2001. *Avian Visual Cognitions*. Tufts University and Comparative Cognition Press.

Cunningham, Derek, and Robert Cunningham. 2018. *The Babel Texts*. Independently published.

Daniels, Gary C. 2012. "Mayan Glyphs on Georgia, Florida Pottery?" Lost Worlds website (March 10).

———. 2019. "Mayan Glyphs at Crystal River Site in Florida." Lost Worlds website (May 19).

David, Gary A. n.d. "The Nagas: Origin of the Hopi Snake Clan?" Ancient Origins website.

de Borhegyi, Carl. 2012. "The Return of Quetzalcoat as Venus." Mayamushroomstone blog (May 10).

Dev Misra, Bibhu. 2016. "The Turtle Supporting Mount Meru in Asian and Mesoamerican Art." Bibhu Dev Misra blog (November 22).

Dobrizhoffer, Martin. 1763. *Historia de los Abipones.*

Douka, Katerina. 2019. "Age Estimates for Hominin Fossils and the Onset of the Upper Paleolithic at Denisova Cave." *Nature* 565: 640.

Doutré, Martin. 2018a. *Ancient Celtic New Zealand.* Auckland: Dé Danann Publishers.

———. 2018b. No title. celticnewzealand.co.nz (May 4).

Dudhane, Rahul. 2021. "Founder of Hinduism." Hinduism facts website (August 20).

Dutchen, Stephanie. 2015. "Genetic Studies Link Indigenous Peoples in the Amazon and Australasia." Harvard Medical School Science Daily (July 21).

Edwards, Alexandra. 2017. "The Archeoastronomy of Kosrae and Pohnpei: An Explorers Club Flag #71 Expedition Report." Pacific Islands Research Institute (PIRI).

Edwards, Edmundo, and Alexandra Edmonds. 2013. *When the Universe Was an Island: Exploring the Cultural and Spritual Cosmos of Ancient Rapa Nui.* Easter Island: Hangaroa Press.

Eilers, A. 1934. *Inseln um Ponape* [in German]. Vol. 8 of *Ergebnisse der Sudsee-Expedition 1908–1910.* Hamburg: Friederichsen de Gruyter.

Elphick, Jonathan. 1995. *The Atlas of Bird Migration.* New York: Reader's Digest Press.

Esteban, César. 2014. "Orientations and Astronomy of Prehistoric Monumental Tombs of Nan Madol." *Studies in Global Archaeology*, no. 20.

Evans, Gary. 2017. "Ancient Acoustic Artifacts and Communication with the 'Gods.'" Ancient Origins website (August 13).

Faure-Brac, Jane. n.d. "Uncovering Ancient Rituals in Polynesia." *ANU Reporter* 50, no. 1.

Fenton, Bruce R. 2018. "The Forgotten Exodus." Forgotten Origin website.

Fiorenza, Nick. 2019. "Nasatras." Lunarplanner website, no longer accessible.

Fredericks, Kásskara. 2017. "Sunken Land of the Hopi Ancestors." Ancient Origins website (December 24).

Genetics Home Reference (now Medline). 2020. "What Does It Mean to Have Neanderthal or Denisovan DNA?" U.S. National Library of Medicine, National Institute of Health website (updated September 18, 2020).

GodElectric.org. n.d. See the pages "Electric Egyptology" and "The Hieroglyphs."

Greer, John. 1997. "El Arte de Rupestre del Sur de Venezuela: Una Síntesis" [in Spanish]. *Sociedad de Investigación del Arte Rupestre de Bolivia,* no. 11: 38–52. Available on the Greer Archeology website.

Gyrus. 2007. *Archaeologies of Consciousness: Essays in Experimental Prehistory.* London: Dreamflesh Press.

Hambruch, Paul. 1910. (NM Map 1910) 1932–1936. Ponape. In *Ergebnisse der Sudsee-Expedition 1908–1910,* edited by G. Thilenius. Hamburg: Friederichsen de Gruyter.

———. 1911. "Die Sogenannten Ruinen von Matolenim auf Ponape." *Korrespondenz-Blatt der Deutsche Gesellschaft fur Anthropologie, Korrespondenzblatt* 42: 128–31.

———. 1936. *Ponape.* Vol. 3 of *Ergebnisse der Südsee Expedition, 1908–1910,* edited by Georg Thilenius. Hamburg: Friederichsen de Gruyter.

Hamilton, Shawn. 2020. "Earth Cataclysms and the Hopi Kachinas, Saviours from Space." Graham Hancock website (April 25).

Hamm, Giles, et al. 2016. "Cultural Innovation and Megafauna Interaction in the Early Settlement of Arid Australia." *Nature* 539 (November 10): 280–83.

Hampson, Jamie. 2016. *Rock Art and Regional Identity: A Comparative Perspective.* U.K.: Taylor & Francis.

Hancock, Graham. 2019. "Response from Graham Hancock to the Society for American Archaeology." Graham Hancock website (November 25).

Hand Clow, Barbara. 2011. *Awakening the Planetary Mind: Beyond the Trauma of the Past to a New Era of Creativity.* Rochester, Vt.: Bear & Company.

Hanebuth, Till, Karl Stattegger, and Pieter M. Grootes. 2000. "Rapid Flooding of the Sunda Shelf: A Late-Glacial Sea-Level Record." *Science* 288 (May), no. 5468: 1033–35.

Hanlon, David. 1988. *Upon a Stone Altar.* Pacific Islands Monograph Series, no. 5. Oahu: University of Hawaii Press.

———. 2004. "Wone Sohte Lohdi: History and Place on Pohnpei." In *Pacific Places, Pacific Histories: Essays in Honor of Robert C. Kiste,* edited by Brij V. Lal, 195–215. Honolulu: University of Hawaii Press.

Hari, D. K, and Hema Hari. n.d. "An Ancient Trail of Lord Ganesha: A Global God Much before Globalization." The Art of Living website.

Heyward, Andrew, Edward Pinceratto, and Luke Smith. 2006. *Big Bank Shoals of the Timor Sea: An Environmental Resource Atlas.* Townsville, Australia: Australian Institute of Marine Science.

Hislop, Alexander. 1858. *The Two Babylons*. Edinburgh: Presbyterian Free Church of Scotland, expanded edition. Originally published in 1853.

Holloway, April. 2015. "Ingapirca: Proof That the Inca Respected the Cultures of Those They Conquered." Ancient Origins website (October 13).

Hutchins, Edwin. 1995. *Cognition in the Wild*. Cambridge, Mass.: MIT Press.

Hutton, J. H. 1921. *Nagaland Naga Art: The Tribal Arts of the Angami Nagas*. London: Macmillan.

Jiang, Peter, and Jenny Li. 2007. "Scientists Confirm Extraterrestrial Genes in Human DNA." Biblioteca Pleyades website (January 26).

Joesting, Edward. 1987. *Kaua'i, the Separate Kingdom*. Honolulu: University of Hawai'i Press and Kaua'i Museum Association.

Joseph, Frank. 2005. *Atlantis Encyclopedia*. Franklin Lakes, N.J.: Career Press.

———. 2006. *The Lost Civilization of Lemuria*. Rochester, Vt.: Bear & Co.

Karim, Ibrahim. 2010. *Back to a Future for Mankind*. Scotts Valley, Calif.: CreateSpace Independent Publishing.

Kawagoe, Aileen. n.d. "Do Japanese Petroglyphs Reveal Prehistoric Connections with the Ancient Sumerian-Akkadian-Elamite or Phoenician Civilizations?" Heritage of Japan blog.

Kelley, David H., and Eugene F. Milone. 2011. *Exploring Ancient Skies: A Survey of Ancient and Cultural Astronomy*. New York: Springer.

Khandavalli, Shankara Bharadwaj. n.d. "Concept of Motherland." Hindupedia website.

King, Serge. 1983. *Kahuna Healing*. Wheaton, Ill.: Quest Books.

Klakring, Jessica, and Cynthia L. Hallen. 1998–1999. "The Tagalog Language from Roots to Destiny." Brigham Young University Linguistics Department website.

Kovalev, Vladimir. 2013. "The Star Gate of Sri Lanka." Vladimir KovalSky blog (October 12).

Krill, Allan. 2017. "Human Evolution in the Sea at Bioko." Gemini: Research News from Norwegian University of Science and Technology and SINTEF (July).

Lawhorn, Richard. 2010. "Petroglyphs at Altavista." Website of Richard Lawhorn. Original site available by using the Wayback Machine (August 27).

Lawler, Andrew. 2002. "Report of Oldest Boat Hints at Early Trade Routes." *Science* 296, no. 5574 (June): 1791–92.

Le Poer Trench, Brinsley. 1960. *The Sky People*. n.p.: Saucerian Books.

Lewis, David S. 2015. "Legends of the Star People Ancestors in High Places." Mountain Pioneer website.

Lewis, Keith, Scott D. Nodder, and Lionel Carter. 2013. "Sea Floor Geology—Zealandia: The New Zealand Continent." Te Ara: Encyclopedia of New Zealand online.

Liller, William. 1993. *The Ancient Solar Observatories of Rapanui: The Archaeoastronomy of Easter Island.* [Los Ojos Calif.?]: Cloud Mountain Press.

Mackenzie, Donald Alexander. 1915. *Myths of Babylonia and Assyria.* London: Gresham.

Malyarchuk, B. A. 2011. "Adaptive Evolution of the Homo Mitochondrial Genome." *Molecular Biology* 45, no. 780.

Masse, W. Bruce. 2007. "Oral Tradition, Myth and Cosmic Impact." In *Comet/Asteroid Impacts and Human Society: An Interdisciplinary Approach,* by Peter Bobrowsky and Hans Rickman, section 2.3, 39–40. New York: Springer.

Mauricio, Rufino. 1998. *Pohnpeian History: The Challenge of Understanding, Using and Preserving Pohnpeian History.* Division of Archives and Historic Preservation Federated States of Micronesia National Government, Pohnpei FSM.

McCulloch, J. Huston. 2016. "Translation of the Cuenca Elephant Tablet using Ohio Decalogue Stone Style." Available online.

Megaliths.net. n.d. "The Dolmens and Megaliths of Korea: Megaliths Dolmens Deciphered as Astronomy." Megaliths.net website. Accessed January 7, 2022.

Mehler, Stephen. 2002. *The Land of Osiris.* Kempton, Ill.: Adventures Unlimited.

———. 2014. *From Light Into Darkness: The Evolution of Religion in Ancient Egypt.* Kempton, Ill.: Adventures Unlimited.

Meijer, Vincent. 2012. "Continuity and Change in Polynesian Visual Symbolic Systems." Ph.D. diss., University College London.

Melville, Leinani. 1969. *Children of the Rainbow: The Religion, Legends, and Gods of Pre-Christian Hawai'i.* Wheaton, Ill.: The Theosophical Publishing House.

Men, Hunbatz. 1990. *Secrets of Mayan Science/Religion.* Translated by Diana Gubiseh Ayala and James Jennings Dunlop II. Santa Fe, N.M.: Bear & Company.

Mkhitaryan, Lilit. 2016. "Celestial Maps of Gegham Mountain: The Unique Rock Art of Armenia." Ancient Origins website (April 16).

Mohan, Praveen. 2020. "Archeologists Unearthed This Stone Turtle! What's Inside Is an Ancient Machine?" YouTube (October 9).

Morgan, Elaine. 1972. *Descent of Woman*. England: Souvenir Press.

———. 1982. *The Aquatic Ape*. New York: Stein & Day.

———. 2002. "Was Man More Aquatic in the Past? What Happens When You Change the Paradigm?" *New Scientist* 16: 23–24.

———. 2008. *The Naked Darwinist*. Leeds, England: Eildon Press.

Morris, Desmond. 1967. *The Naked Ape*. New York: McGraw-Hill.

Morris, Stephen W., and Lydia Sharman. 2005. "Images of Sound: Symmetry Hidden and Manifest in Physics and Art." *idea&s* 2, no. 2.

Morse, Edwin S. 1879. *Traces of an Early Race in Japan*. New York: D. Appleton and Company.

Moulton Howe, Linda. 2001a. "Interview: Frank Joseph, Editor-in-Chief, *Ancient American, Archaeology of the Americas before Columbus,* Colfax, Wisconsin." Future Destinies series, no. 8. Available on the dwij website.

———. 2001b. "Underwater City Reported Off Western Cuba." Earthfiles.com website (May 18). See also "Update on Underwater Megalith," Earthfiles.com website (November 19). See also Moulton Howe's untitled post on free republic.com (November 21, 2001) in response to second article.

Mulloy, William. 1975. "A Soltice Oriented Ahu on Easter Island." *Archaeology & Physical Anthropology in Oceania* 10, no. 1 (April).

Mundkur, Balaji. 1980. "On Pre-Columbian Maize in India and Elephantine Deities in Mesoamerica." *Current Anthropology* 21, no. 5 (October): 676–79.

Nervig, Carole [Carole Jencks, pseud.]. 1970. *Nan Madol*. Trust Territory of the Pacific.

——— [Carole Jencks, pseud.]. 1989. *Nan Madol*. Pohnpei State Tourism.

——— [Caroline Hadley Nervig, pseud.]. 1996. "Journey to Mu." In *Earthwalking Sky Dancers: Women's Pilgrimages to Sacred Places,* edited by Leila Castle. Berkeley: Frog Ltd.

——— 2001a. "Nan Madol: Sacred City of the Pacific." Hawai'i Committee for the Humanities Presentation.

——— 2001b. "Nan Madol: Venice of the Pacific." After Dark in the Park event, Volcanoes National Park, funded by Hawaii Council for the Humanities.

——— Forthcoming. *Nan Madol Revealed*.

Olcott, Jiro. 2013. "Sacred Stones." The Seven Worlds blog (November 7).

Oppenheimer, Stephen. 1998. *Eden in the East: The Drowned Continent of Southeast Asia*. London: Phoenix Press.

Orozco, Lance. 2017. "Significant Archaeological Find in Channel Islands Backs Idea People Lived There 10,000+ Years Ago." KCLU website (June 6).

Oug. 1837. "Traces of Ancient Civilizations among the South Sea Islands." *Sailor's Magazine*. Reprinted by the *Hobart Town Courier*.

Panholzer, Thomas, and Rufino Mauricio. 2003. *Place Names of Pohnpei Island*. Honolulu: Bess Press.

Pasha-Robinson, Lucy. 2016. "Man Searching for Toilet Stumbles across 49,000-Year-Old Evidence of Earliest Human Settlement in Australia." *Independent* website (November 3).

Patterson, Alex. 1992. *A Field Guide to Rock Art Symbols of the Greater Southwest*. Boulder, Colo.: Johnson Books.

Peratt, Anthony. 2003. "Characteristics for the Occurrence of a High-Current, Z-Pinch Aurora as Recorded in Antiquity." *IEEE Transactions on Plasma Science* 31, no. 6 (December).

Petersen, G. 1990. "Lost in the Weeds: Theme and Variations in Pohnpei Political Mythology." Center for Pacific Studies Occasional Paper series, no. 35. Honolulu: University of Hawaii Press.

Piccardi, L., and W. B. Masse, eds. 2007. *Myth and Geology*. London: Geological Society of London.

Pinkham, Mark Amaru. 1997. *The Return of the Serpents of Wisdom*. Kempton, Ill.: Adventures Unlimited.

Pohnpei Vistors Bureau. 2001. *Pohnpei Ecotourism Travel Guide*.

Prieto, Miguel Angel. 1983. "Arqueologia Antropologia e Historia del Pais de Mu" [in Spanish]. Reedición de la Fundación Simón Rodriguez. EBPP. MPPE. Caracas, 2017.

Putnam, Nathan. 2011. "For Turtles, Earth's Magnetism Is a Built-In GPS." National Public Radio.

Putney, Alex. 2014. "Resonance in the Altavista Petroglyphs, Mexico." human-resonance.org (September 25).

Rainbird, Paul. 2002a. "Marking the Body, Marking the Land: Body as History, Land as History: Tattooing and Engraving in Oceania." In *Thinking through the Body*, edited by Yannis Hamilakis, Mark Pluciennik, and Sarah Tarlow, 233–47. New York: Springer.

———. 2002b. "Pohnpei Petroglyphs, Communication and Miscommunication." Abstract, *Indo-Pacific Prehistory Association Bulletin* 22.

———. 2004. *The Archaeology of Micronesia*. Cambridge, U.K.: Cambridge University Press.

Rainbird, Paul, and Meredith Wilson. 1999. "Pohnpaid Petroglyphs, Pohnpei: A Report to the Federated States of Micronesia National Historic Preservation

Office and the Pohnpei State Historic Preservation Office" (June).

————. 2002. "Crossing the Line: The Enveloped Cross in Pohnpei, Federated States of Micronesia (News & Notes)." *Antiquity* 76, no. 293 (Sept.): 635.

Rajagopalan, Ashvin. 2010. "Thiruporur Stone Circles and Burial Cists." The Megalithic Portal website (October 10).

Rehg, Ken. 1979. *Pohnpean Language Dictionary.* Honolulu: University of Hawaii Press.

Revelation Watcher. 2012. "Secret of the Sumerian Tablet." YouTube (March 5).

Richards, Z., C-C Shen, J-P Hobbs, C-C Wu, X. Jiang, and F. Beardsley. 2015. "New Precise Dates for the Ancient and Sacred Coral Pyramidal Tombs of Leluh (Kosrae, Micronesia)." *Science Advances* 1, no. 2 (March 13).

Richey, Clifford C. 2019. "Gobekli Tepe's 'T' Shaped Pillars as Conglomerates as Opposed to Anthropomorphic Entities." Available at Academia.edu.

Roberts, Jane. 1995. *The Education of Oversoul Seven,* San Rafael, Calif.: Amber-Allen.

Royal Society of Victoria. 2019. "Australia's Earliest Humans? The Case for Moyjil." Royal Society of Victoria website (March 4).

Russell, Thembi. 2019. Review of *Rock Art and Regional Identity: A Comparative Perspective,* by Jamie Hampson. *Journal of African History* 59, no. 3: 515–17.

Ryder, Julie. n.d. "Ancient Pictographs: Leon Secatero Translates Ancient Glyphs in Montana." Galactic Facets website.

Saey, Tina Hesman. 2016. "DNA Data Offer Evidence of Unknown Extinct Human Relative." ScienceNews website (October 21).

Sanchéz P., Domingo. 2006a. "The Mesoamerican Venus Symbol in Venezuelan Rock Art." *KACIKE: The Journal of Caribbean Amerindian History and Anthropology* (January).

————. 2006b. "El símbolo de Venus en el arte rupestre de Perú, Chile y norte de Argentina" [in Spanish]. Fundacion de Estudios Indigenistas (FUNDESIN). Paper read at Il National Symposium of Rupestre Art (October), Trujillo, Peru.

Saxe, Arthur. 1980. *The Nan Madol Area of Ponape: Researches into Bounding and Stabilizing an Ancient Administrative Center.* Trust Territory of the Pacific.

Schaefer, Brad. n.d. "Heliacal Rising: Definitions, Calculations, and Some Specific Cases." In *Essays from Archaeoastronomy and Ethnoastronomy News,* the Quarterly Bulletin of the Center for Archaeoastronomy, no 25.

Schoch, Robert. n.d. "Research Highlights: Plasma, Solar Outbursts, and the End of the Last Ice Age." Robert Schoch website, accessed November 1, 2021.

Scranton, Laird. 2015. *Point of Origin: Gobekli Tepe and the Spiritual Matrix for the World's Cosmologies.* Rochester, Vt.: Inner Traditions.

———. 2018. *Decoding Maori Cosmology: The Ancient Origins of New Zealand's Indigenous Culture.* Rochester, Vt.: Inner Traditions.

Selin, Helaine, ed. 2000. *Astronomy across Cultures: The History of Non-Western Astronomy.* Dordrecht, Netherlands: Kluwer Publishers.

Seyfzadeh, Manu, and Robert Schoch. 2019. "World's First Known Written Word at Göbekli Tepe on T-Shaped Pillar 18 Means God." *Archeological Discovery Journal* 7, no. 2: 31–53.

Sigua, Daigu. n.d. "The Concept of Taiwania." Austronesian Origin website.

Silten. n.d. Untitled and unpublished manuscript on the history of Pohnpei. Written circa 1920s. Translated by I. L. Fischer in 1951. In the Tozer Library, Harvard University, Cambridge, Massachusetts.

Silva, Freddy. 2019. *The Missing Lands: Uncovering Earth's Pre-flood Civilization.* Invisible Temple.

Sims, Peter C. 2013. "No Reprieve for Tasmanian Rock Art." *Arts* 2, no. 4: 182–224. Available on MDPI website.

Sjöberg, Katarina V. 1993. *The Return of the Ainu: Cultural Mobilization and the Practice of Ethnicity in Japan.* Netherlands: Harwood.

Smith, Wayne. 2000. "Ancient Hawaiian Celebration of Makahiki Tied to the Stars." Moolelo website (February).

Snow, F. H. 1975. "Swift Creek Designs and Distributions: A South Georgia Study." *Early Georgia* 3, no. 2: 38–59.

Spriggs, Matthew. 1997. *The Island Melanesians.* Cambridge, Mass.: Blackwell.

Strong, Stephen. 2012. "The First Race: Out-of-Australia, Not Africa!" Official website of the Sovereign Union of First Nations and Peoples in Australia (March 12).

Strong, Stephen, and Evan Strong. 2015. "Australia's Stonehenge: Original Elders and Custodians Share the Truth about Ancient Stone Arrangement Site." Forgotten Origin website (September 2).

———. 2019. "Another Block in the Wall." Ancient Origins website (December 10).

Talbot, David. 1980. *The Saturn Myth: A Reinterpretation of Rites and Symbols Illuminating Some of the Dark Corners of Primordial Society.* New York: Doubleday.

Talbot, David, and Wallace Thornhill. 2007. *The Electric Universe*. Portland, Ore.: Mikamar Publishing.

Tambovtsev, Yuri. 2008. "The Phono-Typological Distances between Ainu and the Other World Languages as a Clue for Closeness of Languages." *Asian and African Studies* 17, no. 1: 40–62.

Tarte, Daryl. 2014. *Fiji: A Place Called Home*. Canberra: ANU Press, The Australian National University Press.

Taylor, Christie. 2019. "Relearning the Star Stories of Indigenous Peoples." Science Friday website (September 6).

Taylor, Greg. 2019. "Graham Hancock vs the Archaeological Orthodoxy." The Daily Grail website (December 11).

Temple, Robert. 1998. *The Sirius Mystery: New Scientific Contact 5,000 Years Ago*. Rochester, Vt.: Destiny.

Thompson, Gunnar. 1989. *Nu Sun: Asian-American Voyages*. Pioneer Publishing Co.

Thompson, J. Eric S. 1962. *A Catalog of Maya Hieroglyphs*. Norman: University of Oklahoma Press.

Ueki, T., and M. T. Nena. 1983. "Rediscovering Pohnpei Petroglyphs." *Journal of the Polynesian Society* 92.

University of Leeds. 2008. "New Research Forces U-turn in Population Migration Theory." EurekAlert website (May 23).

Vakoch, Douglas A., ed. 2014. *Archaeology, Anthropology, and Interstellar Communications*. Washington, D.C.: NASA.

Van Der Sluijs, Marinus Anthony. 2011. *Traditional Cosmology: The Global Mythology of Cosmic Creation and Destruction*. Vol. 4, *Disintegration*. London: All-Round Publications.

Van Hoek, Maarten. 2011. "An Overview of a Rock Art Site in La Rioja, Argentina." Available on the Rupestreweb website.

Varner, Gary R. 2012. *Portals to Other Realms, Cup Marked Stones and Prehistoric Rock Carvings*. Raleigh, N.C.: Lulu Press.

Verderame, Lorenzo. 2016. "Pleiades in Ancient Mesopotamia." *Mediterranean Archaeology and Archaeometry* 16, no. 4.

Volker, Judy. n.d. "Star Lore/Pleiades/Part 5 The Americas." Website of Judy Volker.

Von Petzinger, Genevieve. 2017. *The First Signs: Unlocking the Mysteries of the World's Oldest Symbols*. New York: Atria Books.

Weisberger, Mindy. 2019. "Found: First Tibetan Evidence of Neanderthal Cousins, the Denisovans." Livescience website (May 3).

Whipple, Fred L., and Salah El-Din Hamid. 1950. "On the Origin of Taurid Meteors." *Astronomical Journal* 55: 185–86.

Whitley, D. S. 2000. *The Art of the Shaman: Rock Art of California.* Salt Lake City: University of Utah Press.

Więcej, Czytaj. 2019. "A-Mu-Ra-Ca—America." Disclosure News website. (February 28).

Williams, Mark, and Daniel T. Elliot. 2009. *A World Engraved: Archaeology of the Swift Creek Culture.* Tuscaloosa: University of Alabama Press.

Williams-Beck, Lorraine A. 2015. "Limestone Turtle Marks Portal to the Underworld." *The Current: Newsletter of the Island and Coastal Archaeology Interest Group* 3, no. 1 (spring/summer).

Williamson, George Hunt. 1961. *Secret of The Andes.* London: Neville Spearman.

Wisdom Library n.d. s.v. "Narayana, Nārāyaṇa, Nārāyana, Narāyana, Nara-ayana, Nara-yana: 38 Definitions." Wisdom Library website. Accessed January 7, 2022.

Working with Indigenous Australians. Last updated 2020. "History/Australia/60,000 + Years Ago to 1788." Working with Indigenous Australians website.

Yates, Donald N. 2010. "On the Trail of the Spider Woman." DNA Consultants website (December 31).

———. 2015. "Admixture in Pima Includes Greek and Sardinian." DNA Consultants website (March 22).

Index

Page numbers in *italics* indicate illustrations.
Numbers in *italics* preceded by *pl.* indicate color insert plate numbers.